Transforming Political Discourse

To My Mother and the
Memory of My Father

Terence Ball

Transforming Political Discourse

Political Theory and
Critical Conceptual History

Basil Blackwell

First published 1988

Basil Blackwell Ltd
108 Cowley Road, Oxford, OX4 1JF, UK

Basil Blackwell Inc.
432 Park Avenue South, Suite 1503
New York, NY 10016, USA

British Library Cataloguing in Publication Data

Ball, Terence
Transforming political discourse :
political theory and critical conceptual
history.
1. Politics. Concepts. Change
I. Title
320′.01
ISBN 0–631–15821–9

Library of Congress Cataloging in Publication Data

Ball, Terence.
Transforming political discourse : political theory and critical
conceptual history / Terence Ball.
p.   cm.
Includes index.
ISBN 0–631–15821–9
1. Political science—Terminology—History.   2. Political science—
History.   I. Title.
JA61.B35   1988   88–5030
320′.014–dc19   CIP

Typeset in 11 on 13pt Bembo
by Alan Sutton Publishing, Gloucester
Printed and bound in Great Britain
by T.J. Press Ltd, Padstow, Cornwall

What a beautiful book could be written by recounting the
life and adventures of a single word! No doubt it has
acquired different senses from the events in which it has
seen service; it has aroused different ideas in different
places . . . does this not furnish material for an ocean of
reflections?
— Honoré de Balzac, *Louis Lambert*

It may perhaps be censured as an impertinent Criticism in
a discourse of this nature, to find fault with words and
names that have obtained in the World: And yet possibly it
may not be amiss to offer new ones when the old are apt
to lead Men into mistakes . . .
— John Locke, *Second Treatise of Government*

Contents

→ See Seterbery Politics of Definition

(meaning of concepts in
  political science

  ch 4 on
  coercion, force,
  violence

Preface

This is the first volume of a projected trilogy whose general title is 'Political Theory and the Human Sciences'. Each volume outlines and illustrates one of three tasks that I take to be central to political theory in our day. The first advances the view that political theory needs to move beyond 'conceptual analysis' to the construction of 'critical conceptual histories'. The present work is accordingly concerned with the ways in which and the reasons for which the concepts constitutive of political discourse change over time. A second task facing political theorists is to come to grips with the increasingly important role played by the social sciences in the communicative constitution of society. A critical appraisal of the use, abuse and application of social-scientific reason would therefore be a reappraisal of the society in which we live. The second volume, *Positivism, Politics and the Social Sciences*, accordingly consists of a series of critical studies in the history and philosophy of the social sciences. In the third volume, *Reappraisals in Political Theory*, I contend that a third – and, viewed superficially, a rather old-fashioned and traditional – task to be undertaken by political theorists is that of periodically reappraising and criticizing the interpretations and reinterpretations of the classic texts and authors whose discourses both contribute to and differ from our own.

The title of the present work is intended to suggest several things at once. The first is that our political discourses help to transform us, making us who and what we are as political agents and citizens. Language is not and cannot be a morally or politically neutral medium. As we speak, so we are. And as the concepts constitutive of our speech change, so too do we. I also mean to suggest that the concepts constituting political discourse are apt to have, if not essentially contested, then certainly contingently contested, meanings. Which concepts are to figure in such contests, and the ways in which and the reasons for which they are

contested, depends upon the political predicaments in which
political agents find themselves. The variety and complexity of
these situations is indelibly registered in the history of almost any
concept one cares to name, whether it be 'the state' or 'party' or
'power' or any one of a hundred others. Each has 'a past', as the
Victorians were wont to whisper darkly about people whose
probity was questionable and whose careers were chequered or
otherwise suspect. Precisely because these concepts have historically mutable meanings, they necessarily elude fixed or final
definition. 'Only that which has no history', Nietzsche remarked,
'can be defined.' Conceptual change does not come about by
definitional fiat, but through a complex and protracted process of
argumentation in which the proposing of new definitions typically
plays only a very small part. Such argumentation has a double
aspect, inasmuch as it is both *in* language and *about* language; it
must therefore draw upon the resources of a particular language –
rhetorical, metaphorical, allusive and otherwise – in attempting to
change that upon which it draws. Finally, and foremost, the
infelicitous present participle in my title is meant to suggest that
our political discourse is still being transformed, even as – and
because – we speak. The present work is intended in part as a
history of several earlier conceptual transformations and, in equal
part, as a contribution to and an intervention in other contemporary disputes.

This volume is connected with, and is in part an outgrowth of,
other projects with which I have been associated as editor and
contributor. *Idioms of Inquiry* (1987) examines the different idioms
or languages in which social-scientific inquiry has been, is being,
and might yet be conducted. *Political Innovation and Conceptual
Change* (1988), coedited with James Farr and Russell Hanson, is a
collaborative attempt to narrate a number of 'conceptual histories'. *Conceptual Change and the Constitution* (1988), coedited with J.
G. A. Pocock, attempts in a more site-specific way to trace the
particular conceptual changes wrought during the debate over the
writing and subsequent ratification of the United States Constitution.

In the course of writing this book I have accumulated many
obligations. The more formal of these are discharged in the
acknowledgements. Other, more personal debts are a pleasure to

acknowledge. The first is to the University of Minnesota, and to its Department of Political Science, both of which have been generous in providing leave time and research support. I am also grateful to Mary Ellen Otis for turning my ragged typescript into a readable manuscript. To my editor at Blackwell, Stephan Chambers, my special thanks for his initial interest, his continuing support and his exemplary patience. For taking the time to comment critically and helpfully upon earlier versions of individual chapters I thank Elias Berg, Joseph Carens, Stephen Elkin, Peter Euben, J. A. W. Gunn, Alan Gewirth, James Glass, Russell Hanson, Russell Hardin, Jeffrey Isaac, Lorentz Lyttkens, Donald Moon, Joe Oppenheimer, J. G. A. Pocock, Melvin Richter, Naomi Scheman, Quentin Skinner, Gerald Stourzh, William Thomas, James Boyd White, Garry Wills and – most of all – Mary Dietz and James Farr. To my fellow political theorists who are also my friends and climbing companions – Steve Leonard, Jim Farr, John Dryzek and Larry Biskowski – I owe a special debt that is difficult to articulate and impossible to repay. Their support – moral, intellectual and sometimes, at the end of a rope, physical – has given added depth of meaning to the concept of friendship. To my wife Judith and our sons, Jonathan and Stephen, I offer profuse apologies for being so uncommunicative as I sat in my study writing about the communicative constitution of human society.

Every author must wonder where the germ of a guiding idea originated. In his small gem of an autobiography R. G. Collingwood recalls that at the age of nine 'my first lesson in what I now regard as my own subject, the history of thought, was the discovery, in a friend's house a few miles away, of a battered seventeenth-century book, wanting cover and title-page, and full of strange doctrines about meteorology and geology and planetary motions.' In 'reading this old book' he became aware that the history of the natural sciences, no less than that of the human sciences, is the story of more or less continuous conceptual change. In my own less recondite case, the credit must go to my parents. For it was they who made me read the King James version of the Bible from which I must, as I now surmise, have first acquired an interest in the phenomenon of conceptual change. As a child I grappled, in a childish way to be sure, with the difficulties of understanding its archaic, ofttimes puzzling, and strangely beautiful language. Now, as an adult, I am grateful that I was not spared such difficulty or – worse yet – presented with the modernized texts to which some now expose the young in the misguided belief that they are thereby doing them a favour. Not wishing to do the reader any such specious favour, I have in most instances resisted the temptation to modernize spelling or otherwise to simplify the prose of writers long dead. All translations, unless otherwise stated, are my own.

Acknowledgements

Most of the chapters in the present work were, in an earlier incarnation, papers presented to audiences in the United States and abroad. Several have, in earlier and shorter versions, already appeared in print. Chapter 2 is a longer version of a conceptual history of 'party' in *Political Innovation and Conceptual Change*, edited by James Farr, Russell L. Hanson and myself, and published by Cambridge University Press in 1988. Chapter 3 is a considerably expanded version of my essay entitled 'A Republic – If You Can Keep It', in *Conceptual Change and the Constitution*, edited by J. G. A. Pocock and myself and published by the University Press of Kansas in 1988; it began as a paper presented at a conference on 'Conceptual Change and the Constitution of the United States', sponsored by the Conference for the Study of Political Thought and held at the Folger Shakespeare Library in Washington, D.C., in 1987. A slightly amended version of chapter 5 appeared in *NOMOS XXIX: Authority Revisited*, edited by J. Roland Pennock and John Chapman, and published by New York University Press in 1987. A shorter version of chapter 6 appears under the title 'Educative *vs.* Economic Theories of Democracy', in *Democracy, State, and Justice*, a Festschrift for the Swedish political theorist Elias Berg, edited by Diane Sainsbury, and published in Stockholm by Almqvist and Wiksell in 1988. Chapter 7 has a more chequered history. In an earlier and much abbreviated version it was my contribution to a roundtable discussion with Richard Rorty, Michael Walzer and Alan Gilbert, on theories of justice, sponsored by the American Political Science Association in 1984. A later version was presented to audiences at the universities of Chicago and Stockholm, and published in the Norwegian philosophical journal *Inquiry* 28 (September 1986), pp. 321–37. I am grateful to these publishers for granting me permission to reprint portions of these earlier efforts of mine.

1

Political Argument and Conceptual Change

1.1 INTRODUCTION: THE DON'S DILEMMA

This book is about conceptual change, the destruction and reconstruction of the world of words in which we live. In a sense my subject is as old as the biblical story of Babel. It is addressed also in Thucydides' account of the revolution at Corcyra during which 'words changed their meanings', in Hobbes' chilling description of the state of nature, and in Vico's account of the linguistic origins and evolution of the world of nations. But in addressing and appreciating the problematic phenomenon of conceptual change the writers of fiction have heretofore fared better than the philosophers. Indeed, a number of novelists, poets and playwrights have made moral and conceptual change a central and sometimes poignant theme.[1]

Four centuries ago Cervantes showed how the moral codes and concepts of one age are apt to be unintelligible in another. In the novel that bears his name as its title Don Quixote attempts, in vain and with comic results, to resurrect and to follow the code of knight errantry. He does so, however, in an age that thinks and speaks in an entirely different vocabulary. The bookish Don fails to recognize that the concepts constitutive of that code – honour, chivalry, courtly love and the concept of a quest – are out of place in his time and are meaningless to his contemporaries. Because Don Quixote not only speaks and thinks but attempts to act in accordance with this archaic code, his contemporaries see him as a comic character and his quest (we would say nowadays) as a 'quixotic' one.

Don Quixote is at once the archetype and exemplar of a figure who is still rather more in evidence in modern literature than in modern philosophy. He is, to cite but one example, the not-so-distant ancestor of Mark Twain's Connecticut Yankee. Indeed, *A Connecticut Yankee in King Arthur's Court* is *Don Quixote* in reverse. Finding himself technologically transported back into the very period in which Don Quixote fancied himself at home, Twain's hapless Yankee is utterly baffled by the customs, manners and moral language of his new/old contemporaries, and they by him. Although they all speak the same natural language, namely English, they speak different moral languages and live, accordingly, in different worlds.

The theme of conceptual change also pervades the novels of writers as different as Lermontov and Balzac, Jane Austen and Thomas Hardy, George Eliot and Henry James, Tolstoy and Turgenev, Dostoevsky and Dickens, Thomas Mann and Heinrich Böll, George Orwell and Milan Kundera. One need only think, for example, of Lermontov's charting of changes in the concept of heroism when he warns that his hero Pechorin is unheroic by the standards of an earlier age.[2] Or try to imagine what Balzac might mean by making a hero of Louis Lambert, the ambitious amateur philologist who in seeking to unlock all human mysteries uses the history of language as his key.[3] In telling the story of the lost honour of Katharina Blum was Böll suggesting that she had lost her honour or that the concept of honour itself has been lost in a dishonourable age? If the latter, we should not be surprised that her contemporaries, allies and tormentors alike, find her desperate defence of her honour to be utterly unintelligible.[4] Or consider what Mann is doing with the concept of virtue when he has Hans Castorp say of Settembrini, the last survivor and exemplar of an earlier age and culture, 'What a vocabulary! and he uses the word virtue just like that, without the slightest embarrassment. What do you make of that? I've never taken the word in my mouth as long as I've lived; in school, when the book said "virtus", we always just said "valour" or something like that. It certainly gives me a queer feeling inside, to hear him.'[5] This sense of distance, difference, and incomprehension in the face of conceptual change pervades much of modern literature.

No less pervasive is an awareness that our language serves both to link us with our past and to separate us from it. Language, as Orwell and Kundera remind us, is the medium of memory and shared experience. And although language changes, not all changes are for the better. Certain kinds of conceptual change expand and enrich our capacity for remembrance, thereby giving us a degree of critical conceptual distance from present practices and institutions. Others, however, diminish or even destroy this capacity, rendering speakers incapable of criticizing the increasingly closed world in which they live. Such, Orwell warned, would be the unique achievement of a completely closed totalitarian discourse. 'Don't you see that the whole aim of Newspeak is to narrow the range of thought?', says the bureaucrat in charge of compiling the Newspeak dictionary. 'In the end we shall make thoughtcrime literally impossible, because there will be no words in which to express it. Every concept . . . will be expressed by exactly one word, with its meaning rigidly defined and all its subsidiary meanings rubbed out and forgotten.'[6] To remember our language as it once was may enable us to gain a degree of critical purchase on the present. By the same token, of course, our language serves to distance us from the past by enabling us to appreciate the vast differences between past peoples' conceptually constituted practices and our own. To encounter and attempt to understand them in all their strangeness requires the stretching of our own concepts and categories. If philosophy begins in wonder, conceptual history gives us something to wonder about in the first place.

In the chapters that follow I shall suggest, albeit more by example than by argument, that one of the tasks of the conceptual historian is to address this recurring sense of astonishment and incomprehension, not to make it any less astonishing but to make it more comprehensible and, in doing so, to stretch the linguistic limits of present-day political discourse.

1.2 THE LINGUISTIC HALF-TURN

It has long been a truism that our being moral and political creatures presupposes a shared capacity for communication. We therefore live, not as a luxury but as a logical (indeed ontological) necessity, in a world of words.[7] It is by virtue of being communicating creatures that we are tied together not by physical bonds but by the words which are our bonds. Language is, in Locke's

phrase, 'the great bond and common tye of society'.[8] Who and
what we are, how we arrange and classify and think about our
world – and how we act in it – is deeply delimited by the
conceptual, argumentative and rhetorical resources of our language. The limits of my moral and political language, we might
say, mark the limits of my moral and political world. More often
than not, these linguistically imposed limits are invisible to
speakers, serving as something like absolute presuppositions of
intelligible discourse.[9] Sometimes, however, these limits will be
perceived as limitations and our language a prison house from
which one longs in vain to escape, rather than a base from which
to work within and upon the world.[10] And at other times our
common world comes apart at the seams as the concepts constituting our public discourse change their meanings. Over time and
under the pressure of political events, the 'great bond and
common tye' becomes frayed or untied as the concepts composing
it lose old meanings and acquire new ones or, failing that,
disappear altogether. 'Concepts, like individuals,' wrote Kierkegaard, 'have their histories, and are just as incapable of withstanding the ravages of time as are individuals.'[11]

  Although the history of the human species is the story of almost
continuous conceptual change, the political and philosophical
import of this fact has too often been ignored or played down by
modern philosophers. There are of course a number of notable
exceptions. Hegel, Kierkegaard and Nietzsche had a lively appreciation of the historicity and mutability of our moral and political
concepts. And in our century Heidegger, R. G. Collingwood,
Hannah Arendt and Alasdair MacIntyre have been among the
brilliant exceptions to the dismal rule that modern philosophers,
particularly of the Anglo-American 'analytical' variety, have
tended to treat moral and political concepts as though they had no
history, or as though their having a history was a matter of little or
no philosophical interest or importance.

  This neglect seems at first sight surprising, considering that
twentieth-century philosophy has supposedly taken a 'linguistic
turn'.[12] This does not, of course, mean that modern philosophers
are interested in language and their forbears were not, for language has been a perennial source of fascination for philosophers
from Plato onward. The linguistic turn really began with the

realization – reached by thinkers as different as Dewey and Heidegger, Wittgenstein and Austin – that our language does not mirror an independently existing world but is instead partly constitutive of it. Words have meaning by virtue of what speakers do with them, what actions or 'speech acts' they perform with them, whether it be the action of referring, describing, explaining, exhorting, appraising, promising or any of a hundred other actions. None of these is privileged, much less paradigmatic of what meaning (really) is, or should be. Nor does any particular set of linguistic practices, e.g. scientific discourse, set a standard of meaningfulness that all 'inferior' discourses (e.g., moral or aesthetic discourse) should seek to emulate. In these respects the linguistic turn represented a giant step forward.

In other respects, however, it appears that the linguistic turn amounted at mid-century to a half-turn. In emphasizing the minute analysis and clarification of 'the' meaning and use of particular concepts, 'linguistic' or 'ordinary language' philosophy or 'conceptual analysis' as practised in Britain and the United States tended to focus upon the language of one age and culture, namely our own. This narrowing not only blinded philosophers to the fact that meaning and usage change from one age and generation to the next but it also led them to believe their enterprise to be a politically neutral one of clarifying and analysing what 'we' say, as though 'we' were a single speaking subject. In thus assuming that there is a unified 'we', ordinary language philosophy largely ignored the twin issues of political conflict and conceptual change.[13]

This is not to say that the potential for such a focus was utterly lacking in 'linguistic' philosophy, only that the potential was not at first realized. The cases of Wittgenstein and J. L. Austin – two otherwise very different founders of what came to be called ordinary language philosophy – are instructive in this regard. Both paid closer attention to the history of language and conceptual change than did most of the philosophers who followed, as they thought, in their masters' footsteps. Wittgenstein, like his forebears Karl Kraus and Heinrich Hertz, had an acute appreciation of the historical variability and mutability of linguistic meaning. Every concept is the repository of earlier associations and uses. As previous meanings recede into the background, new ones take their place. By way of illustration Wittgenstein invites us to consider 'The concept of a "Festivity". We connect it with merrymaking; in another age it may have been connected with fear and dread. What we call "wit" and "humour" doubtless did not exist in other ages. And both are constantly changing.'[14]

Austin makes a similar point, albeit in a rather different way. Our concepts have histories, he says, and come to us with 'trailing clouds of etymology'.[15] These are the traces left by earlier speakers who have worked and reworked our language, extending its range and pushing its limits by drawing new distinctions, invoking new metaphors and minting new terms. The language we now speak is the result of the most long-lived and successful of those earlier attempts at conceptual revision; it 'embodies all the distinctions men have found worth drawing, and connexions they have found worth marking, in the lifetimes of many generations.'[16] Austin was widely read – or rather, I suspect, misread – as an advocate of conceptual clarification *simpliciter*, and a hidebound conservative who held that our language is already well-nigh perfect and in no need of further revision. If so, he (or at any rate those who read him in this light) makes the same mistake that Marx ascribed to the political economists of his day – the mistake, that is, of assuming that there once was history, but there is no longer any.[17]

Happily, however, there is now every indication that the linguistic turn is being completed. A static and ahistorical view is at last giving way amongst Anglo-American philosophers to a more historical approach to the study of language and in particular the languages of political theory.[18] There is now a noticeable move away from the static and ahistorical enterprise of 'conceptual analysis' to a more dynamic and historically oriented emphasis on conceptual change and the construction of conceptual histories.[19] The present study is offered as a contribution to an emerging genre that I call critical conceptual history, the key features of which will be described below and illustrated in the chapters that follow.

1.3   POLITICAL DISCOURSE AND ITS DISCONTENTS

Since the present work deals with political discourses and the changing meaning of the concepts comprising them, I should say something about the kind of discourse this is and – no less important – is not. Although my approach in some respects resembles that of a number of 'post-modern' deconstructionists or discourse theorists, the resemblance is on the whole a fairly superficial one. At an abstract level we share an interest in language and the ways in which discourses can be said to both enable and constrain their speakers. But if we share several thematic affinities, we differ in a number of important ways.

Firstly, I do not believe that discourses are more or less autonomous entities for which speakers or authors are merely mouthpieces.[20] Speakers are under certain conditions capable of intentionally reconstituting their discourses. I am interested in identifying those intentions and those conditions as they appeared in particular political situations and at specific historical sites. Thus, *pace* some contemporary discourse theorists, one cannot separate practical action from intention. Diane Macdonell, for one, draws a false dichotomy in stressing

> how important practical action, rather than intention is, even in speech or writing. No author and no reader changes the meanings of words. The struggle of discourses changes their meanings, and so the combination in which we put words together matters, and the order of propositions matters: through these, whatever our intentions, words take on meaning.[21]

The claim that intentions are, or conceivably could be, irrelevant to the analysis of political actions – which are preeminently, indeed paradigmatically, publicly performed linguistic actions – is incoherent. For the very identification of a piece of behaviour as a practical action of a particular sort requires that one be able to identify the intention of the agent performing it. Thus, for example, if someone asks what X is doing in repeatedly running round a race-track, the answer might be that 'X is practising for next week's foot-race'. This is a redescription of X's behaviour in terms of X's intentions and beliefs: X intends to win (or at any rate to do as well as possible) and believes that practising beforehand is the best way of fulfilling that intention. Precisely the same point applies to linguistic actions, whether spoken or written. An utterance – for example, 'The ice is very thin over there' – can, depending on the speaker's intention, be a remark, a description, or a warning.[22]

Now it might be objected, and with some justice, that intentional actions often produce unintended consequences. And certainly this is, as we shall see, true of linguistic actions as well: intentional conceptual innovations often yield consequences that were unforeseen, indeed unforeseeable, by the agents who brought them about. But it does not follow from this that intentions can be ignored or dismissed as irrelevant or unimportant. Quite the contrary. For in order to identify an outcome as an unintended consequence one must first know what the agent's (or agents') intention was and then be able to ascertain that the consequence in question was not among those intended by that agent. This rather minor logical commonplace undermines a good many grandiose claims about the irrelevance of intentions to the understanding of human actions and practices.

Because intentions are indispensable in identifying what (kind of) action is being performed by a speaker or writer, one cannot hope to sustain the claim that discourses are self-contained entities that can be studied and understood without reference to human agency, as though the order of words (sic) was all that mattered. While it is true that in ideological and political struggles words can, as Althusser writes, be 'weapons, explosives or tranquilisers and poisons', it does not follow that 'the whole class struggle may be summed up in the struggle for one word against another word. Certain words struggle amongst themselves as enemies.'[23] The way 'in which we put words together' doubtless counts for quite a lot; but to know that and nothing else is not in itself very illuminating. For we also need to know by whom they are put together, in what situation, with what intention(s) and with what effect(s). Otherwise we are left with an utterance whose 'meaning' can be discerned solely by attending to the ordering of the words, phrases and/or propositions of which it is composed. Political utterances, at least, are not 'texts' of that sort.

This in turn points to a further difference between contemporary discourse theory and the approach adopted in the present study. The critical conceptual historian is, for the reasons given in (1.3) less interested in words than in *concepts*, in the kind of actions that these concepts make it possible for agents to perform, and in political arguments as linguistic performances which are intended to preserve, extend, and/or change the concepts constitutive of political discourse. This is not to say, of course, that these intentions are always fulfilled or that these linguistic actions do not produce unintended results. I mean merely to suggest that the ordering of words is apt to be of less interest and importance to the critical conceptual historian than is the attempt by political agents (some of the more innovative of whom we recognize with the honorific title of theorist) to marshal arguments in defence or in defiance of attempts at conceptual-cum-political innovation. My other differences with what passes for discourse theory or discourse analysis will become evident in due course.

The present study shares a somewhat closer affinity with the modern German genre known as *Begriffsgeschichte* or 'conceptual history'. As Reinhart Koselleck, arguably the leading defender and practitioner of this new field, puts it, 'Without common concepts there is no society, and above all, no political field of action.'[24] But which concepts are to be the common coin of discourse becomes, at crucial historical junctures, a veritable field of battle. 'The struggle over the "correct" concepts,' says Koselleck, 'becomes socially and politically explosive.'[25] The conceptual historian attempts to map the minefield, as it were, by examining the various historical turning-points or watersheds in the history of the concepts constituting modern political discourse. This involves not only noting when and for what purposes new and now-familiar words were coined – ideology, industrialism, liberalism, conservatism, socialism and altruism, amongst many others – but tracing the changes in the meaning of older terms such as 'constitution' and 'revolution'. This is just the task outlined and given theoretical justification by Koselleck and undertaken in painstaking detail by the contributors to the massive and still unfinished *Geschichtliche Grundbegriffe* and the *Handbuch politische-sozialer Grundbegriffe in Frankreich 1680–1820*.[26]

In these and other works, German conceptual historians are attempting to test a number of hypotheses. One is that the eighteenth century was a *Sattelzeit*, a period of unprecedented conceptual shifts. Another is that these shifts involved not only the minting of new terms and the reminting of older ones, but that they point to an increased tendency toward ideological abstractions. Thus the late eighteenth and early nineteenth centuries saw the rise of the various 'isms' – socialism, communism, industrialism, etc. – which, by supplying speakers with a new means of locating themselves in social and political space, actually reconstituted that very space. Political conflict accordingly became more overtly ideological, more concerned with questions of principle (or even first principles) than was previously the case. Concepts that had heretofore had concrete class and geographic referents became free-floating abstractions about which one could speak in an ostensibly universal voice. 'Rights', for example, ceased to be the rights of Englishmen and other national or legal groups, becoming instead 'the rights of man' or, as we are apt to say nowadays, 'human rights'. The studies undertaken by Koselleck and his colleagues have, on the whole, tended to confirm these conjectures.

Although I find much to admire in the work of the German conceptual historians, I have not attempted to duplicate it. We have, if I may put it this way, rather different agendas. Firstly, they have so far concentrated their considerable learning in mapping conceptual changes in earlier German and French political and philosophical discourse. My interests here, by contrast, centre almost exclusively on Anglophone political discourse and its antecedents. Secondly, they have attempted to be encyclopaedic in range and scope. My ambitions being altogether more modest, I have been highly selective in my choice of concepts. Even so, our conjectures about conceptual change do occasionally overlap and complement one another. And in a very limited way several portions of the present study amount, in effect, to a comparative test of several of their hypotheses. Thus, for example, my inquiries in chapters 2 and 3 suggest that the eighteenth century was indeed a *Sattelzeit* or period of profound and unprecedented conceptual transformation, at least as regards the concepts of party and republic.

But while the German conceptual historians tend to study the history of the past, I am also inclined to view the present as history. As significant as earlier, and especially eighteenth-century, shifts were, conceptual change is not a phenomenon that is safely confined to the past but is continuing even as, and because, we speak. My own view, which may be more a suspicion than a testable hypothesis, is that we are living through and participating in a period of profound, exhilarating, and in some ways deeply disturbing conceptual shifts. I have attempted throughout the present inquiry to give voice and substance to this suspicion.

Having said how my discourse differs from others', I need now to clarify what I mean by several of the concepts constituting it. In referring to this or that 'language' I do not mean the natural languages analysed by linguistics – Attic Greek, for example, or modern English – but allude to what one might as a first cut call a moral or political language. A language of this sort includes those 'shared conceptions of the world, shared manners and values, shared resources and expectations and procedures for speech and thought' through which 'communities are in fact defined and constituted.㉗ This is immediately complicated, however, by a second consideration. A community's language is not a seamless web or a single structurally unified whole but consists instead of a series of sub-languages or idioms which I call discourses.

A discourse, one might say, is the sub-language spoken in and constitutive of a particular discipline, domain, sphere or sub-community.[28] Examples of such sub-languages might include the discourse of economics, of the law, of medicine, of computer programming, and a score of other disciplines or domains. Paraphrasing Heidegger, we might say that we not only have these discourses but they also have us.[29] This of course runs counter to the Humpty Dumpty view that a speaker is the master of his or her language and may do with it whatever he or she pleases. In reality, of course, one does not step so easily out of one's language or master one's metaphors. 'For we all of us, grave or light,' said George Eliot, 'get our thoughts entangled in metaphors and act fatally on the strength of them.'[30] Some contemporary discourse theorists put the point in a wholly exaggerated way when they say that discourses create their speakers. And yet there is in this, as in any caricature, a grain of truth. It is true, for example, that one becomes, and is recognized as, an economist by virtue of thinking as economists think and speaking as economists speak. An economist or a physician has not only mastered a subject; that subject has, in a sense, mastered him or her. And as we speak, so we are.

Not only, then, are our communities communicatively formed and maintained, but so are our very characters. 'In important ways,' says James Boyd White, 'we become the language we

cf Plato

use.'[31] To transform those sub-languages or specialized discourses is perforce to transform ourselves. And we do change our language, whether by design or inadvertence. To paraphrase what Marx says about making history, we do remake our language, but we do not transform it just as we please; we alter our concepts under circumstances directly encountered, given, and inherited from the past.[32] Our language is also eternally pregnant with the possibility of change. Past and future are present in our language and the specialized discourses out of which it is compounded.

But what of political discourse? Is it merely one discourse amongst many, or does it have distinguishing features of its own? Here matters become much more complicated. One of the key features of political discourse is to be found in its central tension, which may be described in the following way. Political discourse is, or at any rate purports to be, a bridging language, a supra-discourse spanning and connecting the several sub-languages; it is the language that we supposedly share in our common capacity as citizens, not as speakers of specialized sub-languages. But, at the same time, this linguistic-political ideal is undermined in two ways.

First, political discourse borrows from and draws upon more specialized discourses; it is compounded, as it were, out of lesser languages. When the concepts and metaphors constituting the discourse of economics, for example – or of computer programming or law or religion or medicine or any other discipline – enter the field of political meanings they alter the shape and structure of that field by altering its speakers' terms of discourse. This process of transgressing, of leaking across discursive boundaries, is, as we shall see, a prime source of conceptual change.

Second, political discourse characteristically consists of concepts whose meanings are not always agreed upon but are often heatedly contested by citizen-speakers. The possibility of communicative breakdown is an ever-present feature, if not indeed a defining characteristic, of political discourse. As de Jouvenel observes:

> The elementary political process is the action of mind upon mind through speech. Communication by speech completely depends upon the existence in the memories of both parties of a common stock of words to which they attach much the same meanings. . . .

> Even as people belong to the same culture by the use of the same language, so they belong to the same society by the understanding of the same moral language. As this common moral language extends, so does society; as it breaks up, so does society.[33]

Passing this observation through a finer (and less 'mentalistic') mesh one should add that the elementary political process is the action of speaker upon speaker about matters of public or common concern. But of course what is and is not 'public' – and therefore presumably political – is itself a subject of political dispute and argument. Disagreements about the scope and domain of 'the political' are themselves constitutive features of political discourse.

In aim and aspiration, then, political discourse anticipates agreement and consensus even as its speakers disagree amongst themselves.[34] This discursive ideal is as old as Socratic dialogue and as recent as Habermas' ideal speech situation. That this ideal remains unrealized in practice has been taken by some political philosophers to be a defect of political discourse or at any rate a flaw attributable to the speakers engaged in it. From this they conclude that political discourse needs reforming or at any rate that certain sorts of speakers need chastening, either by learning to speak this new language or by being silenced.[35] One of the aims of the present study is to suggest that the hope of ending such disputes and of arresting or even reversing conceptual change is misdirected, inasmuch as it rests upon a misunderstanding of the structure and point of political discourse. In focusing exclusively upon the anticipation of consensus, one grasps only one of the poles of political life. By grasping the pole of anticipated consensus and playing down conceptual conflict one denatures political life and the language that makes that life both possible and necessary. Disagreement, conceptual contestation, the omnipresent threat of communicative breakdown, and the possibility of conceptual change are, as it were, built into the very structure of political discourse.

Several contemporary political philosophers have attempted to articulate and analyse this feature of political discourse by suggesting that moral and political concepts are 'essentially contested'. A concept is essentially contested if it has no single definition or criterion of application upon which all competent speakers can agree.[36] For reasons that will, I hope, become clear in the course of our inquiries, I do not believe that the thesis of essential contestability takes us very far in any analytically useful direction. For to claim that a particular concept is essentially contested is to take an ahistorical view of the character and function of political concepts. Not all concepts have been, or could be, contested at all times. Conceptual contestation remains a permanent possibility even though it is, in practice, actualized only intermittently.) The now-ubiquitous disputes about the meaning of 'democracy', for instance, are of relatively recent vintage, while the once-heated arguments about 'republic' have cooled considerably since the late eighteenth century. We might say, then, that the essential contestability thesis holds true not as a thesis about individual concepts but as a valid generalization about political language as a species of discourse. The language of political discourse is essentially contestable, but the concepts comprising any political language are contingently contestable.[37] Which concepts are believed to be worth disputing and revising is more often a political than a philosophical matter. In some situations it becomes important for political agents to take issue with their opponents' and/or audience's understanding of 'party' or 'authority' or 'democracy'. Out of these challenges, or some of them anyway, come the conceptual changes that comprise the subject-matter of critical conceptual history.

1.4   CRITICAL CONCEPTUAL HISTORIES

The task of the critical conceptual historian is to chart changes in the concepts constituting the discourses of political agents living and dead. The kinds of questions to be asked about the transformation of political discourses will typically include the following. How might one identify or describe these discourses and the specific changes made in them? Which concept(s), in particular, had their meanings altered? How and why did these changes come about? Who brought them about, and what rhetorical strategies did they use? And, not least, what difference did (or does) it make?

The first of these questions will characteristically, though not always, be answered by pointing to a particular political tradition or, if one prefers, a tradition of discourse.[41] Examples of such traditions might include republicanism, liberalism and Marxism, amongst many others. And these can in turn be further divided into sub-traditions such as classical and Renaissance republicanism, Soviet Marxism, Manchester liberalism, and the like.

Political discourses, and the concepts that constitute them, have histories that can be narratively reconstructed in any number of ways. Such histories would show where these discourses functioned and how they changed. These changes may, moreover, be traced to the problems perceived by particular (classes of) historical agents in particular political situations. Conceptual changes are brought about by political agents occupying specific sites and working under the identifiable linguistic constraints of a particular tradition as it exists at a particular time. The vocabularies within and upon which these agents work are to some degree flexible although not infinitely malleable. They can to some extent transform their language; but it also subtly transforms them, helping to make them the kinds of creatures they are. The ways in which speakers shape and are in turn shaped by their language are the subject-matter of critical conceptual history.

An understandably impatient critic might at this point raise two questions. Why speak of concepts instead of words, of conceptual change rather than linguistic change, and of conceptual history rather than linguistic history?[39] And what, after all, is critical about critical conceptual histories?

The first question is easily answered. A political vocabulary consists not simply of words but of concepts. To have a word for X is to be in possession of the concept of X. Yet one may possess a concept without having a word to express it. It is, for instance, clear that Milton knew about, and valued, 'originality', otherwise he would not have thought it important to try to do 'things unattempted yet in prose or rhyme'. But although Milton quite clearly possessed the *concept* of originality, he had no word with which to express it, for 'originality' did not enter the English language until a century after his death.[40] Much the same is true of moral and political concepts. For example, the concept of rights long predated the word.[41] Moreover, the same word can, in different periods, stand for quite different concepts. The 'rights' of Englishmen, for example, were quite unlike the 'rights' of man or the 'human rights' defended or violated by modern regimes. Nor did 'the state', or at any rate *lo stato*, mean for Machiavelli what it means for us.[42] Nor did 'revolution' mean for Locke and his contemporaries what it means for us. They understood a revolution to be a coming full circle, a restoration of some earlier uncorrupted condition; we understand it to be the collective overthrow of an old regime and the creation of an entirely new one.[43] 'Ideology' was originally, in the eighteenth century, the systematic scientific study of the origins of ideas; now it refers to a more or less tightly constrained set of political ideas and ideals.[44] A 'patriot' – nowadays an uncritical supporter of his country's government – was once one who dared to be an opponent and critic of his government.[45] These and many other examples suggest that words do not change, but concepts and meanings do. In an important sense, then, words do not have histories but concepts do. The history of *political* concepts (or more precisely, concepts used in political discourse) cannot, however, be narrated apart from the political conflicts in which they figure. What distinguishes critical conceptual history from philology or etymology is its attention to the *arguments* in which concepts appear and are used to perform particular kinds of actions at particular times and at particular political sites. Histories of political concepts are, in short, histories of political arguments and the conceptual contests and disputes to which they give rise.

A second and more complicated question still remains to be answered: What, exactly, is critical about 'critical conceptual histories'? Several answers can be given. The first is that these are histories written with a critical intention of showing that conceptual change is not only possible but is virtually a defining feature of political discourse. Second, such histories will, if successful, show how particular political agents became aware of the subtle and heretofore unrecognized ways in which their discourses had transformed them (and their contemporaries) before setting about the task of transforming political discourse. Third, a critical conceptual history shows how these agents actually transformed the discourse of their day. This requires that the historian identify the processes and mechanisms by means of which specific agents brought about particular changes. These include, preeminently, the discovery, exposure and criticism of ostensible contradictions

rhetorical analysis

and incoherencies in dominant discourses, and the arguments and rhetorical stratagems employed for that critical purpose and for the more positive purpose of constructing an alternative discourse.[46] Far from being the domain of detached armchair philosophers, this kind of critical activity affects the ways in which political agents themselves think and act. What Alasdair MacIntyre says of the role of criticism in changing moral concepts is no less true of its role in changing political ones:

> philosophical inquiry itself plays a part in changing moral concepts. It is not that we have first a staightforward history of moral concepts and then a separate and secondary history of philosophical comment. For to analyze a concept philosophically may often be to assist in its transformation by suggesting that it needs revision, or that it is discredited in some way. Philosophy leaves everything as it is – except concepts. And since to possess a concept involves behaving or being able to behave in certain ways in certain circumstances, to alter concepts, whether by modifying existing concepts or by making new concepts available or by destroying old ones, is to alter behaviour. A history which takes this point seriously, which is concerned with the role of philosophy in relation to actual conduct, cannot be philosophically neutral.[47]

Nor, by the same token, can conceptual histories be politically neutral. This is not to say that they are necessarily partisan in any narrow sense, but rather that they alert their audience to the ways in which and the means by which their communicatively constituted world has transformed them and how they in their turn may yet transform it.

1.5   PLAN OF THE PRESENT WORK

Five interrelated conjectures connect the following chapters. The first is that politics, understood as a species of argumentation, is a conceptually constituted activity. Secondly, the concepts constituting political arguments, although not essentially contestable, are nevertheless contingently contestable and have historically mutable meanings. Thirdly, insofar as political-cum-theoretical arguments are not only necessarily stated in language but are in part about language, they serve the important function of making agents and audiences aware of the ways in which a particular political discourse can constrain or empower them. Fourthly, as political arguments are ever more frequently recast as technical or scientific ones conducted by and for experts, the discourses of the several social sciences have become a prime source of conceptual mutation. And finally, the construction of conceptual histories like these, far from being a politically neutral enterprise, can reopen and reinvigorate the possibilities of political argument by creating a critical distance between citizen-speakers and the increasingly closed conceptual universe that they inhabit. Each of the following chapters traces and attempts to account for critical changes in the meanings of a number of concepts constitutive of political discourse.

The concepts whose histories (or portions thereof) I have chosen to examine do not, of course, constitute an exhaustive list. To reconstruct and narrate the histories of all political concepts would be an impossibly tall order for any individual to fill. As Balzac's Louis Lambert recognized with dismay, more than a lifetime of learning would be required for one to tell the story of a single concept, much less the whole array of the concepts constituting political discourses past and present. I have had, therefore, to be highly selective. While my choice of concepts has doubtless been dictated in part by personal, and perhaps even idiosyncratic, interests, greater weight has been given to two other considerations.

I have tried, first of all, to narrate the histories, or more often episodes therein, of concepts that have been overlooked or neglected by others. The history of the concept of liberty, for example, forms no part of my present inquiries, not because it is unimportant – quite the contrary – but because its history has been better narrated by others.[48] I prefer to focus instead on the obvious, the workaday and the commonplace. That is why my inquiries begin with 'party', a concept so commonplace that its history has yet to be written. I have also tried to select concepts that exhibit politically and/or historically problematic features. What was at issue in the controversy over the meaning of 'republic' during the American founding? In what ways has the meaning of 'power' changed and in what ways is it changing even now? Why has the concept of authority been so problematic for modern political thinkers, and what help, if any, have the social sciences supplied in rendering it less so? What happens to 'democracy' when the concept is recast in the idiom of economics, and what might we learn from the attempt? Why does 'justice' become peculiarly problematic when we try to talk about justice between generations? These are among the questions that have dictated my choice of concepts and the order of the chapters. I begin by showing how agents in earlier times constructed their transformative arguments as a prelude to showing how we might yet construct ours. Thus the order of the present discourse proceeds from the longer and ostensibly detached and 'historical' earlier chapters to the more contemporary interventions attempted in the later ones. The present work is intended, in other words, not only to be about the transformation of political discourse but to form a series of exercises in and contributions to such transformation. Chapters 2 and 3 deal with past conceptual controversies, chapter 4 with a continuing one, and chapters 5, 6 and 7 are attempts to intervene in ongoing disputes. Chapter 4 therefore marks a kind of watershed or pivot in the organization of this book and also between two ways of doing critical conceptual history.

In chapter 2 I reconstruct the prehistory of the distinctly modern concept of 'party'. By tracing the submerged metaphors in whose terms the concepts of 'faction' and 'sect' were traditionally understood, we can see how the modern concept of the political party – understood as an organized, loyal and legitimate opposition – became a possibility for the first time only in the eighteenth century. So long as the polity was conceived in organic or bodily terms – as a 'body politic' – the idea of a legitimate opposition party was well-nigh incoherent. But when in the eighteenth century politics came to be understood in contractual terms, polities were at last acknowledged to have a place for, and indeed to need, 'parties'.

In chapter 3 I reconstruct a portion of the history of 'republic', a concept that loomed large in early American political discourse. A good deal of controversy has centred of late on what the American Founders meant by 'republic'. Was it that of Machiavelli and the Florentine republican tradition, as adopted and amended by James Harrington and the eighteenth-century English Commonwealthmen? Or did the concept undergo a radical change of meaning in revolutionary America? I argue that the debates over the ratification and adoption of the Constitution revolved to a very large degree around the meaning of the term 'republic', and allied notions like 'corruption' and 'virtue'. In other words, 'republic' was at that time a contested concept whose meaning rival arguments were meant to reveal and fix. By reconstructing the relevant portions of the political arguments between Federalists and Antifederalists we can cast new light on ongoing historiographical and hermeneutical controversies.

Chapter 4 traces the history of 'power', showing how its meaning changed in the seventeeth century and is changing even now. Tracing its history from Hobbes, Locke and Hume through Weber and twentieth-century social scientists, I show that 'power' was until very recently understood as the political equivalent of efficient causation. This understanding of power has lately come under attack from various quarters. By looking closely at the otherwise very different analyses provided by Hannah Arendt, Jürgen Habermas, Michel Foucault, and certain metascientific 'realists', I attempt to show how this conception of power is being displaced, and perchance replaced, by an alternative account which views power as a constitutive feature of social life.

Chapter 5 begins by considering the claim that the concept of authority has all but disappeared from the modern world, in part because the paradigms of post-Enlightenment political and religious thought have no place for it. I then examine two recent social-scientific attempts to reconstruct 'authority'. According to the 'emotivist' model, authority is extensionally equivalent to power, influence, coercion, or anything else that 'makes people obey'. Thus one's acknowledgment of someone as an authority or of a policy or command as authoritative is merely a matter of feeling for which no rational grounds can be given. According to the 'epistemocratic' model's reconstruction, authority is what experts possess by virtue of their superior scientific or technical knowledge. Nineteenth-century Positivists such as Saint-Simon and Comte, and the present-day prophets of a coming post-industrial 'knowledge society', are alike in reconstructing authority according to the requirements of the epistemocratic model. Chapter 5 concludes with a critique of these attempts at conceptual reconstruction.

In chapter 6 I examine two quite different ways of constituting democratic discourse. The 'educative' view holds that democracy requires a special sort of citizen, namely one who has been educated to adopt the perspective of people other than himself; to advance, and to listen to, arguments about the common weal or public good; and to have acquired an ability to deliberate about and to judge between competing perspectives and arguments. The point of democratic participation is to learn how to be a citizen of this sort. The 'economic' view, by contrast, holds that the requirements of the educative theory are unrealistic, not to say irrelevant and unnecessary. All that is required, according to this alternative perspective, is to know about and to act upon one's own preferences or interests, leaving to impersonal 'market' processes the task of aggregating these preferences. The latter view has been championed by some social scientists, and by economists and rational-choice theorists in particular. After exploring the contradictions and civic costs resulting from reconstructing democratic discourse along 'economic' lines, I conclude by suggesting that the economic approach is nevertheless not without value.

Finally, in chapter 7 I argue that the phenomenon of conceptual change has heretofore unnoticed implications for the ways in which we think about, and act toward, future generations. Our moral intuitions tell us that all people, including our distant descendants, ought to be treated justly. But if past history serves as any guide, their understanding of what constitutes or counts as 'justice' is likely to be very different from ours. Thus, for example, Plato, Aristotle and their contemporaries were in no position, logically speaking, to act justly toward us, because their concept of 'justice' is not ours. This of course raises the spectre of relativism in its most radical – and presumably most pernicious – form, namely a thoroughgoing nihilism that bids us take no account of the welfare of future generations. I conclude by suggesting that relativistic arguments need not yield the sorts of nihilistic conclusions that they are often said to produce. The upshot of my argument, if successful, is to force us to confront the possibility that we are treating our distant descendants in ways that are unjust, even by our lights.

2

The Prehistory of Party

2.1 INTRODUCTION

Surely no institution is a more ubiquitous feature of the modern
political landscape than the political party. Every modern system,
indeed, has at least one. So common is the concept of party that
we nowadays regularly classify systems and regimes according to
the number and kinds of parties they have. Yet it was not always
so. 'Party' – the concept if not the word – is a relatively recent
addition to the vocabulary of politics. Perhaps because it is widely
believed to be an institution instead of a concept, 'party' has been
largely ignored by historians of ideas. As J. A. W. Gunn observes,
'Liberty, justice and equality – not to mention representation, the
majority, and the separation of powers – all have their intellectual
histories; but party seems to be an institution singularly bereft of
intellectual parentage.'[1] To trace its ancestry would be to tell an
important and heretofore largely missing part of the story of
political theory and practice in the West.[2] A comprehensive
history of 'party' being well beyond the bounds of the present
chapter, I shall merely sketch some of the more noteworthy
contours of the concept's prehistory, focusing in particular upon
the changing imagery and distinctions that preceded its emergence
in Anglophone political theory and practice in the late seventeenth
and eighteenth centuries. My prehistory of 'party' therefore ends
just where one would expect a proper conceptual history to begin,
with the recognizably modern conception of party as a principal
and loyal opposition.

My archaeological excavation of a series of long-abandoned
political sites proceeds in the following way. After briefly outlin-
ing the approach against which I shall be arguing, I go on to show
that the modern idea of a loyal opposition party emerged haltingly

and haphazardly from a long prehistory in which an older political vocabulary was gradually transformed. This transformation in its turn permitted a series of shifts in political perceptions. These stemmed not only from arguments about what is legitimate and permissible but from a changing stock of political metaphors, among which the shift from organic or bodily imagery to contractual notions proves to be particularly important. Finally, I conclude by examining the changing place of 'party' in late eighteenth-century American political discourse.

[margin note: Organic vs. contractual.]

2.2   A FALSE START

One way of writing the history of 'party' would be to take the ahistorical tack of suggesting that parties have always existed even though they were until quite recently regarded as an illegitimate species of political organization. The history of 'party' would then become, not the story of conceptual-cum-political change and innovation, but an account of changing attitudes toward something that has always existed. This is the view advanced, for example, by Harvey Mansfield, Jr., who holds that 'Parties are universal, but party government is the result of the recent discovery that parties can be respectable. Because the reason for partisanship is so simple and compelling, the respectability, not the existence, of party is the distinguishing mark of party government.'[3] Two things are presupposed in such an account. The first is the nominalist view that political concepts – in this case 'party' – have meanings merely by virtue of being names or labels attached by convention to independently existing phenomena. The second supposition is that an emotivist theory of meaning offers an adequate account of the way in which moral and political terms actually function in discourse. According to the emotivist view, what matters for purposes of political analysis and historical understanding are not names but the changing feelings or attitudes of political agents toward the thing named. Thus the difference denoted by calling some grouping a 'party', instead of, say, a 'sect' or a 'faction', is a psychological difference of feeling or attitude. Simply stated, a party is a faction of which one approves, and a faction a party of which one disapproves. The history of party is

[margin note: affective, not cognitive]

therefore a nominalist story about changing labels and a psychological story about changing attitudes toward the phenomenon to
which these labels have been attached.

In the case of 'party', however, the foregoing account gets
matters exactly backward. Far from functioning as labels attached
to independently existing phenomena, as suggested by the nominalist theory of meaning, political concepts are themselves partially *constitutive* of those phenomena. And, contrary to the
emotivist theory, feelings and attitudes are more the products than
the sources of our conceptually constituted world. Thus, for
example, we don't call an action 'unjust' because we disapprove of
it; rather, we disapprove of it because we have reason for believing
it to *be* unjust. And we do not designate an organization as a
political party because we approve of it (or, conversely, as a
faction because we disapprove of it); rather, we mean to mark an
actually existing, politically pertinent – and distinctly non-
psychological – difference between parties and factions.

To see how this process might work let us imagine an eminently rational political agent who is eager to exhibit his behaviour
as legitimate.[4] Let us further imagine that he wishes to act in some
new or otherwise untoward way. If he is to satisfy both *desiderata*
he must be able to describe the latter in terms recognizable within
the limits set (however loosely) by the former. It then follows that
linguistic form constrains political content; linguistic limitations
limit political possibilities. As a speaker or writer who wishes to
communicate with others our ideally rational agent cannot, like
Humpty Dumpty, make words mean whatever he wants them to
mean. And this, for a *political* agent, is a consideration of
surpassing importance. For, *qua* political agent, he necessarily
wishes not only to communicate but if possible to persuade others
to follow his new route. Hence he needs to be able to call upon an
already existing stock of concepts, if his appeal is to be at all
intelligible, much less persuasive. By argument, analogy, metaphor, and other means he might, with sufficient skill, be able to
alter or extend the range of reference of some of the concepts
constitutive of the political discourse of his day. But however
skilful he is, he will not be able to create concepts *ex nihilo* but
must instead work within an already established universe of
discourse. Hence, as Skinner notes, 'the problem facing an agent

who wishes to legitimate what he is doing at the same time as gaining what he wants cannot simply be the instrumental problem of tailoring his normative language in order to fit his projects. It must in part be the problem of tailoring his projects in order to fit the available normative language.'[5] Although the 'ordinary language' that a theorist inherits is rarely his last word, it must of necessity be his first word, lest he be unintelligible to himself and to others.

Even so, conceptual change is not reducible to or identical with linguistic change – that is, the making of new distinctions, the coining of new terms or extending or altering the criteria used in applying older terms. Conceptual change and political innovation are as much a matter of non-discursive myths, metaphors, symbols, images, and over-arching world pictures as of linguistic extension. As Isaiah Berlin reminds us:

> Men's beliefs in the sphere of conduct are part of their conception of themselves and others as human beings; and this conception in its turn, whether conscious or not, is intrinsic to their picture of the world. This picture may be complete and coherent, or shadowy or confused, but almost always . . . it can be shown to be dominated by one or more models or paradigms: mechanistic, organic, aesthetic, logical, mystical, shaped by the strongest influence of the day – religious, scientific, metaphysical or artistic. This model or paradigm determines the content as well as the form of beliefs and behaviour.[6]

Indeed, as George Armstrong Kelly notes, 'One may observe throughout the long history of political science that it periodically, perhaps even paradigmatically, attaches itself to root metaphors from other surrounding bodies of knowledge and achieves its discourse in them.'[7] Political innovation and conceptual change are therefore linked, inevitably and inextricably, to large-scale, and often gradual and unconscious, shifts in the models and metaphors that dominate our discourse and thereby our lives and our thought.[8]

Until the late seventeenth century there was neither the vocabulary nor the necessary stock of images in which anything like the recognizably modern concept of party could be conceived, much less publicly articulated and defended. The appropriate imagery,

along with an allied vocabulary – including the ideas of an
irreducible plurality of political interests, a legitimate and loyal
standing opposition, and the like – was a long time in the making.

2.3   BODIES POLITIC

The ancients had no concept corresponding to our 'party'. Even
though democratic Athens in the fifth century B.C. was well
acquainted with factions of various stripes, it knew nothing of
parties as we understand them. 'There were [in Athens] no parties
in anything like the modern sense,' writes A. H. M. Jones, 'either
among the politicians or among the general public.' Although
'there were groups or cliques among the politicians', these 'were
probably based on personalities rather than principles, and seem to
have been temporary'.[9] And while there were also the more
persistent factions formed along class lines, as described by
Aristotle in *The Politics*, these were by no means parties. The polis
is a compounded whole that is greater than the sum of its several
'parts' (*meros* or *morion*), including individuals, families, and other
partial associations whose interest coincides with that of the
whole. A 'faction' (*stasis*), by contrast, aims at its own good rather
than the community's and acts to the detriment of the whole.
Thus faction or *stasis* represents an unnatural reversal of the proper
ordering of the whole and its several parts.

   Later writers were long content to follow Aristotle's lead on this
matter. Even among Roman writers such as Cicero we find no
significant departure from this feature of Aristotelian doctrine.
The *res publica* was said to embody the shared or public interest of
the whole, not the partial interest of any individual 'part' or
'party'. Significantly, the terms 'party' and 'faction' have entirely
different origins. 'Faction' derives from *factio*, making, which is
connected to the verb *facere*, to do or act. Thus a faction was any
group bent on taking matters into their own hands and making
them conform to their own designs. By contrast, 'party', which
comes from *partire*, to partition or divide, originally had no
distinctly political meaning. A 'party' was simply a 'part' of some
larger association composed of several parts or parties. Although
there were in the Roman republic factions and intrigues aplenty,

these were not political parties, properly speaking. *Optimates* and *Populares* did not correspond to oligarchs and democrats or to conservatives and progressives but referred instead to groups consisting of 'leading political figures and their followers'. Such unprincipled personal entourages and familial factions scarcely deserve to be termed parties.[10]

Christian writers (Augustine to the contrary notwithstanding) were not inclined to doubt the wisdom of Aristotle's analysis of faction and tyranny. So far as faction is concerned, they were in the main content to repeat the teachings of 'the philosopher', or, as Dante called him, 'the master of them that know'.[11] The end of wisdom, says Thomas, is the bringing of order into human affairs. This order may be of two types. The first consists of arranging separate parts into a coherent and useful whole; this is the sort of order that the builder imparts in constructing a dwelling. A second and altogether 'different sort of order exists between things which are united by some common end'. Such is the order of the commonwealth. And since the whole is prior to the parts (*partis*), the latter cannot properly be said to exist except insofar as they serve and help to constitute the whole. Thus 'there is no action of the parts which is not also action of the whole', and vice versa.[12] Should any individual 'part' seek its own advantage instead of the good of the whole it ceases to be a part, properly speaking, and becomes instead a faction intent upon tyranny.

Even as late as the fourteenth century, in the writings of Remigio de' Girolami, Bartolus of Saxoferrato and Marsiglio of Padua, Aristotle's account of faction remains essentially unchanged. All are agreed that internal divisiveness or 'faction' poses the single greatest threat to the liberty and security of city-republics, and all see the prevention or elimination of faction as the surest means of muting civil strife and promoting the public good.[13] Moreover, they took very seriously – and sometimes quite literally – the classical imagery of a unified political body. The body politic could be healthy only as long as its 'members' or 'parts' cooperated and fulfilled their respective functions. No body, corporeal or political, could long survive if its members constantly worked at cross purposes.

The point is perhaps made most vividly in Marsiglio's *Defensor Pacis*. Invoking the authority of Aristotle's *De motu animalium*

Marsiglio writes that 'the well-ordered animal' cannot move in response to conflicting commands. 'For if there were many of these principles and they gave contrary or different commands at the same time, the animal would either have to be borne in contrary directions or remain completely at rest.' In either case 'it would . . . lack those things, necessary and beneficial to it, which are obtained through motion.' And, as with animal bodies, so with political ones: 'The case is similar in the state properly ordered, which [is] analogous to the animal well formed according to nature. Hence, just as in the animal a plurality of such principles would be useless and indeed harmful, we must firmly hold that it is the same in the state'. The moral that Marsiglio draws is that factions or partial associations, each attempting to impart motion and direction to the political body, can only bring chaos and disorder. A well-ordered body politic must therefore have a single unified government. Justice is the harmonious ordering of the several parts or members for the good of the whole.[14]

Renaissance writers continued to maintain that the presence of factions, sects and cabals tended to undermine the unity and security of the state. Guicciardini, for one, reiterated the traditional view that factions are disruptive of civic stability and a prime source of political corruption.[15] In his *Ricordi* he hails the 'praiseworthy and useful citizen' who 'renders good service to his country' by eschewing 'faction and usurpation' (*sette e usurpazione*).[16] Machiavelli's account is rather more complex and ingenious. Some 'divisions' (*divisioni*), he maintains, are injurious and others not. The former include all factions or sects formed for private purposes; the latter include any portion, part, or partisans (*partigiani*) of the society 'which maintains itself without cabals or factions [*sette*]'.[17] And while Machiavelli traced the creation and maintenance of Roman republican liberty to the conflict between the nobles and the plebeians, these contending *divisioni* or 'parts' were by no means parties in any of our several modern senses. Nor were they factions or sects in the sense familiar to Machiavelli and his contemporaries. Nobles and plebeians were not small, short-lived sectarian factions but were, rather, larger, longer-lived natural divisions within Roman society, each exemplifying different 'tempers' within the body politic. Out of the clash of these 'two different tempers [*umori diversi*]' came the compromises and 'the laws favourable to liberty'.[18]

Medical analogies connect Fed Papers to
classical tradition even in they work out of it
(Wolin)

The Prehistory of Party   29

The venerable imagery of a civic body made medical analogies featuring physicians and remedies almost as commonplace among Renaissance writers as they were among classical authors. Guicciardini in his *Dialogo* complains of the difficulty of finding the *medicina appropriata* for curing the ailments afflicting different parts of the political body.[19] And Machiavelli develops his medical metaphors in even more lurid detail. Just as leeches may be required to relieve the human body of its blood-borne ill-humours, he says, so may the ills of the body politic require equally drastic remedies. Factions are most likely to be formed when this natural outlet is blocked; 'and when these ferments cannot in some way exhaust themselves, their promoters are apt to resort to some extraordinary means, that may lead to the ruin of the republic.' By contrast, 'nothing renders a republic more firm and stable, than to organize it in such a way that the excitement of the ill-humours that agitate a state may have a way prescribed by law for venting itself.' One of the sources of faction being the absence of legal remedies for 'enabling the people to exhaust the malign humours that spring up among men', the wise republic will provide legal home remedies to prevent any disgruntled sectarians from calling upon the even more malign ministrations of foreign physicians.[20] Like Guicciardini, Machiavelli warned that 'there is no surer way of corrupting the citizens, and to divide the city against itself than to foment the spirit of faction that may prevail there'. If it is to be long-lived a republic must be 'united and without antagonistic parts (*unite e senza parti*)'.[21] Even as he reiterates the traditional warnings about the evils of faction, Machiavelli avers that controlled conflict among the 'parts' can have beneficial consequences, including the prevention of political corruption and the promotion of liberty.[22]

Despite his fulminations against Aristotle and his repeated railings against 'the darknesse of School distinctions', Thomas Hobbes did not doubt that factions or formed oppositions of any kind are among 'those things that weaken, or tend to the dissolution of a commonwealth'. It is ironic that Hobbes, who derided any thinker who relied upon metaphors and other 'abuses of speech', should himself have had recourse to that hoariest of metaphors, the body politic, and its accompanying medical imagery, in a way that exceeds even Machiavelli. The 'infirmities of the commonwealth', Hobbes insisted, 'resemble the diseases of a naturall body'. Such 'internall diseases' and 'intestine disorder' weaken, and eventually kill, the political body. Political convulsions 'not unfitly may be compared to the Epilepsie, or Falling-sickness . . .. For as in this disease there is an unnaturall spirit, or wind in the head that obstructeth the roots of the nerves, and moving them violently, taketh away the motion which naturally they should have from the power of the soule in the brain, and thereby causeth violent, and irregular motions, which men call convulsions, in the parts . . . so also in the Body Politique', which internal convulsions must 'either overwhelm . . . with oppression, or cast . . . into the fire of a Civil Warre'. From this it follows that 'mixed government' is a contradiction in terms; for 'such government, is not government, but division of the common-wealth into . . . independent factions.' This results in a monstrously misproportioned body: 'To what disease in the naturall body of man, I may exactly compare this irregularity of a Common-wealth, I know not. But I have seen a man, that had another man growing out of his side, with an head, arms, breast, and stomach, of his own: If he had had another man growing out of his other side, the comparison [with mixed government] might then have been exact'. Associations whose presence is perceived to pose a threat to sovereign authority 'are as it were many lesser Common-wealths in the bowels of a greater, like wormes in the entrayles of a naturall man'. These 'little wormes, which physicians call ascarides', must be expelled lest the political body perish.[23]

Anyone who expects unity to emerge from faction, Hobbes says in *De Cive*, is as deluded as the daughters of Pelias:

> They going to restore the decrepit old man to his youth again, by the counsel of Medea they cut him into pieces, and set him in the fire to boil; in vain expecting when he would live again. So the common people, through their folly, like the daughters of Pelias, desiring to renew the ancient government, being drawn away by the eloquence of ambitious men, as it were by the witchcraft of Medea; divided into faction they consume it rather by those flames, than they reform it.[24]

Here Hobbes is of course speaking of 'faction', not 'party'. But even when he does use the word 'party' – as in 'the king's party' – he refers merely to those who took the king's part, or side, in the

English Civil War.[25] That even an apparently radical innovator like Hobbes did not envision anything like 'party' in our sense is scarcely surprising. For he – no less than the dreaded Schoolmen, much less Marsiglio, Machiavelli and Guicciardini – remained wedded, with subtle reservations, to the traditional idiom and imagery of the body politic, with its attendant aversion to anything that threatens its health and organic integrity. Just how subtle, and how momentous, these reservations were, we shall see shortly.

More surprising, perhaps, is that Hobbes' *bêtes noires* – Levellers like Lilburne and Overton, Diggers like Winstanley, and other radical sectarians – neither favoured faction nor formulated any notion of a legitimate opposition party. To peruse Puritan tracts in search of some recognizable precursor of the political party is to look in vain. The body politic and its allied imagery remained pretty firmly intact in Puritan political discourse. Even the most utopian tracts – Winstanley's *The Law of Freedom* foremost among them – envisioned a good society in which no provision was made for parties or organized opposition. Hence it is anachronistic to suggest that Winstanley wrote 'the first socialist utopia formed in the hopes of becoming a party program'.[26] And although the Levellers were without doubt a democratically organized political movement it is surely stretching credulity to claim that theirs 'was the first political party . . . to organise itself on a pattern of democratic self-government'.[27] An opposition movement it surely was, and some of the organizational features of the modern party it surely had; but there is little evidence to suggest that the Levellers operated with anything like our modern understanding of party.

What is true of radical English puritans was by and large true of their more moderate American brethren. Describing 'a due forme of Government both civill and ecclesiasticall', John Winthrop repeats the old maxim that 'the care of the publique must oversway all private respects . . .; for it is a true rule that perticuler estates cannott subsist in the ruine of the republique.'[28] Winthrop went so far as to sanctify the body politic, comparing the Christian commonwealth to the body of Christ:

> There is noe body but consistes of partes and that which knitts these partes together gives the body its perfeccion, because it

because it makes eache parte soe contiguous to other as thereby they doe mutually participate with eache other, both in strengthe and infirmity in pleasure and paine, to instance the most perfect of all bodies, Christ and his church make one body: the several partes of this body considered aparte before they were united were as disproportionate and as much disordering as soe many contrary quallities or elements but when Christ comes and his spirit and love knitts all these partes to himself and each to other, it is become the most perfect and best proportioned body in the world.[29]

It is precisely because individual Christians and their communities are 'partes' of one body – the body of Christ – that there is in their discourse no place or function for disputatious parties, sects or factions. Nor, despite the deep internal schisms occasioned by the Antinomian controversy, were sectaries like Roger Williams wont to question this piece of conventional wisdom. Far from repudiating the older organic imagery, orthodox Puritans and Antinomians alike accepted and even embellished it.

2.4 CONTRACTING PARTIES

Given the widespread agreement about the evils of faction, one might well wonder how the modern political party ever appeared at all. At least part of the answer is to be found in the various ways in which the older organic imagery began to give way to newer ways of picturing the political association. To put it crudely, the idea of the body politic as a natural body began to give way to the notion that it was an artificial body created by contract and agreement. The beginnings of this shift can be seen already in the Puritans, with their resurrection of the old Hebrew idea of a community created by covenant. But the shift is perhaps more readily discernable in their arch-foe Hobbes, whose account of the commonwealth combines elements of the older and newer pictures.

Hobbes' subtle shift in perspectives begins with his admission that the ills of the body politic 'resemble' those of the natural body. This amounts to saying that the body politic is – *pace* Aristotle – not a natural body at all, but a 'body' of an altogether different sort. While the body politic may 'resemble' a natural body in some respects – having, for example, 'members', a 'head', and 'arms', and being liable to 'intestine disorders' – it is in fact an artificial body. Men are not only 'members' but the 'makers and orderers' of the commonwealth. And the way in which they create this artificial body is by entering into a covenant. By human art and artifice is created the great Leviathan. The irony is that this 'mortall god' is itself the creation of its own devotees and worshippers. Little wonder, then, that Hobbes the absolutist should have been suspected by many monarchists of being a seditious wolf attired in royal purple. For he made the bond between Sovereign and subjects conditional, resting upon an agreement among his subjects that they would obey him only as long as he is able to protect them.

It is scarcely an exaggeration to suggest that the emergence of this picture – of a political society created consciously and by contract – marks a momentous shift in political self-understanding in the West.[30] Instead of depicting a society founded by the solitary lawgivers and heroic founders of antiquity, Hobbes paints a picture of many individuals joining together for the purpose of self-preservation. Far from merging their individual identities into some greater organic whole, each member remains readily identifiable. This is perhaps most vividly portrayed in the original frontispiece to the 1651 edition of *Leviathan*, in which the body of the Sovereign is shown to consist of the clearly discernable bodies of the individual members. His body exists by virtue of their agreeing to create it. And this they do by making a covenant among themselves.

But what, exactly, does all this have to do with the conceptual history of 'party'? Just this: one of the crucial characteristics of a covenant, or contract, is that there must be 'parties' to it, i.e., people who take part or participate in making and keeping it. This is the sense in which the term is used, even today, in ostensibly nonpolitical activities. Thus lawyers, for example, draw up contracts referring to the signers or participants as 'parties' (as in 'the party of the first part agrees to convey to the party of the second part . . .') And when reserving a table in a restaurant one will quite likely be asked how many people are in one's party. The question is not, of course, a political one.[31]

In fact, 'party' was not much used in political contexts until the seventeenth century. I want to suggest that one – though by no means the only – reason why 'party' came to be conceived as a political concept was that politics came in some quarters to be pictured in England after 1660 increasingly in contractual terms. Whereas bodies – including bodies politic – have parts, contracts have 'parties'. Although contractual relations are relations among parties, these are not yet parties in our modern sense(s) of the term. The contracting parties are, rather, still understood as 'parts' of the larger society which, despite their disagreements, agree to live according to some rule of common equity. If these are not yet 'parties' in our sense, neither are they properly describable as factions or sects. The danger, however, is that one of the parties will break faith with the others and attempt to dominate them for its own private purposes. Such a party would then have ceased to be a party or 'part', becoming instead a faction in the older sense.

This distinction became increasingly clear in the course of the Exclusion Crisis of 1679–80, during which the names of Tory and Whig were heard for the first time.[32] Most Tories took the older Cavalier view that the king, ruling as he did by Divine Right, was not party to any contract and could not be bound by its terms. The Whigs – the name comes from the Whiggamores, radical Scots covenanters of the 1640s – argued that by allowing the accession of his Catholic brother James II to the throne, Charles II had violated the terms of the Restoration Settlement of 1660. Charles' several attempts at compromise having failed, he dissolved Parliament in 1681, ruling until his death in 1685 without one. When James succeeded his brother he in effect attempted to repeal not only the specific terms of the Settlement but the very idea that the relations between Crown and country could be pictured in anything remotely resembling contractual terms. The Glorious Revolution of 1688 amounted to a militant reaffirmation of the Whiggish or contractarian view that monarchs too are 'parts' who are as it were parties to an agreement by which they are constitutionally bound. It was this principle, more than any other, that gave rise to and served to sustain the distinction between Whigs and Tories, the first divisions even remotely resembling modern political parties.

Perhaps the most subtle, abstractly theoretical, and radical defence of the Whig picture is to be found in Locke's *Second*

Treatise. 'Tis not a change from the present state,' says Locke, 'which perhaps Corruption, or decay has introduced, that makes an Inroad upon the Government, but the tendency of it to injure or oppress the People, and to set up one part, or Party, with a distinction from, and an unequal subjection of the rest.'[33] Any 'part, or Party' attempting such a move ceases to be a proper party to the contract and becomes a 'rebel'. The rebel, in effect, makes his part or party into a faction inimical in its operation to a previously agreed conception of the common good. This, says Locke in a faint but audible allusion to the older organic imagery of the body politic, is the justification for 'cutting off those Parts, and those only, which are so corrupt, that they threaten the sound and healthy.'[34] That Locke, himself a doctor, should have relied so infrequently upon medical analogies surely says a good deal about the demise of the older organic imagery and its replacement by newer notions of contract, consent, and agreement amongst distinct 'parties' or 'parts'.

2.5   LIBERTY AND FACTION

The somewhat less theoretical tracts of the late seventeenth and early eighteenth century also suggest that, so far as party and partisanship were concerned, a subtle shift in political self-understandings was beginning to take place. To be sure, there was as yet no defence of party *per se*, nor was there any well-articulated idea of a loyal opposition. 'Party' is sometimes taken to be virtually synonymous with faction, whose mischiefs are frequently decried, and political opposition is often equated with treason. This mainstream view is found, for example, in 'The Trimmer' Halifax's 'Political Thoughts and Reflections' (*c.*1690). 'The best Party', wrote Halifax, 'is but a kind of a Conspiracy against the rest of the Nation.'[35]

This and other oft-repeated warnings were turned by 'Real Whig' polemicists in a different direction. Invoking the names of Machiavelli, Harrington and Locke, among others, the Real Whigs or Commonwealthmen sought to consolidate and extend the English libertarian tradition.[36] John Toland's *The Art of Governing by Partys* (1701) begins conventionally enough by resurrecting the imagery of the political body racked by the disease of partisanship: '. . . of all the Plagues which have infested this nation . . . none has spread the contagion wider, or brought us nearer to utter ruin, than the implacable animosity of contending Partys . . . it is the most wicked masterpiece of tyranny purposely to divide the sentiments, affections, and interests of a people.'[37] But Toland then goes on to argue that partisan divisions, though often evil, need not always be so. It is not parties *per se* but their 'implacable animosity' that poses the greatest political threat to the nation. What may therefore be needed is not the abolition of parties but their being put to some better public purpose. Factiousness and freedom go hand in hand; the point is to keep both from getting out of hand. This view Toland developed in his *Memorial of the State of England* (1705) and at greater length in *The State Anatomy of Great Britain* (1716). 'Every division,' he wrote in *The State Anatomy*, 'is not simply pernicious: Since Parties in the State, are just of the like nature with Heresies in the Church: sometimes they make it better, and sometimes they make it worse; but held within due Bounds, they always keep it from stagnation.'[38]

In warning of the dangers of stagnation Toland echoed the Machiavellian (and Harringtonian) view that divisions or 'parts' are not inherently evil but can, under the appropriate circumstances, be beneficial in allowing the political body to vent its ill humours. This, minus the medical imagery, had also been the central theme of Robert Molesworth's *Account of Denmark* (1694). Molesworth saw in the factionless state of Denmark the peace of the grave. 'Where there are no Factions, nor Disputes about Religion which usually have a great influence on any Government,' he wrote, the possibilities for political reform and renewal were stifled. Though this uniformity of opinion be a 'vast convenience to any Prince', it precludes popular reform and leads inevitably to political stagnation.[39] In a similar spirit Walter Moyle asked, 'who is there that would not prefer a factious liberty before a settled Tyranny?'.[40]

Although such unorthodox views met with widespread opposition, we see in this period the first glimmerings of the idea that at least some political divisions are based upon principles of some sort, however odious or mistaken or disingenuously proclaimed,

and that such divisions, however dangerous, may even be unavoidable in a free state. More significant still, some writers were
going so far as to suggest that honest and honourable men might
disagree about what the common interest was and how it might
best be served. Thus while warning of the evils of faction the
anonymous author of *The State of the Parties* (1692) averred that the
differences between Whigs and Tories stemmed not from one's
serving the common interest and the other's not; but from their
having different conceptions of the common interest of the nation
to which both were loyal after their fashion. Such partisan
contentiousness came to be taken by some as an identifying feature
of the English national character. The unnamed author of *The
Political Sow-Gelder* (1715) averred that Englishmen were and
would remain as varied in their politics as England was in her
climate. And the author of *The Freeholder's Alarm to his Brethren*
(1734), usually attributed to Henry Fielding, remarks that parties
and partisans were inevitable in a political climate in which
freedom and liberty prevailed.[41]

Among political philosophers like Hobbes and Locke one
expects a certain degree of self-consciousness about conceptual
change. Perhaps surprisingly, however, one finds among political
pamphleteers of the period a remarkably similar sensibility. John
Toland, for example, notes that 'Patriots and loyalists, court and
country-parties, tho in themselves words significant enough, yet
they are become very equivocal, as men are apt to apply them:
whereas Whig and Tory cannot be mistaken; for men may change,
and words may change, but principles never.'[42] Along with the
emerging idea that parties, properly understood, stand for principles of some sort came an appreciation of the mutability of our
moral and political concepts and an awareness that meanings, like
minds, can be changed through political argument.

The arguments in favour of party were neither legal nor logical
but political and rhetorical ones in which actions were redescribed,
new distinctions made, and old ones recast or abandoned. Chief
among these was, of course, the distinction between faction and
party. To defend faction and factiousness, as Molesworth and
Moyle had done, doubtless had a certain shock value; but such a
defence could scarcely be sustained, given the prevailing views
about the evils of faction. Hence the importance of drawing the

distinction in ways that might prove politically acceptable. The distinction was drawn in different ways, some writers preferring to focus upon their respective members' motives, others upon organizational features or political functions, and still others upon some combination of these. In *An Enquiry into The State of the Union of Great Britain* (1717), for example, William Paterson reports on the (perhaps imaginary) meeting of 'the Wednesday's Club in Friday-street', as follows:

> You say you are for Parties; Are you for Factions too?
> By no means (reply'd Mr. Grant) these are wicked things.
> A very nice Distinction (reply'd Mr. Ford) pray wherein do your parties and factions differ? Since I confess my self so wise as not to know.
> The difference is manifest several ways (said Mr. Grant) particularly your natural Parties are things consisting only of Members without Heads, but your Factions, or in other Words provoked unnatural Parties, have Heads.
> By what other Properties can we distinguish them? (said Mr. Ford)
> Your natural Parties are pretty tame, . . . (reply'd Mr. Grant) but the others are always wild and voracious; the first is capable of Good, as well as Hurt, of Love as well as Hatred, and frequently produce Emulation, a very good thing. But instead thereof, your unnatural Parties [or factions] hate, but love not, are hurtful in the Nature, and chiefly produce Enmity, a dangerous Quality in Men.[43]

Although other defenders of party drew the distinction in other ways, the central point, politically speaking, was that distinctions were being drawn and that party was accordingly coming to be viewed by some as a novel, acceptable, and even a valuable English political institution.

Opponents of party, by contrast, were intent upon reinstating and defending older distinctions or at any rate disputing new ones. This strategy consisted, in the main, of attempting to show that parties were nothing new under the sun, but an old phenomenon parading under a new name. Numerous anti-party pamphleteers purported to show that parties were really factions after all, or, failing that, that parties tended to degenerate into factions. But it remained for Bolingbroke, 'the classic anti-party writer' and 'fountainhead of anti-party thought',[44] to construct a last-ditch defence against the encroachment of party.

Bolingbroke ingeniously deployed an array of 'Old Whig' arguments to criticize parties and partisanship. The Crown having been captured by the corrupt ministry of Walpole and the 'new whigs', Bolingbroke appealed to earlier Whig defences of the Glorious Revolution, in hopes of creating a 'Patriot King' freed from the snares of party politics and partisan narrowness. Such a king could 'defeat the designs, and break the spirit of faction, instead of partaking in one and assuming the other'.[45] And while he might temporarily favour one party over another, he would remain aloof from both. The irony in this defence of royal prerogative is that the conditions that make it possible must be brought about by a new kind of party – a 'country party' devoted not to narrow partisan interests but to 'principles of common interest'. Cutting across the distinction between Whig and Tory, Bolingbroke's country party would include men of good will from both parties and therefore would not be a party, strictly speaking. 'A party thus constituted,' he maintained in *A Dissertation upon Parties* (1748), 'is improperly called party. It is the nation speaking and acting in the discourse and conduct of particular men.'[46]

Bolingbroke's idea of a nonpartisan party was advanced as a temporary expedient and a necessary evil, not an inevitable feature of constitutional government. But in advancing and defending the idea of a party to end all parties Bolingbroke conceded the necessity, the importance – and the justifiability – of such an institution. And in doing so he had to acknowledge that there could, in principle, be 'parties' of different kinds and that party was not necessarily synonymous with faction. Indeed he further reinforces the latter point by asserting that 'parties' inevitably 'degenerate into absolute factions'.[47] Since, strictly speaking, something (an acorn, a party) can hardly be said to be identical with the thing that it eventually becomes (an oak, a faction), it therefore follows, contrary to Bolingbroke's intentions, that parties are not factions. He cannot, in the end, have it both ways. Too ingenious by half, Bolingbroke's argument against parties proved in the end to be singularly self-subverting.

In 'Of Parties in General' and 'The Parties of Great Britain' (1742) David Hume brought together a number of earlier argu-

ments in a novel synthesis. Hume's argumentative and rhetorical
strategy was to concede that 'parties' were 'factions' but that
factions came in several different varieties, not all of which are
equally noxious. He began by reaffirming the traditional view that
factions are evil 'weeds'. But like Molesworth and the Real Whigs,
Hume held that factions are 'plants which grow most plentifully in
the richest soil', i.e., 'they rise more easily, and propagate
themselves faster in free governments'. Different forms of free
government give rise to factions of quite different kinds. 'Personal
factions,' for example, 'arise most easily in small republics. Every
domestic quarrel, there, becomes an affair of state.' Such personal
or familial factions as those of republican Rome and Florence are
increasingly rare in the modern state. More common nowadays
are 'parties' or 'real factions' which 'may be divided into those
from *interest*, from *principle*, and from *affection*'. The first, says
Hume, 'is the most reasonable, and the most excusable'.[48] Parties
of the third type – 'parties from affection' – 'are founded on the
different attachments of men towards particular families and
persons, whom they desire to rule over them' even though 'they
are in no wise acquainted . . . and from whom they never
received, nor can ever hope for any favour.'[49] But it is the second
sort of party which is truly novel. 'Parties from principle,
especially abstract speculative principle, are known only to
modern times, and are, perhaps, the most extraordinary and
unaccountable *phenomenon*, that has yet appeared in human
affairs.'[50] Parties professing to stand for some set of political or
philosophical principles represented an entirely new wrinkle.
Hume was among the first to note that this development was
rapidly becoming commonplace. Indeed, as he remarks in 'Of the
Original Contract', 'no party, in the present age, can well support
itself, without a philosophical or speculative system of principles,
annexed to its political or practical one.'[51] Such parties being
unavoidable in a free state, the cure would then be worse than the
disease. Like it or not, parties from principle were becoming a
familiar feature of the political landscape. Hume ably described, if
he did not altogether approve of, this development.[52]

By the time Samuel Johnson published his *Dictionary of the
English Language* in 1755, his definition of party was already out of
date. Swimming against an ever stronger current of conceptual

change Johnson defined 'party' as 'a number of persons confederated by similarity of designs in opposition to others, a faction; . . .
side, persons engaged against each other, as, of your party; cause,
side.'[53] Then as now, dictionaries follow fashion; they do not
dictate it. Johnson, however, followed political and philosophical
fashion at an ever-increasing distance.

The phenomenon that Hume found extraordinary and unaccountable and Johnson ordinary and unacceptable was presently
justified by means of an argument at once principled and prag-
matic. In *Thoughts on the Cause of the Present Discontents* (1770)
Edmund Burke defended the practice of partisan 'connexion'
against the anti-party fulminations of the Earl of Chatham (William Pitt).[54] As Prime Minister Chatham claimed to be interested
in 'measures, not men', and had had some success in luring
partisans away from their parties, including the Rockingham
Whigs with whom Burke was affiliated. Once separated from
their party they then became more susceptible to manipulation by
the Chatham ministry. Seeing through this strategy of divide and
conquer, Burke proceeded to denounce nonpartisanship and to
defend the idea of principled opposition.[55] This was now practicable in part, Burke argued, because the older and politically
disastrous division between monarchists and parliamentarians no
longer existed. But although 'the great parties which formerly
divided and agitated the kingdom are known to be in a manner
entirely dissolved', there remains a politically ambitious and
corrupt 'court faction' or 'cabal' which while hiding behind a
facade of nonpartisanship seeks to advance its own interests at the
country's expense.[56] 'This cabal has, with great success, propa-
gated a doctrine which serves for a colour to those acts of
treachery.' That 'doctrine', says Burke, is 'That all political
connexions are in their nature factious, and as such ought to be
dissipated and destroyed; and that the rule for forming administra-
tions is mere personal ability, rated by the judgment of this cabal
upon it'. The wilful failure to distinguish between faction and
party 'connexion' is politically pernicious:

> That connexion and faction are equivalent terms, is an opinion
> which has been carefully inculcated at all times by unconstitutional
> statesmen. The reason is evident. Whilst men are linked together,
> they easily and speedily communicate the alarm of any evil design.

They are enabled to fathom it with common counsel, and to oppose it with united strength. Whereas, when they lie dispersed, without concert, order, or discipline, communication is uncertain, counsel difficult, and resistance impracticable. Where men are not acquainted with each other's principles nor experienced in each other's talents, . . . no personal confidence, no friendship, no common interest, subsisting among them; it is evidently impossible that they can act a publick part with uniformity, perseverance, or efficacy.[57]

Part and party are intertwined, in that one cannot reasonably hope to 'act a publick part' outside of one's party:

In a connexion, the most inconsiderable man, by adding to the weight of the whole, has his value, and his use; out of it, the greatest talents are wholly unserviceable to the publick. No man . . . can flatter himself that his single, unsupported, desultory, unsystematick endeavours are of power to defeat the subtle designs and united cabals of ambitious citizens. When bad men combine, the good must associate; else they will fall, one by one, an unpitied sacrifice in a contemptible struggle.[58]

The 'parties from principle' which Hume had found so unaccountable are for Burke paradigmatic of party *per se*. 'Party', as Burke defines it, 'is a body of men united, for promoting by their joint endeavours the national interest, upon some particular principle in which they are all agreed.'[59] Needless to say, Burke's definition of 'party' hardly met with universal acceptance. Clearly, however, a momentous if still subtle shift in the terms of Anglophone political discourse was well under way.

2.6 'PARTY' IN AMERICA

Nowhere was this shift more rapid or more pronounced than in the fledgling American republic. As I attempt to show in chapter 3, the new Constitution was defended and criticized in the idiom of republican discourse. And the discourse of republicans from Machiavelli to Moyle and the English Commonwealthmen exhibited an ambivalent attitude toward divisions within a republic.

On the one hand, factions were divisive and posed a danger to the body politic; on the other hand, however, the tensions and struggles between such groups could help to keep the body politic vigorous and fit. Which of these consequences came about depended upon how that body was constituted. In a well-ordered body the tensions were useful and healthy; in an ill-ordered body they were destructive of the very sinews of civility.

This tension within republican discourse was clearly evident in the 1780s, and especially in the 1787–8 debate over the ratification of the Constitution. Federalist friends and Antifederalist foes of the Constitution were virtually unanimous in agreeing about the dangers of party and faction, which they tended to treat as synonymous terms. This synonymy began to break down, however, as it was realized that partisan divisions may well be a by-product of political liberty. In 1786, Benjamin Franklin, for example, decried 'the infinite mutual abuse of parties, tearing to pieces the best of characters'. And yet, Franklin acknowledged – as had Hume and, earlier still, Molesworth and Toland – that some good can come out of party wrangling. Parties, wrote Franklin, 'will exist wherever there is liberty; perhaps they help to preserve it. By the collision of different sentiments, sparks of truth are struck out, and political light is obtained.'[60] A similar tension is present in the thought of John Adams and others among the American Founders.[61] But it is in the thought of James Madison that the tension is most ingeniously resolved, not once but twice.

In 1787 Madison and his co-author Alexander Hamilton mince no words in condemning the evils of faction or party, which they take to be interchangeable terms. In *Federalist 10*, Madison equates party and faction, decrying the designs of 'the most numerous party, or, in other words the most powerful faction'. But then, like Franklin (and Hume, his probable source), Madison goes on to suggest that the formation of factions is inevitable in a free state. 'Liberty is to faction what air is to fire, an aliment without which it instantly expires.' 'But', Madison immediately goes on to say, 'it could not be less folly to abolish liberty, which is essential to political life, because it nourishes faction, than it would be to wish the annihilation of air, which is essential to animal life, because it imparts to fire its destructive agency.' The 'latent causes of faction' being 'sown in the nature of man', it is neither possible nor desirable to eliminate them. The secret, Madison argued, lay in controlling the harmful effects of faction. And that could best be done by constitutionally creating the conditions under which factions would multiply and proliferate. Only in this way, Madison maintained in 1787, could the most dangerous faction of all – 'a majority . . . of the whole, . . . united by some common impulse or passion, or of interest, adverse to the rights of other citizens, or to the permanent and aggregate interests of the community' – be effectively prevented from coming into existence.[62]

With the ratifying of the Constitution in 1788 the Federalist ranks were split. Siding with Jefferson against Hamilton, Congressman Madison sought in the early 1790s a second solution to the problem of parties. The first feature of this solution was that the old equation of 'party' and 'faction' ought now be dispensed with. In Madison's hands 'party' loses its negative associations and becomes instead a more or less neutral term for designating opposing political groups. From now on, it is not the term party *per se* that carries some sort of negative (or positive) connotation, but the adjective specifying the *kind* of party to which one is referring. Madison, moreover, periodizes the history of political parties in America in a novel way. Finally, and most significantly of all, Madison refers to his own political association as a party. Let us examine each of these argumentative moves more closely.

'In every political society,' writes Madison in 'Parties' (1792), 'parties are unavoidable. A difference of interests, real or supposed, is the most natural and fruitful source of them.' Parties may be either 'natural' ones 'aris[ing] out of the nature of things', or 'artificial' ones resting upon unnatural divisions among men.[63] Madison makes it clear that this is precisely the distinction to be drawn between his and Jefferson's party – 'the Republican party, as it may be termed' – and Hamilton's 'anti Republican party'.

Armed with this new understanding of 'party', Madison in 'A Candid State of Parties' proceeds to periodize the political history of America in a novel fashion. 'The most interesting state of parties in the United States may', Madison says, 'be referred to three periods.' From 1776 to 1783, 'Those who espoused the cause of independence and those who adhered to the British claims, formed the parties of the first period; *if, indeed, the disaffected class were considerable [i.e., numerous and important] enough to deserve the name of a party.'* That is to say, the American revolutionaries constituted a 'party' – a significant concession, and certainly one that neither Madison nor most of his contemporaries would have made several years earlier. 'From 1783 to 1787,' he continues, 'there were parties in abundance, but being rather local than general, they are not within the present review.' The second significant period occurred in 1787–8, the years of the ratification debate, which saw the contest between two new 'parties, the Federalists and the Antifederalists'. Now that this contest has been decided in favour of the former, these parties no longer exist. The third period, he holds, is the present one in which Hamilton's Federalist party is opposed by 'the Republican party' of Jefferson and Madison. Unlike earlier, short-lived divisions, the division between 'the antirepublican party, as it may be called' and 'the Republican party', he observes, 'is likely to be of some duration'.[64]

Madison does not flinch from speaking of 'the Republican party', though he never once calls it a faction. In this way party loses its older association with 'faction' and becomes, depending upon the adjective used to designate it, an honourable or dishonourable political affiliation.

The extent to which the distinction between 'party' and 'faction' was now clearly and definitively drawn is dramatically underscored by Jefferson's fury at Hamilton for 'daring to call the republican party *a faction*'.[65] The rapidity with which this crucial distinction was drawn is, in retrospect, remarkable. For like most of his contemporaries Jefferson had begun by equating party and faction, which he condemned as divisive and out of place in a free society. As late as 1789 he denied being a party man. To belong to a party 'is the last degradation of a free and moral agent. If I could not go to heaven but with a party, I would not go there at all.' 'I am', he said, 'neither federalist nor antifederalist; . . . I am of neither party, nor yet a trimmer between parties.'[65] But it was not long before the ostensibly nonpartisan Jefferson was speaking of 'our party' and acknowledging that 'Wherever there are men there will be parties and wherever there are free men they will make themselves heard'. So long as no party places itself above the law, 'all will be safe . . . and you need never fear anarchy or tyranny'.[67]

It is scarcely an exaggeration to suggest that Madison and Jefferson in word and deed reconstituted the concept of party. In their discourse it became a relatively long-lived political organization devoted to the furthering of its own aims and principles in peaceful and law-abiding opposition to other parties. It was just this conceptual shift that made it possible for Jefferson and Madison to be the co-founders of the first modern political party.[68] With this the prehistory of 'party' ends and we enter a world recognizably modern and more clearly akin to our own.

3

Reconstituting Republican
Discourse

3.1 INTRODUCTION

The political and conceptual controversies of yesteryear have a
way of becoming the historiographical disputes of today. Historians have wrangled with such questions as whether the American founding was a genuinely republican rather than a protoliberal
or perhaps even a Humean–Scottish one, and there is to date no
successful resolution in sight.[1] As one commentator observes with
some understatement, 'The true nature of early American republican thought remains a topic of fierce dispute among historians.'[2]
  My purpose in the present chapter is not to reopen, much less to
resolve, that controversy, but to add a small footnote to it. I want
to suggest that the search for 'the true nature of early American
republican thought' is misguided from the outset, since the true
nature of republicanism was itself very much in dispute during the
founding. Indeed it is probably fair to say that no concept was
more hotly contested during that period than that of 'republic'.
And with good reason. 'Republic' was central to the rhetorical
appeals and arguments of all the parties to the dispute over
ratification. One's understanding of 'tyranny', or 'liberty', or
'virtue' or 'corruption' was deeply dependent upon what one took
a 'republic' to be. Federalists and Antifederalists alike claimed to
be the 'real' republicans, and each decried the other's misunderstanding – or worse, their deliberate and malicious misrepre-
sentation – of what a 'republic' really was. Disputants on both
sides believed themselves, rightly enough, to be engaged not in a
verbal dispute but in a political controversy of the highest
importance. What was at issue were not merely the meanings of
certain key terms but the competing conceptions of citizenship,

liberty, and civic responsibility lodged in and constituted by alternative political vocabularies. In the debates over ratification two competing accounts met in rhetorical and argumentative combat, each vying for the allegiance of an American public that was still politically fluid and very much in the throes of self-formation. Theirs was at once a choice between competing political vocabularies and ways of life, not only for themselves but for many generations to come.

I propose to view the ratification debate of 1787–8 as a case study of conceptual change. My aim is to look at this conceptual-cum-political controversy with an eye to discerning the argumentative and rhetorical resources used by both sides to preserve old meanings or, alternatively, to create new ones. I shall for the sake of brevity begin with a very short sketch of the history of 'republic', before focusing upon competing conceptions of 'republic' as understood and defended by Federalist friends and Antifederalist foes of the new Constitution. To further simplify matters, my inquiry will be concerned with three questions around which conceptual controversy centred, most memorably in the debate between 'Brutus' and 'Publius' in New York.[3] The first question is, what bearing does the size or extent of its territory have upon a polity's claim to be a republic? Second, how and by whom are the citizens of a republic to be represented? Third, what is to be the meaning and place of virtue in an American republic? My reason for retreading this oft-trod ground is to bring into bold relief the conceptual dimensions of the ratification controversy. Finally, I conclude by showing how the ratification debate took a 'linguistic' turn as the protagonists became increasingly aware of the conceptually constituted character of their respective views of politics and citizenship.

3.2 'REPUBLIC' IN HISTORICAL PERSPECTIVE

The word 'republic' comes originally from the Latin *res publica*, meaning 'public thing'. The *res publica* was for the Romans the most comprehensive of all human associations, being concerned, as we saw in chapter 2, not with the well-being of this or that single party or 'part' but with all of the parts, that is, with that of the 'public' as a whole. But although the word is Latin, the *concept* is older still, stemming from Greek sources. Inasmuch as the traditional division of governments into 'pure' types – monarchy, aristocracy and democracy – was predicated upon one particular part ruling the others, each was to that extent partial, partisan and unrepresentative of the whole. So long as governments continued to be one or another of these unalloyed species, they would be unstable, short-lived, and subject to revolutionary overthrow. We find in Plato's *Laws*, in Aristotle's *Politics*, and more clearly still in Polybius' *Histories*, the argument that stability could be ensured by giving each of these parts an active role in constituting the government, whose existence and legitimacy is underwritten by a body of law accepted by all. The wider public could, in short, be best served by means of a mixed constitution consisting of a combination of pure types. Despite their differences, the interests of the several parts could be served simultaneously by a mixed government or commonwealth. In this mixture lay the secret, Polybius thought, of the longevity of the Roman republic.

This vision of how government may be structured so as to serve a shared or common interest became the stock in trade of later Roman writers. As Cicero says in *De Re Publica*:

> The commonwealth [*res publica*] is the people's affair [*populi res*]; and the people is not every group of men, associated in any manner, but is the coming together of a considerable number of men who are united by a common agreement about law and rights and by the desire to participate in mutual advantages.[4]

And Augustine, accepting the view of 'republic' taken from 'the Roman authors', repeats Cicero's remarks almost verbatim.[5] Later scholastic writers, including Ptolemy of Lucca, Remigio de' Girolami, Bartolus of Saxoferrato, Marsiglio of Padua, and the Florentine politician-priest Fra Girolamo Savonarola, defended republican 'liberty'. Echoing Aristotle and other classical authors, they decried 'faction' and its attendant corruption, understood as the pursuit of private interests without any regard for the public good.[6] The most important source of this emerging, or reemerging, republican discourse were the fifteenth-century Italian humanists, particularly those frequenting the Florentine Orti Oricellari.[7] The most original and important member of this select circle of anti-Medician writers was Niccolo Machiavelli.

This is not the place to reiterate the intricacies of Machiavelli's analysis of the rise and demise of republican liberty – a task that has, in any case, already been better undertaken by others.[8] Suffice it to say that Machiavelli's achievement lay in his having brought together, in a novel synthesis, a number of themes that were to become watchwords and guideposts for later generations of republicans, including the idea that the public good can best be discovered and promoted by free and active citizens who are on their guard against any threat to their liberties. Chief among these is the freedom from despotic rule, along with the corollary liberty of the citizen to take an active part in deciding matters of public or common concern. Such citizens must subscribe to a manly or heroic code of civic *virtù*, which requires the *virtuoso* citizen not only to rule and be ruled in turn, but to be prepared to defend his and his city's liberties with his life. From this follows Machiavelli's abiding interest in matters military, and more particularly his concern with the arming and training of citizen militias and his unremitting hostility to standing armies and any reliance on foreign mercenaries. Only a corrupt citizenry would fail to promote the public happiness by protecting their liberties. Corruption is thus understood as a kind of civic lethargy or laziness – a turning away from political affairs because of the siren song of wealth or luxury or ease. Corruption is, in short, the collective falling away from civic *virtù*. Although history shows that corruption is inevitable and that all free republics are in consequence doomed to decline and perish, a well-ordered republic can stave off corruption and decay for a very long time indeed, as the examples of Sparta and Rome show. That even these exemplars eventually perished shows the fragility of all things human. Happily, however, liberty can in time be restored, corruption overcome, and *virtù* renewed by means of a return to the principles upon which republics are founded. This requires that republican citizens share a capacity for remembrance, a common stock of memories, and in particular a memory of foundings, founders and first principles.[9] With the recalling of, and the return to, first principles, the cycle then begins all over again. The task of the theorist then becomes to discover the means by which republican liberty might be prolonged. These include the laying of strong foundations that will ensure the rule of law, the prevention of undue concentrations of power in any single party or part, and the proper balancing of the polity's several parts or orders so as to contain conflict in a constructive way.[10]

Much of Machiavelli's originality resides in the novel way in which he addresses the problem of how best to contain and control political conflict. Unlike earlier republican writers who had taken as their model *Venezia serenissima* – the supremely serene republic of Venice – and had decried the tumultous politics of republican Rome, Machiavelli maintained that these tumults were actually the source of Roman vitality and *virtù*. Internal rivalries and the almost ceaseless conflict among the classes served the politically useful function not only of ensuring that the citizens remained actively involved in the affairs of their city but of preventing any single class or faction from concentrating all power in its hands. It was in the mixture of the parts and the dynamic tension between them that the strength of the whole resided.

These themes reappear, in somewhat altered but readily recognizable form, in the utopian commonwealth envisioned in James Harrington's *Oceana* (1656). Like Machiavelli an admirer of 'ancient prudence', Harrington combined an interest in classical republican ideals with an astute analysis of military might, property ownership and political organization. Wherever standing armies are at the beck and call of rulers, the liberty of the subjects is insecure. Hence Harrington calls for the formation of a militia composed of free citizens, always at the ready to defend their liberties. Since no citizen can be free if he is dependent upon others for his livelihood, Harrington's ideal commonwealth is also characterized by relatively widespread property ownership. By limiting the size of landed estates, an agrarian law checks any tendency to return to a feudal aristocracy. Just as concentrations of arms and wealth are inimical to liberty, so too is the concentration of political power in the hands of a single individual or class. To preclude such concentrations, Harrington engineers an elaborate constitutional system of balances and checks. Taking to heart Aristotle's dictum that the citizen is one who rules and is ruled in turn, Harrington prescribes a 'rota', a system in which officeholders are rotated in and out of office at regular intervals, thereby preventing the formation of a permanent ruling class or oligarchy.

The legislature is, moreover, to consist of two branches, a senate consisting of wealthier citizens which proposes legislation, and an assembly of small freeholders empowered to accept or reject such proposals. By means of such constitutional engineering corruption can be checked and the life of the republic prolonged indefinitely.[11]

After the Restoration in 1660 these republican themes were taken up by 'Real Whigs' or 'Commonwealthmen', including Algernon Sidney and Henry Neville, and later by Walter Moyle, Robert Molesworth, John Toland, John Trenchard and Thomas Gordon and by Bolingbroke, who turned republican or 'old' Whig arguments against Walpole's commercial or 'new' Whigs. This English 'country'-party or opposition ideology, though largely ineffectual against Walpole's ministry, was to prove particularly important in the formation of an American republican ideology.[12] By the middle of the eighteenth century the stage was set for the influential synthesis supplied by Montesquieu.

Montesquieu divides governments into three types – republican, monarchical and despotic – each of which is animated by a different principle or ruling passion. In the meanest of these, 'despotic government, . . . a single person directs everything by his own will and caprice'.[13] Its ruling passion is fear. The two remaining forms are non-despotic. Monarchy is not the rule of whim or caprice, but a system 'in which a single person governs by fundamental laws'. Its animating principle is 'honour'.[14] In the third species of government, republicanism, 'the body, or only a part of the people, is possessed of the supreme power'. If the former, it is called 'democracy'; if the latter, 'aristocracy'.[15] In both instances the main animating principle is 'virtue', by which Montesquieu means an austere and self-sacrificing regard for the public good. 'Virtue in a republic is a most simple thing; it is a love of the republic. . . that may be felt by the meanest as well as by the highest person in the state. When the common people adopt good maxims, they adhere to them more steadily than those we call gentlemen.' The love of one's country 'is conducive to a purity of morals' inasmuch as it curbs the selfish passions. In a democratic republic, the civic virtues inculcated by its laws include the love of equality and frugality.[16] Such a system can come about and thrive only under certain conditions, one of the most important of which is the limited extent of its territory:

It is natural for a republic to have only a small territory; otherwise it cannot long subsist. In an extensive republic there are men of large fortunes, and consequently of less moderation . . . . In an extensive republic the public good is sacrificed to a thousand private views. . . In a small one, the interest of the public is more obvious, better understood, and more within the reach of every citizen; abuses have less extent, and, of course, are less protected.[17]

Large republics, Montesquieu goes on to say, are more likely than small ones to succumb to tyranny and despotism. Small republics, on the other hand, are likely to be conquered by external enemies. The solution to this dilemma is to be found in 'a confederate republic', which 'has all the internal advantages of a republican, together with the external force of a monarchical government'. A confederated league of adjoining small republics is 'able to withstand an external force [and to] support itself without any internal corruption'.[18]

If these individual republics are to remain free from internal corruption, their respective constitutions must prescribe a system whereby powers are divided among mutually checking branches. Borrowing from Bolingbroke's and Rapin de Thoiras' idealized accounts of the English constitution, Montesquieu traces that country's long-lived liberties to its 'mixed' constitution. It is in the constitutional division of powers among the executive, the legislative and the judicial that the secret of English liberty lies.

I conclude this short conceptual history with Montesquieu's concept of *république* because his *L'ésprit des Lois* was in America accorded a respect bordering on reverence. Indeed, American patriots regularly cited not only eighteenth-century Commonwealthmen and the Tory Bolingbroke but also Montesquieu in defence of their rights as Englishmen, rights that they believed were being trampled upon by an increasingly corrupt Crown and Parliament.[19] Forrest McDonald scarcely stretches the truth in suggesting that 'American republicans regarded selected doctrines of Montesquieu's as being on a par with Holy Writ' whose 'central points' they 'could recite . . . as if it had been a catechism.'[20] The hegemony of earlier republican discourses – classical, Machiavellian and Montesquieuian – was soon to be challenged, however, and the discourse of republicanism radically changed by the creation of a new kind of 'republic' and the discourse through which it was explained, sustained and justified.

3.3 FROM REVOLUTION TO RATIFICATION

Immediately before and during the American Revolution Thomas Paine and other pro-revolutionary writers revived and lauded the idea of 'republican' government limited and checked by the power of a virtuous and vigilant citizenry, including its popular or 'democratical' part.[21] Revolutionary pamphleteers borrowed republican themes from classical writers, from Machiavelli, Harrington and Sidney, from eighteenth-century Commonwealth-men like Trenchard and Gordon, and even from the Tory Bolingbroke who had turned Old Whig arguments against the 'new' Whig ministry of Walpole. The energies – and the suspicions – that fuelled this ideological ferment were evident in the tone, tenor and provisions of the various state constitutions drafted during this period and even in the Articles of Confederation themselves.[22] By the mid-1780s, however, the political climate had begun to alter appreciably. Shays' Rebellion and other local protest movements looked to some like parts of a larger and more ominous conspiracy being hatched by democrats and debtors. This lent an air of urgency to the call for a convention to amend the Articles of Confederation.[23]

What came out of that meeting was not, of course, an amended version of the Articles but an altogether different document. Despite their differences, proponents and critics of the new Constitution were agreed that it would, if adopted, reconstitute the American body politic in a radically new way. The ratification debate of 1787–8 reopened a veritable hornets' nest of questions: What is a republic? What are republican liberties? How are they best protected, and how can they be corrupted? How can corruption be stemmed? By what constitutional means might a republic be maintained and its life prolonged?

The dispute over ratification was remarkable in many respects. Not the least of these was the way in which political arguments and rhetorical stratagems were deployed by Federalists and Anti-federalists in attempting to alter or preserve the meanings of older political concepts. As Gordon Wood rightly notes, 'Under the pressure of this transformation of political thought old words and concepts shifted in emphasis and took on new meanings.' Thus, for example, 'tyranny' ceased to refer to the illegitimate exercise of power by a despotic ruler, and came to refer to 'the abuse of power by any branch of the government, even . . . by the traditional representatives of the people'. Likewise, 'liberty' ceased to mean 'public or political liberty, the right of the people to share in the government'. 'The liberty that was now emphasized,' says Wood, 'was personal or private, the protection of rights against all governmental encroachments, particularly by the legislature. . .'[24] In addition to 'tyranny' and 'liberty,' other concepts acquired new meanings as they lost their older significations. Not the least of these was the concept of republic itself.

To reconstruct the world of words within which Federalist argued against Antifederalist is to enter a world both different from and yet formative of the one we now inhabit. The late Herbert Storing was surely right in suggesting that the new American Republic was the joint creation of Federalist and Antifederalist alike.[25] It was a new political system, created not by the dictates of a lone legislator, but argued into existence and quite literally constituted out of an intense debate between partisans of different political persuasions and theoretical convictions. During this debate Antifederalist criticism brought forth Federalist defenses that not only clarified but in some measure constituted the meaning and theoretical justification of the new Constitution. In looking again at that debate one is bound to be struck by the degree to which it revolved around the meanings of the concepts constitutive of republican discourse – liberty, tyranny, virtue, corruption, representation, even 'republic' itself. Although Antifederalists and Federalists often used the same words, they often meant quite different things by them. Although both may be said to have inhabited essentially the same 'universe of republican discourse', it is worth noting that while one wished to maintain the boundaries of that universe, the other wished to redraw them.[26]

Even the merest glance at *The Federalist Papers* and at Antifederalist rejoinders is sufficient to show how centrally important the concept of republic was during the debate over ratification.

As one Antifederalist pamphleteer, the pseudonymous Federal
Farmer, saw it, the issue was not so much between 'federalist' and
'antifederalist' but between 'real republicans' and 'pretended' ones:

> . . . if any names are applicable to the parties, on account of their
> general politics, they are those of republicans and anti-republicans.
> The opposers are generally men who support the rights of the body
> of the people, and are properly republicans. The advocates are
> generally men not very friendly to those rights, and properly anti
> republicans.[27]

By the same token, Federalist defenders of the new design
presented it as 'wholly and purely republican'.[28] And so it was –
but only if one was first persuaded by the Federalists' revision of
the concept of republicanism. America as redesigned and quite
literally reconstituted by the Constitution, and as defended in *The
Federalist Papers*, was not only a new republic but a new *kind* of
republic, the likes of which had not been seen before.

3.4   AN EXTENDED REPUBLIC?

Few issues were more heatedly debated than that of the optimal –
or rather, perhaps, the permissible – size of any republic deserving
the name. Federalists and Antifederalists alike agreed that the
American Republic represented a new wrinkle in the annals of
republicanism. It was to be an extended republic, taking in a large
territory and an ever-increasing population, with the prospect of
still further extension to the south and west. Antifederalists were
quick to seize upon what they took to be a rank contradiction.
Citing Montesquieu, they argued that an extended republic is no
republic at all, but, on the contrary, a veritable contradiction in
terms. One of the ablest Antifederalists, New York's Brutus
(probably Robert Yates), held that if we consult 'the greatest and
wisest men who have ever thought or wrote on the science of
government' we shall have to conclude that 'a free republic cannot
succeed over a country of such immense extent, containing such a
number of inhabitants, and these encreasing in such rapid pro-
gression as that of the whole United States.' The first of 'the many
illustrious authorities' cited by Brutus is none other than Montesquieu, and more particularly his observation that 'It is natural to a

republic to have only a small territory, otherwise it cannot long subsist.' Large territories, having heterogeneous populations, diverse interests and immoderate men of large fortunes, are by their very nature incapable of self-government. They are, there-fore, more naturally governed either by monarchs or despots.[29]

Hamilton and Madison were prepared for attack from this quarter. They had read their Hume and had rehearsed their arguments in advance of Brutus' assault.[30] They soon countered with a one-two punch in *Federalist* Nos 9 and 10, published on 21 and 22 November. Not to be outdone by Brutus' reference to 'the science of government', Publius in No. 9 raises the ante, averring that Brutus' science is outmoded, if indeed it is scientific at all. 'The science of politics,' Hamilton sniffs, 'like most other sciences, has received great improvement'. Thanks to discoveries made in the interim, Rome and Athens will no longer suffice as examples of republican rectitude and longevity. And inasmuch as the Roman republic provided Machiavelli's paradigm, Machiavelli and his heirs – English, French, and American – are all equally passé.[31] Publius thus echoes Hume's remark that Machiavelli lived in too early an age to have been a truly scientific thinker:

> . . . the world is still too young to fix many general truths in politics, which will remain true to the latest posterity. We have not as yet had experience of three thousand years; so that not only the art of reasoning is imperfect in this science [of politics], but we even want [i.e., lack] sufficient materials upon which we can reason. . . . MACHIAVEL was certainly a great genius; but having confined his study to the furious and tyrannical governments of ancient times . . . his reasonings . . . have been found extremely defective . . . [T]he errors of that politician proceed . . . from his having lived in too early an age of the world, to be a good judge of political truth.[32]

Thus those who follow in Machiavelli's footsteps – including, eventually, even Montesquieu himself – are still steeped in the ignorance and error of that earlier age.

Hamilton continues to press the claim that theirs is an age of new developments and novel discoveries. Indeed, he has the temerity to 'venture, however novel it may appear to some, to add one more' truth to an already expanding body of scientific knowledge. 'I mean the ENLARGEMENT of the ORBIT within which such systems are to revolve. . ..'[33] Taking a larger and less localized view of the American political universe, Publius thereby plays Copernicus to the benighted Brutus' Ptolemy. The rhetorical intent is to undercut the force of any appeal to antiquity or to arguments from authority, which Publius disavows because they are unscientific. Publius thereby portrays his opponent as a mere autodidact, an amateur describing after the fact the scientific discoveries of an earlier age, and himself as a scientist adding new contributions to an ever-expanding body of scientific knowledge.

By the time Publius gets round to Brutus' confident reference to 'many illustrious authorities' and 'the opinion of the greatest men' – including the untouchable Montesquieu – the damage has already been done. 'The opponents of the PLAN proposed have with great assiduity cited and circulated the observations of Montesquieu on the necessity of a contracted territory for a republican government,' Hamilton allows with an air of anti-climax. As if mention of their outdated second-hand science were not sufficient rebuke, Publius adds articulate insult to inarticulate injury when he suggests that the Antifederalists not only assume an uncritical and unscientific attitude toward traditional authority but have failed even to read their authorities aright. Although they cite Montesquieu, 'they seem not to have been apprised of the sentiments of that great man, expressed in another part of his work, nor to have adverted to the consequences of the principle to which they subscribe, with such ready acquiescense.'[34]

Publius makes two points. The first is that the Antifederalists cannot legitimately employ Montesquieu's arguments about the restricted size of republics inasmuch as his very scale or standard of measurement is, in America, already outdated:

> When Montesquieu recommends a small extent for republics, the standards he had in view were of dimensions, far short of the limits of almost every one of these States. Neither Virginia, Massachusetts, Pennsylvania, New York, North Carolina, nor Georgia, can by any means be compared with the models, from which he reasoned and to which the terms of his description apply.

From this it follows that Montesquieu's terms of political discourse – including, by implication, his understanding of 'republic' itself – are inapplicable in America, not only under the new Constitution but even under the Articles of Confederation. Indeed, 'if we take his ideas on this point, as the criterion of truth, we shall be driven to the alternative, either of taking refuge at once in the arms of monarchy, or of splitting ourselves into an infinity of little, jealous, clashing, tumultous commonwealths, the wretched nurseries of unceasing discord and the miserable objects of universal pity or contempt.'[35] (The political choice is thus rhetorically recast in mathematical terms: an unacceptable unity ('monarchy') or an intolerable 'infinity'.) Publius' genius resides in his having shown that the Antifederalist equation can be solved for two unknowns, both of which, when known, prove equally unacceptable. A new standard and a new scale are accordingly called for.

Publius' second point is that this new standard or scale is to be found, ironically, in Montesquieu's notion of a 'confederate republic'. Had the Antifederalists read their chief authority aright they would have seen already what Publius must now show them. Montesquieu, he explains, 'explicitly treats of a CONFEDER-ATE REPUBLIC as the expedient for extending the sphere of popular government and reconciling the advantages of monarchy with those of republicanism.' After an extensive citation of the relevant passages – passages routinely quoted by Antifederalists for contrary purposes – Publius admits to having 'thought it proper to quote at length these interesting passages, because they contain a luminous abridgement of the principal arguments in favour of the Union.' Having turned the Antifederalists' chief ally against them, Hamilton concludes No. 9 by turning against Montesquieu, whose authority, however welcome it might be, is not needed. His various distinctions and discriminations are in the end more scholastic than scientific. The 'distinctions insisted upon were not within the contemplation of this enlightened civilian' and must therefore be dismissed as 'the novel refinements of an erroneous theory'.[36]

Hamilton's countering of the restricted-size argument in *Federalist* No. 9 paves the way for the conceptual revision of 'republic' offered on the following day in No. 10. Without mentioning Montesquieu by name, Madison rejects the heretofore unchallenged Montesquieuian idea that a republic can be democratic. By insisting upon a sharp distinction between a 'democracy' and a 'republic' Madison redraws the conceptual map in a radically new way. There is of course nothing novel about his description of democracy as a system of direct rule by an assembly of citizens who inhabit a relatively restricted territory; Montesquieu himself had said as much. What is novel is Madison's two-fold insistence that, *pace* Montesquieu, a democracy cannot be a republic and – more strikingly still – his radical redefinition of 'republic' itself. A democracy, in Madison's view, is neither more nor less than a system in which the numerically largest group rules. Calling this ruling part 'the majority' does not alter the fact that it is capable of degenerating into a faction ruling unchecked in its own interest. A 'pure democracy', therefore, 'can admit of no cure for the mischiefs of faction'. An altogether different form – a republic – 'opens a different prospect, and promises the cure for which we are seeking'.[37] A republic, as Madison (re)defines it, is characterized by two key features. The first is its system of delegation or representation; the second, its enlarged extent (or 'orbit' in No. 9).

 Madison of course knows, though he omits to mention, that the kind of pure or direct democracy he decries – and also the kind of democratic republic described by Montesquieu – is likely to be practicable only on the scale of a town or a city. But this is scarcely what his Antifederalist foes were alluding to in defending the sovereignty of the several state-republics and arguing against the new constitution's creation of an extended republic. They were, so to speak, defending an entirely different position and performing an altogether different series of speech-acts. Despite the caricature presented by Publius, Brutus and his fellow Antifederalists were hardly simple democrats defending direct democracy; many saw themselves, rather, as republicans of a classical stripe.[38] And being good republicans they posted their warnings about the future by turning to the past. 'History,' says Brutus, 'furnishes no example of a free republic, anything like the extent of the United States. The Grecian republics were of small extent; so also was that of the Romans.' And when they 'extended their conquests over large territories of country' they ceased to be republics, 'their governments [having] changed from that of free governments to those of the most tyrannical that ever existed in the world'.[39] As if 'the opinions of the greatest men, and the experience of mankind' were not enough to show how misbegotten 'the idea of an extensive republic is', Brutus adds that 'reason and the nature of things [are] against it':

> In every government, (the will) of the sovereign is the law. In despotic governments, the supreme authority being lodged in one, his will is law, and can be as easily expressed to a large extensive territory as to a small one. In a pure democracy the people are sovereign, and their will is declared by themselves; for this purpose they must all come together to deliberate, and decide. This kind of government cannot be exercised, therefore, over a country of any considerable extent; it must be confined to a single city, or at least limited to such bounds as that the people can conveniently assemble, be able to debate, understand the subject submitted to them, and declare their opinion concerning it.

Brutus goes on to suggest that a 'free republic' represents a *via media* between these extremes. It is neither large enough to make despotism necessary nor small enough to make direct democracy possible. The 'true criterion between a free government and an arbitrary one' is that the former requires that 'the people must give their assent to the laws by which they are governed', and this they do through their representatives.[40]

Brutus is, thus, defending not direct democracy but state sovereignty while at the same time warning his audience of the danger of despotism that extended territory brings to a republic. 'I have attempted to shew,' he says, 'that a consolidation of this extensive continent, under one government, for internal, as well as external purposes . . . cannot succeed without a sacrifice of your liberties.' Hence, he concludes, 'the attempt is not only preposterous, but extremely dangerous.'[41] Brutus is warning, in short, of the danger of creating an American empire ruled by despots rather than duly elected representatives.

3.5 TWO CONCEPTS OF REPRESENTATION

Far from being a defence of 'direct democracy' – a rhetorical red herring of Madison's own devising – Antifederalist arguments about size and scale are actually about the conditions under which representative government can be said to be truly representative. Their disagreements about the criterion of true representativeness and about the kind and quality of representation afforded by the new constitution stem from their subscribing to two quite different, indeed incommensurable, theories of representation. Following Hanna Pitkin, I propose to call these the 'mandate' and the 'independence' theories.[42] According to the mandate view, the task of a representative is to mirror the views of those he represents; he does as they would do, were they in his place. His function is not merely to represent their interests but to share their attitudes and feelings as well. He is to be their 'actual' representative. The independence view, by contrast, holds that the representative is a trustee who must make his own judgements concerning his constituents' interests and how they might be best served. He is to be their 'virtual', not their 'actual', representative. The constituents' feelings and attitudes are, from this perspective, largely irrelevant.[43]

In the main, and depending upon which governmental body was being discussed, the Antifederalists subscribed to the mandate view, and the Federalists to the independence view. To be sure, they did not all speak with a single voice on this, or any other, issue. But most were agreed on at least three points. The first was that the House of Representatives, but not the Senate, should be a representative cross-section or microcosm of the larger society. Secondly, members of the House should be guided by the actual or 'mandate' theory of representation, even if Senators did (or should) not do so. Thirdly, they were agreed that the House did not in fact meet the first two requirements and was therefore not a genuinely representative body. Like many of his fellow Antifederalists Brutus believed that the new constitution created two representative bodies that were so in name only. His harshest words were reserved for the House of Representatives, which he thought misnamed. 'The more I reflect on this subject, the more firmly am I persuaded, that the representation is merely nominal – a mere burlesque . . .'[44] And, given the master metaphors and controlling imagery of Antifederalist discourse, and their theory of representation in particular, this charge comes as no surprise. In attempting to picture the relationship between a constituent and

his 'actual' representative, mandate theorists often employ the
pictorial imagery of 'resemblance', 'reflection' and 'mirroring',
and Brutus is no exception:

> The very term representative implies, that the person or body
> chosen for this purpose, should *resemble* those who appoint them –
> a representation of the people of America, if it be a true one, must
> be *like* the people. It ought to be so constituted, that a person, who
> is a stranger to the country, might be able to form a just idea of
> their character, by knowing that of their representatives. They are
> the *sign* – the people are the thing signified. It is absurd to speak of
> one thing being the *representative* of another, upon any other
> principle. . . . [T]hose who are placed instead of the people, should
> possess their sentiments and feelings, and be governed by their
> interests, or, in other words, should bear the strongest *resemblance*
> of those in whose room they are substituted.[45]

From this pictoral or mandate view of representation Brutus
derives what he takes to be a mathematically warranted conclusion:

> It is obvious, that for an assembly to be a true likeness of the people
> of any country, they must be considerably numerous. – One man,
> or a few men, cannot possibly represent the feelings, opinions, and
> characters of a great multitude. In this respect, the new constitution
> is radically defective.[46]

It is important to note that Brutus is *not* suggesting that representatives should, or even can, represent each of their individual
constituents in their uniqueness. Clearly that would be impossible, for the number of representatives would then equal the
number of people represented. The result would then be, not
representative government, but direct democracy. And that, as we
have already seen, is not the system that Brutus and most of his
fellow Antifederalists were defending.

What system, then, were the Antifederalist defending? It is a
system of representation resting, as we have seen, upon the
mandate theory of 'actual' representation, to which is added yet
another earlier republican conception, namely, representation not
of individuals but of 'orders' or 'ranks' or 'classes' (this last not
referring to socioeconomic classes in the later nineteenth-century

sense). As Brutus puts it: 'This extensive continent is made up of a number of different classes of people; and to have a proper representation of them, each class ought to have an opportunity of choosing their best informed men for the purpose.' If there is to be a 'just resemblance' between 'the several classes of people' in the society and those they elect to speak on their behalf in the representative assemblies – and the House of Representatives in particular – then

> the farmer, merchant, mecanick, and other various orders of people, ought to be represented according to their respective weight and numbers; and the representatives ought to be intimately acquainted with the wants, understand the interests of the several orders . . ., and feel a proper sense and becoming zeal to promote their prosperity.[47]

The mode of election and system of representation mandated by the new constitution are designed not only to thwart the representation of the various orders or ranks, but to ensure their exclusion:

> The great body of the yeomen of the country cannot expect any of their order in this assembly [namely, the House of Representatives] – the station will be too elevated for them to aspire to – the distance between the people and their representatives, will be so very great, that there is no probability that a farmer, however respectable, will be chosen – the mechanicks of every branch, must expect to be excluded from a seat in this Body.[48]

The result will be that 'in reality there will be no part of the people represented, but the rich, even in that branch of the legislature, which is called democratic.' The Federalists' claim that those elected will disinterestedly serve all the people, including the 'democratical part', is 'specious' in the eighteenth-century sense, i.e., attractive but erroneous. 'The well born, and highest orders in life, as they term themselves,' warns Brutus, 'will be ignorant of the sentiments of the midling class of citizens, strangers to their abilities, wants, and difficulties, and void of sympathy, and fellow feeling.' Theirs 'will literally be a government in the hands of the few to oppress and plunder the many.'[49]

This is republican rhetoric about the recognition and representation of orders and ranks, not populist rhetoric about how naturally virtuous and pure 'the people' or 'the masses' are. For all their talk about how important it is that 'the democratical part' be represented in a well-ordered republic, most Antifederalists were far from sympathetic to pure or direct democracy, much less to narrow partisan politics, and still less to mob rule. To argue otherwise is to accept the caricature painted for partisan purposes by their Federalist opponents. Had the Antifederalists couched their arguments not in the idiom of classical republicanism but in that of undifferentiated mass democracy, they would have succeeded only in shooting themselves in their collective foot. In the 1780s 'republic' was by and large a term of approbation and 'democracy' a term of opprobrium.[50] Had the Antifederalists been democrats and their arguments democratic, they would hardly have called forth, or even required, the concentrated rhetorical firepower of *The Federalist*. But they were not, by their lights at least, democrats; they were republicans constructing and propagating republican arguments for an audience that they expected, not without reason, to share their republican sympathies.[51]

It was precisely because the arguments of Brutus and of other Antifederalists were bound to strike deeply resonant republican chords that they had to be met, if not head-on, then at least sideways. Brutus' paper of 15 November was met one week later by Madison's most powerful broadside, the justly famed *Tenth Federalist*. After attempting to tar the Antifederalists with the brush of direct democracy, the real choice, as Madison finally acknowledges, is not between democratic and republican forms, after all. The choice facing Americans is actually between two types of republic and the kinds of representatives likely to be chosen in them. Is a small (or classical or Montesquieuian) republic to be preferred to a large (modern or Humean) one? The answer one gives will, he allows, depend less upon *who* is to be represented than upon *what* is to be represented. The choice is between representing the private interests of the various orders – rhetorically redubbed 'factions' – or the public good. If we subscribe to the mandate view, he suggests, our legislation will consist of an impure amalgam of narrow factional interests, not a duly filtered distillation of pure public interestedness. Assuming that real republicans will want the latter rather than the former, the only question remaining is how that result might best be achieved. 'The question resulting,' says Madison, 'is, whether small or extensive republics are most favorable to the election of proper guardians of the public weale.' The issue is 'clearly decided in favour of the latter' by 'two considerations,' both of which, he allows, are 'obvious'. The first, which is indeed crashingly obvious, is that the pool of 'fit characters' is likely to be larger in a large society than in a small one. The second consideration is rather less obviously true. It amounts to saying that the greater the number of voters in any given election, the more difficult it is for 'unworthy candidates to practice with success the vicious arts, by which elections are too often carried'.[52]

The point of Madison's argument is to counter the charge of corruption in the event that the wealthy acquire undue influence. If wealth brings one kind of corruption, as Brutus and the Antifederalists charge, a 'numerous representation' would result in corruption of another, and far worse, sort. Where Brutus had decried the actions of unrepresentative representatives, Madison decried the stratagems of 'unworthy candidates' who were likely to triumph in a popular free-for-all. Bribery, bombast, demagoguery, and the various 'vicious arts' would be their stock-in-trade. In other words, while Brutus and the Antifederalists focused on what representatives are apt to do after they are elected, Madison and his fellow Federalists focused initially on what candidates might do in order to be elected in the first place, and secondarily upon what wicked and improper projects they might pursue after they took office.

The issue of 'actual' versus 'virtual' representation could not be so easily disposed of, however, and Hamilton returned to face it head-on in No. 35. The Antifederalist argument in favour of actual representation he portrays as 'specious and seductive' and 'altogether visionary', consisting only of 'fair sounding words' which are 'well calculated to lay hold of the prejudices of those to whom [they are] addressed'. Hamilton counters with arguments of two sorts. The first we might call the arithmetical, the second the sociological, argument. The arithmetical argument is simply a reminder that such a system would, by greatly increasing the number of representatives, be well-nigh impossible to put into practice. For if the Constitution should require 'an actual representation of all classes of the people by persons of each class,' then 'each different occupation' would have to 'send one or more members' to the Congress. This would require a representative body so large and unwieldly that 'the thing would never take place in practice.' Not only is such a scheme 'impracticable'; it is also 'unnecessary' for reasons that we might today term sociological. There is a 'natural' tendency for persons of lower social standing to defer to, and to rely upon, those possessing higher social status:

> Mechanics and manufacturers will always be inclined . . . to give their votes to merchants in preference to persons of their own professions or trades. Those discerning citizens . . . know that the merchant is their natural patron and friend; and they are aware that however great the confidence they may justly feel in their own good sense, their interests can be more effectually promoted by the merchant than by themselves. . . .. We must therefore consider merchants as the natural representatives of all these classes of the community.

To talk of the efficiency with which their 'interests' may be 'promoted' might appear to miss the point, as Hamilton acknowledges. The Antifederalists believe it 'necessary that all classes of citizens should have some of their own number in the representative body, in order that their feelings and interests may be the better understood and attended to.' But this, Hamilton says in effect, is to overlook the likelihood that their 'feelings' are apt to be of inadequacy, inferiority and incompetence. The lower orders would therefore be understandably reluctant to send people like themselves to Congress to represent their 'feelings and interests'! The 'altogether visionary' hope of creating a system of actual representation 'will never happen under any arrangement that leaves the votes of the people free'.[53]

Significantly, however, Hamilton omits to mention, much less to answer, the recurrent Antifederalist charge that the new constitution would exacerbate and intensify these feelings of civic incompetence, leading inevitably to popular apathy, political corruption, and the loss of civic virtue.

3.6 CORRUPTION AND VIRTUE

We have seen already how 'corruption' in the republican tradition of discourse refers to a condition in which rulers and citizens have ceased to know or care about the common good, preferring instead to seek their own private (and especially pecuniary) interests. Just as the human body becomes 'corrupt' with age, so likewise must the body politic sooner or later lose its unity and organic integrity, its 'parts' becoming partisan, self-seeking, and ceasing to work together for some greater shared purpose. To have lost interest in the common good is to have ceased to be a citizen, or at any rate a virtuous one. Corruption is, in short, the loss or absence of civic virtue.[54]

The concepts of corruption and virtue, as used by many Antifederalist writers, have deep republican roots. The Antifederalist critique echoes many of the themes to be found in the earlier English republican and radical Whig warnings of the dangers of corruption, especially those sounded by eighteenth-century English 'country' party ideologists against the 'court' ideology of Walpole and the new Whigs.[55] Thus, for example, the Real Whig warnings about the dangers of political appointees or 'placemen' is repeated by Brutus when he decries 'that kind of corruption, and undue influence, which will arise from the gift of places of honor and emolument'. This, combined with other forms of 'influence', is certain to corrupt the executive and the legislature. Indeed,

> when it is considered what a number of places of honor and emolument will be the gift of the executive, the powerful influence that great and designing men have over the honest and unsuspecting, by their art and address, their soothing manners and civilities, and their cringing flattery, joined with their affected patriotism: when these different species of influence are combined, it is scarcely to be hoped that a legislature, composed of so small a number, as the one proposed by the new constitution, will long resist their force.[56]

Without 'an equal and full representation in the legislature' there could be 'no security against bribery and corruption'.[57]

The corruption of officials or representatives was one thing, but the corruption of the citizenry another, and arguably more serious, matter. In the Antifederalist view, these were linked in either of two ways. On the one hand, if the members of the various orders should agree that 'fit characters' not of their order were by nature or disposition better able to represent their interests, they might then be willing to consign their liberties to the doubtful safekeeping of the 'natural aristocracy' of their social superiors. On the other hand, should the citizens feel themselves to be powerless and voiceless, they would lose interest in public affairs. In either event they would concentrate on their own purely personal or private affairs and grow lazy or lax as regards the good of their own order and, by implication, of the common good as well. Either would result inevitably in the corruption of the citizenry and, ultimately, in the destruction of their liberties.

As depicted by Antifederalist critics, the new constitution embodied both defects. Suspecting a massive Federalist conspiracy against republican ideals and institutions, many Antifederalists felt that the new constitution was designed precisely for the dual purpose of making citizens trust their social superiors even as they themselves forgot the Spirit of '76 and became inward-looking and inattentive to matters of common concern. The new constitution could therefore be viewed, in the idiom of classical republicanism, as a medium or instrument of civic corruption and a destroyer of the people's liberties.

In the discourse of Antifederalist republicanism, moreover, a properly constructed constitution is more than a set of rules. Inspiring, informing and educating the citizenry about their rights and duties, a constitution is also a medium of civic character-formation and public instruction. However hastily drafted and ill-written the various state constitutions may have been, they purportedly fulfilled that educative function. They admonished governors and representatives even as they reminded the citizens that republican liberties are too easily lost when the public is inattentive.[58] From this perspective one can more readily appreciate the Antifederalists' antipathy toward the document drawn up in Philadelphia.

One of the Antifederalists' main complaints was that the new constitution sent the wrong sort of message to the citizenry. Not only did its implicit theory of representation imply that their views did not much matter and that the protection of their and the public's interest was best left to an elite; it also failed to inculcate the all-important sense of civic virtue. These defects were said by many Antifederalists to be most painfully obvious in the absence of a Bill of Rights. Such an addition would serve as a reminder to all – rulers and citizens alike – that the government's authority was limited by its citizens' inviolable liberties. Did not the Glorious Revolution result in a Bill of Rights agreed to by King William? Did not the still more glorious revolution of 1776 deserve no less a guarantee? What was it fought for, if not to preserve American rights and liberties? If they are to be properly protected, the nature and extent of those liberties must be fixed from the outset. The good will or solicitude of rulers or representatives was not to be relied upon for very long, if at all.[59] Those who have power are bound to abuse it, unless checked by the law and an active and alert citizenry.

Even in a well-ordered republic there exists an inevitable tendency toward corruption. And to Antifederalist eyes this new American republic seemed to be singularly ill-ordered, its tendency toward corruption hastened at its birth by a constitution that encouraged corruption by empowering rulers and representatives at the national or federal level even as it emasculated the citizenry at a more local level. This emasculation was effected in part by making the individual citizen and his order smaller by enlarging the scale on which national action was to be taken by an unrepresentative elite. At the very least, then, some 'declaration of rights' must be written into the new plan, lest the people be deceived and led into a trap from which there would be no escape.[60] Without such a declaration to protect the rights of 'the democratical part', says Brutus, 'the plan is radically defective in a fundamental principle, which ought to be found in every free government; to wit, a declaration of rights.'[61] Because the arguments in favour of such a declaration are so compelling, its omission is an ominous portent, revealing the true colours of Publius and his fellow Federalists: 'so clear a point is this, that I cannot help suspecting, that persons who attempt to persuade people, that such reservations were less necessary under this constitution, than under those of the states, are willfully endeavouring to deceive, and to lead you into an absolute state of vassalage.'[62] Again and again the Antifederalists hammered the point home with all the repetitive intensity of the Anvil Chorus: without a bill of rights the new system scarcely deserved the name republican.

Finally, in No. 84, Publius was compelled to answer, although reluctantly and under the heading of 'miscellaneous points' to be dealt with as though they were mere afterthoughts and scarcely on a par with the truly important issues discussed earlier. 'The most considerable of these remaining objections,' writes Hamilton, 'is, that the plan of the convention contains no bill of rights.' By way of reply he notes that several state constitutions, including New York's, are also without bills of rights. Acknowledging the force of the Antifederalists' answer to this objection – namely, that no separate bill of rights is needed because provisions for protecting those rights are incorporated into the texts of the state constitutions – Hamilton asserts that the same is true of the new federal constitution as well. 'The truth is, after all the declamation we have heard, that the constitution is itself in every rational sense, and to every useful purpose, A BILL OF RIGHTS.'[63] Yet the bill of rights that Hamilton teases out of the text is a rather motley amalgam of legal guarantees, prohibitions and definitions. The 'priviledges' of *habeas corpus* and jury trials are affirmed (although there is no requirement that the jury be composed of one's peers); 'treason' is defined; and the prohibition of titles of nobility, of which Madison had made so much in No. 39, is again presented as proof positive of the republican character of the new constitution:

> Nothing need be said to illustrate the importance of the prohibition of titles of nobility. This may truly be denominated the corner stone of republican government; for so long they are excluded, there can never be any serious danger that the government will be any other than that of the people.[64]

Well aware that 'A Countryman' and other Antifederalists had earlier denied that there was any necessary connection between the two,[65] Hamilton then goes on to play his ace. The Antifederalists had often charged their opponents with attempting to alter the meanings of key concepts. Now it is Hamilton's turn. Playing the part of conceptual historian, he turns the tables by charging the Antifederalists with having attempted to alter the very meaning of the concept of a bill of rights – a concept as old as the Magna Carta and as recent as the Bill of Rights to which William of Orange had agreed. Because 'bills of rights are in their origin, stipulations between kings and their subjects,' says Hamilton, they have no place in a republican charter. 'Here, in strictness, the people

surrender nothing, and as they retain every thing, they have no
need of particular reservations.' The Preamble, he sniffs, affords 'a
better recognition of popular rights than volumes of those
aphorisms . . . in several of our state bills of rights, and which
would sound much better in a treatise of ethics than in a
constitution of government.'[66]

In thus downplaying 'ethics' Publius did not so much deny the
importance of virtue and character as he proposed to *relocate* them.
Henceforth virtue would not be an individual but a systemic
property. It is the virtue and character of the *system*, not the
citizenry, that Publius praises repeatedly. The citizen is, at best, a
weak reed bending easily before the wind of self-interest. If the
individual be weak, the system must be strong. 'Ambition must be
made to counteract ambition.' The appropriate 'policy' must
therefore be one 'of supplying by opposite and rival interests, the
defect of better motives'.[67] Here again Publius follows Hume:

> Political writers have established it as a maxim, that, in contriving
> any system of government, and fixing the several checks and
> controuls of the constitution, every man ought to be supposed a
> knave, and to have no other end, in all his actions, than private
> interest. By this interest we must govern him, and, by means of it,
> making him, notwithstanding his insatiable avarice and ambition,
> co-operate to public good.[68]

The corruptibility of the citizenry is, in short, to be stemmed by the
incorruptibility of the system.

In thus relocating virtue, Publius redefines its role and changes
its meaning. And in changing the meaning of 'virtue' and its proper
place within a 'republic', Publius partially reconstituted the concept of republic. Yet this and other conceptual changes can hardly
be discounted, much less dismissed, as so much semantic quibbling
or rhetorical window-dressing; they were, rather, rational strategies in a hard-fought conceptual-cum-political struggle.

3.7   PUBLIUS' LINGUISTIC TURN

As the ratification debate intensified, the protagonists focused not
only upon individual issues but also, and increasingly, upon the
appropriate language in which to frame and discuss these very

issues. <u>Madison, in particular, recasts the conflict over ratification as a competition between tongues, languages and voices.</u> 'Hearken not,' he admonishes,

> to the voice which petulantly tells you that the form of government recommended for your adoption is a novelty in the political world; that it has never yet had a place in the theories of the wildest projectors; that it rashly attempts what it is impossible to accomplish.

#14

In an uncharacteristically emotional appeal the calm and 'candid' Madison adds: 'No, my countrymen, shut your ears against this unhallowed language.' Even this might not seem so odd, were it not that Madison then goes on to take that very language for his own. He admits that the critics are right, after their fashion: The system *is* new; it is untried. 'But why,' he asks, 'is the experiment of an extended republic to be rejected merely because it . . . is new?'[69]

But since the Antifederalists had not objected to the new constitution merely because it was new and untried, but because it was by their lights not truly 'republican', Publius returned repeatedly to the defence of his, and the new constitution's, republican *bona fides*. In *Federalist 14* Madison once again felt compelled to defend the distinction drawn in No. 10 between a democracy and a republic, but this time with a new logical-cum-linguistic twist that was to become even more pronounced as the ratification debate wore on through the waning months of 1787 and well into 1788. Due to a 'fallacy' stemming from 'the confusion of names,' Madison avers, 'it has been an easy task to transfer to a republic, observations applicable to a democracy only,' including the oft-heard contention that a republic 'can never be established but among a small number of people, living within a small compass of territory.' 'Such a fallacy,' he adds on an apparently conciliatory note, 'may have been the less perceived as most of the governments of antiquity were of the democratic species.' What he omits to note, of course, is what Machiavelli and Montesquieu accepted without question, namely that those 'democracies' were in fact 'republics'. Without mentioning either republican theorist by name, Madison reiterates and reinforces the 'Humean' point made by Hamilton in No. 9: Earlier thinkers – Machiavelli and Montesquieu among them – lived in too early an

age to see what can now be seen clearly by all but the most
benighted and prejudiced. Not wishing to pit any of the founders
against those republican paragons, he attributes this new
'discovery' not to the genius of any man or small band of men but
to that of an entire nation. 'America,' says Madison, 'can claim the
merit of making the discovery [of 'the great principle of representation'] the basis of unmixed and extensive republics.'[70] Thus
Madison invokes the classical republican notion of 'glory' not for
the framers, as Publius had proclaimed in No. 9, but now for the
people themselves. 'Is it not the glory of the people of America,'
he asks, 'that whilst they have paid a decent regard to the opinions
of former times and other nations, they have not suffered a blind
veneration for antiquity, for custom, or for names, to overrule the
suggestions of their own good sense. . .?' It is to this forward-
looking 'manly spirit' of innovation that 'posterity will be indebt-
ed'.[71] Madison omits to mention that the innovation is above all a
conceptual one. For it is after all the concept of republic itself that he
(like Hume before him) has subtly if not altogether convincingly
tried to transform.

It is scarcely surprising, then, that Brutus and other critics were
quick to charge Publius with abusing the hallowed language of
republicanism.[72] Madison responded by taking his own version of
the linguistic turn. All language, republican or otherwise, he
complains, is an inherently imperfect medium. His exasperation is
especially evident in No. 37, where he decries the opacity and
recalcitrance of language itself:

> [T]he medium through which the conceptions of men are conveyed
> to each other, adds a fresh embarrassment. The use of words is to
> express ideas. Perspicuity therefore requires not only that the ideas
> should be distinctly formed, but that they should be expressed by
> words distinctly and exclusively appropriated to them. But no
> language is so copious as to supply words and phrases for every
> complex idea, or so correct as not to include many equivocally
> denoting different ideas. Hence, it must happen, that however
> accurately objects may be discriminated in themselves, and how-
> ever accurately the discrimination may be considered, the defi-
> nition of them may be rendered inaccurate by the inaccuracy of the
> terms in which it is delivered. And this unavoidable inaccuracy

must be greater or less, according to the complexity and novelty of the objects defined.

Imprecision and 'inaccuracy' are 'unavoidable', the more so as 'the objects defined' are complex or novel, or both. The object of an extended republic having been admitted (in No. 14 and elsewhere) to be both novel and complex, Madison reflects upon the difficulty facing any conceptual innovator. Machiavelli and Rousseau had asked how a human but god-like legislator can hope to communicate with ordinary mortals, given the limitations of their language.[73] Madison wonders aloud whether God Almighty himself might fail to make his meaning clear, were he to speak to us even in our own tongue. 'When the Almighty himself condescends to address mankind in their own language,' says Madison, 'his meaning, luminous as it must be, is rendered dim and doubtful, by the cloudy medium through which it is communicated.'[74]

Madison goes on to list 'three sources of vague and incorrect definitions' – namely 'indistinctness of the object, imperfection of the organ of conception, [and] inadequateness of the vehicle of ideas' – any one of which 'must produce a certain degree of obscurity'. In remarking that the framers of the new plan had 'experienced the full effect of them all', Madison implied that mere mortals had been saddled, as Rousseau had remarked, with the responsibility of gods. In Madison's hands, however, this was not a proclamation of superiority, but a plea for sympathy and understanding of the difficulties faced by legislators who are also conceptual innovators. Not the least of these difficulties involved the problems presented by Publius' newly minted concept of republic.

Madison therefore felt compelled to return in No. 39 to the bold promise made in No. 1 and to the question that he had attempted to answer in Nos 10, 14 and 37. In No. 1 Publius had promised to demonstrate 'the conformity of the proposed constitution to the true principles of republican government'.[75] In No. 10 he had offered 'a Republican remedy for the diseases most incident to Republican Government'.[76] In No. 14 he reiterated and reinforced the argument of No. 10. And in No. 37 he had adverted to the inadequacy of language as a medium of political communication. One senses in his linguistic turn a growing sense of desperation. In the six weeks that had passed since the appearance of the first number of *The Federalist* he had failed to convince his critics that the new government would be republican in form and spirit; and he could only fear that his wider audience must share their scepticism.

And so, already nearly halfway through the series, Madison begins No. 39 with a question that should have been settled earlier. 'The first question that offers itself is, whether the general form and aspect of the government be strictly republican?' For, he admits,

> It is evident that no other form would be reconcileable with the genius of the people of America; with the fundamental principles of the revolution; or with that honorable determination, which animates every votary of freedom, to rest all our political experiments on the capacity of mankind for self-government. If the plan of the Convention therefore be found to depart from the republican character, its advocates must abandon it as no longer defensible.[77]

The stakes are higher now. Madison must prove the republican character of the new constitution or repudiate it. But how?

Publius' two-fold strategy might best be characterized as a linguistic or conceptual counterattack. His first task is to show that the term 'republic' has been applied indifferently and indiscriminately, even by the greatest authorities – and thus, by implication, by those lesser authorities who cite them, the Antifederalists. This done, he can then defend not only the legitimacy but also the superiority of his alternative understanding. He begins by asking what 'the distinctive features of the republican form' are. He then proceeds to show that there is no single feature or set of features shared by all polities designated as 'republics'. Holland, Venice, Poland and England have all been called republics at one time or another. Yet 'these examples, which are nearly as dissimilar to each other as to a genuine republic, show the extreme inaccuracy with which the term has been used in political disquisitions.'[78]

About Madison's first move we might pause to note two objections that his Antifederalist opponents did not, and indeed could not, have raised. The first is that Madison's criticism is, from a linguistic point of view, misconceived, not to say misleading. It is a little like asking, as Wittgenstein does in another context and for another purpose, what single feature or set of features are common to all the things we call games. What do board games, games played on fields, with and without balls or other objects, by teams or by individuals or by solitary players, etc., have in common? The answer, of course, is nothing – and everything. There are, as Wittgenstein remarks, 'family resemblances' between and among all those things we call 'games'.[79] Just as no single feature – nose shape, hair colour, complexion, etc. – is shared by all members of one family, so too, we might say, no single feature is shared by all those polities called republics. To raise this objection would, however, be unfair, not to say anachronistic.

A second objection, however, suffers from neither of these liabilities. Translated into more modern terms, it amounts to this. There is today no political system that has not been described by someone, somewhere, as 'democratic'. Chile, South Africa, South Korea, North Korea, East Germany, West Germany, the Soviet Union and the United States have all been described as 'democracies'. From this fact, neither of two conclusions follow. The first – that their systems of government are essentially similar if not identical – is self-evidently absurd. The second – that the term 'democracy' is meaningless – does not follow either. The most that can be concluded from this fact is that 'democracy' is a 'contested concept' whose criteria of application are disputed by partisans of different political persuasions.[80] And, as with 'democracy' in our day, so too with 'republic' in Publius' time.

Were this the sum and substance of Publius' argument in No. 39, the case for the 'republican character' of the plan would hardly have been proved. But once again Madison has warmed up, so to speak, by setting fire to a straw man. His second and weightier argument is about the priority of principles in political discourse. Names or labels, he maintains, count for less than principles. The former are applied by partisans of various ages in the heat of passion and political intrigue; the latter, by contrast, constitute the acid test of the validity of those claims. Thus, if we try to define a republic, 'not by recurring to principles, but in the application of the term by political writers, to the constitutions of different States, no satisfactory one would ever be found'.[81]

But when in No. 39 Publius sets out to 'define a republic' in 'principled' terms, he plays down the ostensibly crucial distinction – introduced in No. 10 and reiterated in No. 14 – between 'democracy' and 'republic.' Those particular institutional forms, he admits, apparently have no essential bearing upon the defining 'principle' of republicanism:

> [W]e may define a republic to be, or at least may bestow that name on, a government which derives all its powers directly or indirectly from the great body of the people; and is administered by persons holding their offices . . . for a limited period, or during good behaviour. It is *essential* to such a government, that it be derived from the great body of the society, not from an inconsiderable proportion, or a favored class of it; otherwise a handful of tyrannical nobles, exercising their oppressions by a delegation of their powers, might aspire to the rank of republicans, and claim for their government the honorable title of republic. It is *sufficient* for such a government, that the persons administering it be appointed, either directly or indirectly, by the people.[82]

There would now appear to be no reason 'in principle' why a democracy could not be a republic (though perhaps not a very harmonious or long-lived one, as Hamilton had charged in No. 9) and every reason why a system ruled by 'tyrannical nobles' cannot be. Publius must then show that, contrary to the charges levelled by some Antifederalists, the new system would not be a tyrannical aristocracy, either in principle or in practice. Publius points out that all the officers in the new government have their terms in office limited either by periodic elections or by good behaviour, adding that any of them can be removed from office at any time. Even the President can be impeached. And, as though this were not enough, Publius offers a final and apparently conclusive proof. 'Could any further proof be required of the republican complextion [sic] of this system,' he maintains, 'the most decisive one might be found in its absolute prohibition of titles of nobility, both under the Federal and the State governments; and in its express guarantee of the republican form to each of the latter.'[83]

The only decisive proofs in politics derive not from our language but from those principles whose meanings our language tries, too often in vain, to capture and hold. If the word 'republic' be mutable, Madison contends, the principles of republicanism are timeless and above the partisan fray. Ironically, in maintaining that principles, unlike terms, are timeless, Madison echoes John Toland's contention that 'men may change, and words may change, but principles never.'[84] What neither Toland nor Madison recognized, however, is that 'words' are no more mutable than 'principles', for there can be no principle that is not expressed in words. In revising the meaning of 'republic' Publius had not merely changed the meaning of a word. He had helped to reconstitute a concept and had thereby constituted a world. Whether or in what sense that world was any longer recognizably 'republican' remains a matter of dispute. Significantly enough, however, that dispute rages today amongst historians and not amongst citizens.

4

The Changing Face of Power

4.1 INTRODUCTION

Few concepts are more commonly encountered in political discussion and social-scientific discourse than 'power'. Yet, like many of the concepts constitutive of political discourse, 'power' has been the subject of considerable controversy. The apparent intractability of these disputes has led some to suggest that power is an 'essentially contested concept' whose meaning and criteria of application are and must remain forever unsettled.[1] It is doubtless because 'power' is such a central concept in political discourse that its meaning has been and continues to be so hotly contested. Yet, despite their disagreements, most of the disputants appear to agree that 'power' refers, at a minimum, to one agent or agency's ability to affect the attitudes and/or actions of another. The disputes have centred, as we shall see, on what kinds of entities can count as agents or agencies, and in what sorts of ways they must affect one another if an interaction is to count as a power relation.

My aim in this chapter is not to narrate a comprehensive history of the concept of power but to focus on several episodes that would occupy a central place in such a history. By these means I hope to bring into bolder relief the contours of this continuing conceptual controversy and to suggest something about the new direction(s) in which it may now be headed. My argument proceeds in the following way. I begin by briefly sketching an outline of the origins of the word (if not the concept of) power, saying something about its place in Roman political discourse. Next I contrast this earlier understanding with one which is in part traceable to developments in the seventeenth century, and particularly to the New Science as adapted by Hobbes and his successors to civil or political philosophy. My contention is that the New Science supplied the metaphors and the imagery in whose terms the discourse of twentieth-century social science is still largely constructed (and, arguably, constricted). In making this case I focus, for the sake of brevity and clarity, upon the 'three faces of power' debate in American political science. This ostensibly methodological and epistemological debate was in no small part an exercise in and a contribution to conceptual change. By tracing the internal dialectic of this debate we can, I think, discover the limits and the limitations of the discourse in which it was conducted and, in so doing, can be led to look for newer, more critical, and possibly more fruitful ways of talking and thinking about power. I conclude by examining the ways in which three alternative discourses construct the concept of power.

4.2 'POWER' IN HISTORICAL PERSPECTIVE

The English word 'power' comes by way of the French *pouvoir* which in turn derives from the Latin *potestas* or *potentia*, meaning 'ability' (both from the verb *potere*, to be able). For the Romans, *potentia* referred to the capacity or ability of one person or thing to affect another. *Potestas*, having a more narrowly political sense, referred to the particular kind of *potentia* possessed by people communicating and acting in concert. The kind of communicative action in which the people at large were capable of engaging was not, however, to be confused with the kind of careful judgement and deliberation that those in public office presumably possessed and were capable of exercising. The latter possessed not power but authority (*auctoritas*), understood as the capacity to begin, initiate and augment.[2] *Potestas* was the capacity of the people to empower those in authority. *Potestas*, like *auctoritas*, was thus identifiable and definable according to the kinds of agents who had and exercised it and what social space or office they occupied. This piece of conceptual-cum-political differentiation can be seen, for instance, in Cicero's maxim, *Potestas in populo, auctoritas in senatu*, 'Power in the people, authority in the Senate'. When today we say that there is power in numbers we capture something of the sense of that earlier understanding of 'power'.

To explain why this classical understanding of power did not survive into the modern age would be well beyond the scope of the present chapter, which is scarcely more than a sketch of several prominent features of a changing historical landscape. A more complete conceptual history would presumably cite several explanations, including such apparently disparate developments as the emergence of the modern state, the Protestant Reformation, and the scientific revolution of the seventeenth century. The scale and structure of the modern state brought with it changes in the understanding of the very nature of political power.[3] The Reformation removed the individual from an enfolding community of the faithful and placed him, isolated, before his God.

Nowhere, however, was this process of dissolution more dramatic than in the discourse and imagery of the New Science. Old landmarks and points of reference, once thought to be fixed and firm, were set into motion. The earth was displaced as the centre of the cosmos and sent whirling through the void in an orbit around the sun. The newly felt sense of loss and disorientation was well captured in Donne's tortured exclamation:

> And new Philosophy calls all in doubt;
> The Element of fire is quite put out;
> The Sun is lost, and th'earth, and no mans wit
> Can well direct him where to looke for it.
> And freely men confesse that this world's spent,
> When in the Planets and the Firmament
> They seeke so many new; they see that this
> Is crumbled out againe to his Atomies.
> 'Tis all in peeces, all cohaerence gone.[4]

And since the divinely ordered and earth-centred cosmos had been the source of a good deal of political symbolism, its dissolution presaged a new political imagery in which men were pictured as social atoms and self-interested calculators. This new imagery, in its turn, served to undermine older meanings and to give shape and credence to a new, or at any rate radically reworked, stock of concepts – including 'power'.

Amongst the first to adapt the discourse of the New Science to politics – and to 'power' in particular – was Thomas Hobbes. Borrowing the mechanistic imagery of the new science, Hobbes pictures power in terms of contacts and collisions in which some bodies ('agents') push other bodies ('patients'). Power is redefined as a causal relation between an actively pushing agent and a patient:

> Power and Cause are the same thing. Correspondent to cause and effect, are POWER and ACT; nay, those and these are the same things. . . . For whensoever any agent has all those accidents [i.e., combined features] which are necessarily requisite for the production of some effect in the patient, then we say that the agent has the power to produce that effect, if it be applied to a patient. . . . Wherefore the power of the agent and the efficient cause are the same thing.[5]

Hobbes' reconceptualization of power in causal terms entails also a reconceptualization of human agency. Human beings are reconceptualized as material entities who by their very nature are disconnected social atoms driven by desire and self-interest.

The central difficulty in Hobbes' attempt to reconceptualize 'power' within the framework of a materialist and determinist discourse lay in the fact that the possession and exercise of political power involves sentient subjects who have goals or aims and who are given to evaluating and appraising their situation in light of those aspirations. Human beings are, in short, not mute material objects but creatures who communicate, compare, criticize and make judgements. Thus, despite Hobbes' hope of redescribing human actions in the new 'scientific' idiom of mechanistic pushes and pulls, he could not expunge all traces of the older Aristotelian view that all things aim at some end and that human action necessarily involves some view of the good. This is especially evident in the exercise of power. So far as human beings are concerned the acquisition and exercise of power are inevitably connected with an agent's having some view of the good and an intention to bring it about. (There is of course no counterpart to this in the natural sciences.) Living in a world of scarcity, Hobbesian egoists will attempt to bring about their own good, which each equates with the satisfaction of his desires.[6] Each will therefore attempt to increase his power, which Hobbes defines as 'his present means, to obtain some future apparent Good'.[7] And 'because he cannot assure the power and means to live well, which he hath present, without the acquisition of more', Hobbes 'put[s] for a generall inclination of all mankind, a perpetuall and restlesse desire of Power after power, that ceaseth onely in Death.'[8] Power is, in sum, the ability of an agent in a relation of conflict to alter his and/or others' situation so as to promote his individual interests.

John Locke attempts to trace the origins of our 'simple [i.e., uncompounded] idea' of power which he, like Hobbes, understands essentially in causal terms. Like 'cause', the idea of power originates in our awareness of changes in sensory 'impressions':

> Power is one of those simple ideas which we receive from sensation and reflection. For, observing in ourselves that we do and can think, and that we can at pleasure move several parts of our bodies which were at rest; the effects, also, that natural bodies are able to produce in one another, occurring at every moment to our senses, – we both these ways get the idea of power.[9]

It is, Locke insists, only our awareness of observable change and movement that gives rise to the idea of power:

> . . . whatever change is observed, the mind must collect a power somewhere able to make that change, as well as a possibility in the thing itself to receive it. . . . A body at rest affords us no idea of any active power to move; and when it is set in motion itself, that motion is rather a passion than an action in it. For, when the ball obeys the motion of a billiard-stick, it is not any action of the ball, but bare passion. Also when by impulse it sets another ball in motion that lay in its way, it only communicates the motion it had received from another, and loses in itself so much as the other received: which gives us [an] idea of an active power of moving.[10]

Varying his imagery only slightly, Locke then trades his billiard balls (which Hume later inherits) for tennis balls. Human beings, Locke suggests, are rather like tennis balls, variously at rest or in motion. But tennis balls, unlike human agents, cannot think and therefore cannot express any 'preference of motion to rest, or vice-versa'.[11]

Locke, like Hobbes, has some difficulty in translating the language of human action into the idiom of the new science. The older Aristotelian language of entity-specific 'powers' lurks in the background, as when he speaks of 'a power' that is 'able to make [some] change' and of the recipient's 'power' to be acted upon in the requisite way ('passive power' in Hobbes' terms). Moreover Locke, like Hobbes, tries to rework the concept of 'communication' in a nonlinguistic way, so that one ball is said to 'communicate' its 'motion' to another.[12] As we shall see, the tension between what we might call two discursive poles – that of mechanistic-causal talk about matter in motion and that of intentional-action talk about (and by) sentient speaking subjects – has come back to haunt late twentieth-century social scientists.

David Hume's reworking of the concept of power was even more uncompromising than his predecessors'. He attempted to bring about conceptual changes by way of a series of conceptual conflations and radical reconceptualizations. While he agreed with Hobbes and Locke that power is a causal concept, he held that the concept of causation needed to be revised along the lines that we now call empiricist. And in revising the concept of causation he revised the concept of power as well. The causal relation, he averred, was not a matter of natural necessity but of regular succession or 'constant conjunction'. For Hume 'the idea of power is relative as much as that of cause; and both have reference to an effect, or some other event constantly conjoined with the former.'[13] Causation, and hence power, is a purely contingent, not a necessary, relation between independently identifiable entities. It therefore follows that 'power' cannot be understood as a dispositional property, or, in the language of Aristotle (and latterly, but much more faintly, of Locke), of an entity-specific capacity or potential ('a power'). Heaping ridicule upon the language of essential properties or 'powers', Hume maintains that 'the distinction . . . betwixt power and the exercise of it is . . . without foundation.'[14]

Although begun by philosophers, this series of ontological and epistemological claims and conceptual changes eventually found their way into the discourse of twentieth-century social scientists. Excercises of power involve relations of conflict in which self-interested causal agents work their way against hapless patients. Thus Max Weber, for example, defined power as 'the probability that one actor in a social relationship will . . . carry out his own will' against the resistance of others.[15] Likewise, Lasswell and Kaplan contended that politics consists of 'acts considered as affecting or determining other acts, a relation embodied in the key concept of power'.[16] Although hardly a key concept in all the social sciences, 'power' is clearly central to the discourse of political science.[17] It is to a conceptual dispute within that discipline that I now turn.

4.3   THREE FACES OF POWER

Various episodes in the history of the social sciences suggest that philosophers' metaphors may, in time, become behavioural scientists' 'models'.[18] If nothing else, an examination of the discourse of behavioural political science in the third quarter of the twentieth century suggests that the rule of metaphor is most powerful (sic) when it is least recognized.[19] By looking closely at the behaviouralists' treatment of 'power', we can see how concepts that had formerly functioned in one discourse leaked into, and transformed, the language of another. This episode also allows us to see how the contradictions and limitations inherent in the newly transformed discourse were exposed and criticized, thereby preparing the way for the reconstruction of 'power' by alternative discourses.

The debate about 'power' can be narrated as a tale of conceptual transfers and transformations from one 'face' or 'dimension' to another.[20] It began with the equation of 'power' with 'cause', the latter being understood in Humean terms as an observable constancy of conjunction between contingently related events. Recalling in the mid-1950s the route by which he came to view political power in mechanistic-causal terms, Herbert Simon says that he turned

> to the task of defining political power, only to find myself . . . unable . . . to arrive at a satisfactory solution. The difficulty appeared to reside in a very specific technical point: influence, power, and authority are all intended as asymmetrical relations. When we say that A has power over B, we do not mean to imply that B has power over A. . . . When I had stated the question in this form – as a problem of giving operational meaning to the asymmetry of the relation between independent and dependent variable – it became clear that it was identical with the general problem of defining a causal relation between two variables. That is

to say, for the assertion, 'A has power over B,' we can substitute the assertion, 'A's behavior causes B's behavior.' If we can define the causal relation, we can define influence, power, or authority, and vice-versa.[21]

Apparently unaware that this solution was already three centuries old by the time he proposed it, Simon's lead was followed by others.[22] Robert Dahl, for example, acknowledged that his 'way of thinking about power or influence is analogous to the concept of force in mechanics. In mechanics object A exerts a force on object B if A produces a change in the velocity of B.' While warning that 'we ought not to push such analogies very far', Dahl nevertheless insisted that 'our ideas about underlying measures of [power or] influence rest on intuitive notions very similar to those on which the idea of force rests in mechanics.' The 'underlying idea in both cases' is essentially the same.[23]

Perhaps, *pace* Dahl, we do not ordinarily push our analogies and metaphors so much as they push us.[24] The early behaviouralists' attempt to transfer the language of mechanics to the description and explanation of political phenomena raised a host of further questions. Amongst the more difficult of these is the question of interdiscursive translation, which arises in the following way. If one wishes to employ the discourse of mechanics to talk about politics, then one must find conceptual equivalences for 'translating' between discourses. Hence Hobbes' (and Simon's) equation of 'power' with efficient 'cause'. Hence also Hume's series of conceptual collapses or equations. We see this also in the tendency of behavioural political scientists to treat 'power, influence and authority' as synonyms.[25] Still other concepts, such as 'communication', are relocated in conceptual space and made to do new work. Thus, for example, Simon, working backward from the newer idiom into the old, asks, 'What corresponds, in the social sciences, to the postulate of "no action at a distance"?' The 'direct analogue,' he answers, 'is "no power or influence without communication".' Although '"communication" cannot be taken quite literally as "verbal communication",' he adds, 'the principle remains an important and probably indispensable tool for the identification of power or influence mechanisms.'[26] Once again, Simon's lead is followed by others whose shared view is succinctly summarized by Dorwin Cartwright. 'Communication,' he says, 'is the mechanism by which interpersonal influence is exerted.'[27]

One of the difficulties that arise in talking about 'communication' in purely mechanistic terms stems from the fact that human beings, unlike billiard balls, are language-using creatures. For, to put the point crudely, human beings do not ordinarily 'communicate' their 'motion' or exercise power by bumping into other human beings but by communicating with them through a system of signs or gestures or words. Locke recognized this by saying that human beings, unlike tennis balls, are capable of expressing 'preference of motion to rest, and vice-versa'.[28] And behaviourally oriented political scientists acknowledged this by having recourse to the 'mechanism' of a 'preference communication' or a 'persuasive communication' between agent A and patient B. A exercises power over B if and only if A communicates a preference to B and B complies with A's expressed preference. The paradigmatic power-wielder thus becomes the policeman directing traffic, and the paradigmatic preference (or persuasive) communication the command. If policeman A succeeds in getting motorist B to do what A commands, namely stop (or go), then A has exercised power over B.[29]

Early behaviouralists further stipulated that A and B be individuals and that A's action and B's response must be observable events isolated in space and time, with A's preference communication preceding B's response; there must, that is, be a 'time lag' between the two events.[30] Thus an exercise of power can be said to have occurred only if A makes an observable attempt to cause B to do what A intends but what B would not otherwise do. If A's 'power attempt' succeeds, then A is said to have power over B with respect to the particular 'issue area' over which they openly disagreed.[31]

During the second phase of the debate the behavioural construal of power was criticized less because it is mistaken than because it is partial and one-sided or 'one-dimensional'. According to the 'two-dimensional' account advanced by Peter Bachrach and Morton Baratz, political power is Janus-faced. They readily conceded that the pluralists were right in viewing power as a causal relation between individual actors and that power is sometimes exercised in an overt and observable way. Sometimes, but not always; for power has another, hidden face. Power may in some instances be exercised covertly and in ways that are not directly observable but can only be inferred indirectly. For instance, A might exercise power by controlling the agenda, thereby limiting discussion, debate and decision-making to 'safe' issues which do not threaten A's interests. Or A might be able to take advantage of biases built into the political system that tend to favour A's interests over B's. Or again B, anticipating defeat and/or reprisal, might be unwilling to challenge A on a particular issue. The fact that there is no observable conflict – no direct challenges or overt 'power attempts' – does not necessarily mean that no power is being exercised. On the contrary, it may well mean that a dominant person or group is exercising power in a particularly efficient and effective way.[32]

Although an improvement over its predecessor, the two-dimensional critique and alternative, Steven Lukes argued, does not go far enough. While Lukes agrees that 'The absolutely basic common core to, or primitive notion lying behind, all talk of power is the notion that A in some way affects B,' he adds that 'in applying that primitive (causal) notion to the analysis of social life, something further is needed – namely the notion that A does so in a non-trivial or significant manner.'[33] The sort of significant affecting picked out by the concept of power involves one agent's ability not only to affect another, but to do so in a way that adversely affects his or her interests. Lukes' 'three-dimensional' alternative accords a central place to the concept of interest. 'A has power over B,' Lukes contends, 'when A affects B in a manner contrary to B's interests.' Of course the one- and two-dimensional construals of power also, as Lukes notes, presuppose some conception of interests.[34] But defenders of the one- and two-dimensional views are alike in sharing an unduly narrow and naive understanding of 'interest'. Specifically, both simply assume that would-be challengers do in fact know what their real interests are, simply because they know what they want or prefer. One's interests are, in short, reducible to one's preferences, whether they be revealed through participation (as in the one-dimensional view) or concealed (as in the two-dimensional view).

This, Lukes claims, will not suffice. For interests, unlike preferences or wants, are the sorts of things that one can be

mistaken about. One may have mistaken beliefs about what is and
is not in one's interest. Indeed, the most effective way in which A
can exercise power over B is to shape B's very beliefs about what
is and is not in B's interest. To the degree that A can instil and/or
take advantage of B's false or mistaken interpretation of B's
interests, A's power is well-nigh complete, and all the greater for
its being virtually invisible to those over whom it is exercised. Is it
not, Lukes asks, 'the supreme exercise of power to avert conflict
and grievance by influencing, shaping, and determining the
perceptions and preferences of others?'[35]

Lukes' emphasis on 'objective' interests is reminiscent of the
Marxian notion of 'false consciousness'. Someone suffering from
false consciousness labours under the illusion that his 'subjective'
or perceived interests – those instilled by, and benefiting, a ruling
class, caste or group – are in fact his real or 'objective' interests,
and more especially the economic interests of the class to which he
belongs. But there is also, Lukes insists in a manner more
reminiscent of Kant than of Marx, a transcendental interest in
autonomy which we possess simply by virtue of being human.
Whether aware of it or not, individual human beings have an
interest in being or becoming autonomous agents. Thus the slave
who sees his lot as normal and natural, or the wage-labourer who
is utterly uncritical of the capitalist system, or the Indian 'Untouchable' who accepts his lowly status within the Hindu caste
system, are arguably unaware of their objective interests.[36]

Although Lukes' three-dimensional view of power has led to
some interesting and important research,[37] it has come under
sharp attack from several directions. Some critics have charged
that in equating 'exercising power' with 'causing harm' Lukes has
unduly restricted the range of 'power', ruling out instances in
which power can be exercised through rational persuasion and
even in beneficial or benevolent ways.[38] Other criticisms have
centred upon his defence of the concept of objective interests,
either because one has no way of knowing what they are or
because the analyst's belief that he knows what they are leads to
'paternalism' or 'vanguardism'.[39] And other critics focused on his
claim that 'power' is an 'essentially contested' concept. They
contended that Lukes cannot coherently claim that power is
essentially contestable and that his three-dimensional view is

superior to alternative conceptualizations.[40] For our purposes, however, the more interesting challenges are those directed against the very discourse in which the 'three faces' of power debate was framed in the first place.

4.4   NEW FACES OF POWER

The challenges to which I refer have come from several quarters. These include, to mention only a few, Critical Theory, realist metascience, Neo-Marxist theories of the state, structuralism, deconstructionism, and feminist theory.[41] Here I shall, for the sake of brevity, consider only three of these attempted conceptual reconstructions, which I call the communicative, the realist and the deconstructionist. Despite their differences, all are alike in expressing profound dissatisfaction with the way in which social scientific discourse has heretofore constructed, analysed and applied the concept of power. It is as yet too early to tell whether these alternative discourses will remain divergent or whether they might yet prove to be mutually compatible and capable of merging.

Let us consider first the challenge posed by the communicative construal of power. We saw earlier how the concepts of power, cause and communication were linked by behaviouralists (and their philosophical forebears): before A can be said to exercise power over B (= cause B to do something that B would not otherwise do), A must have communicated something – a 'motion' or a 'preference' – to B. If B, having a different motion or preference, then changes in the wake of A's communication, A can be said to have exercised power over B with respect to the content of that communication. Early behaviouralists were wont to illustrate the point by referring to colliding billiard balls or, in the case of human agents and patients, to policemen and motorists.

A communicative perspective on power invites us to take a closer look at what is being presupposed in such exercises of power. In order to exercise power, two conditions – neither of which was central to the behaviouralist account – must already have been satisfied. The first is that the agent must be capable of communicating certain things in certain ways; he or she must, in short, be a competent speaker. The second is that the 'patient' or recipient of such a 'persuasive communication' be capable of understanding it and knowing what kind of speech-act it is. The motorist must, for example, know that a particular communication from a policeman is an order or a command rather than, say, a suggestion, a plea or a request.[42] Both must possess a common stock of concepts, such as 'command' and 'obedience', which are partly constitutive of their discourse, and are the precondition of their being able to communicate and thus to be members of the same community. As Peter Winch observes,

> . . . it does not make much sense to suppose that human beings might have been issuing commands and obeying them before they came to form the concept of command and obedience. For their performance of such acts is itself the chief manifestation of their possession of those concepts. An act of obedience itself contains, as an essential element, a recognition of what went before it as an order.[43]

Both must, in short, have 'power' of a certain sort, the power of speech. From a communicative or linguistic perspective, then, a 'power relation' can best be characterized not as an agent-patient but as an agent-agent relation. In this respect, at least, relations of power are relations between (ontological) equals.

This can be seen even more clearly if we look not at the power of policemen but at the power of agents acting as citizens. For it is in the role of citizen, Hannah Arendt argued, that people act as free and equal agents who create power collectively through their communicative action and interaction. In making this case Arendt began by re-making several crucial distinctions. Above all, political power had to be carefully distinguished from force, violence, coercion, authority and other concepts that behaviouralists had told us to treat as synonyms, inasmuch as each ostensibly refers to some sort of causal relationship. Such conceptual conflation represents a politically disastrous loss of precision:

> It is, I think, a rather sad reflection on the present state of political science that our terminology does not distinguish among such key words as 'power', 'strength', 'force', 'authority', and, finally, 'violence' – all of which refer to distinct, different phenomena and would hardly exist unless they did. . . . To use them as synonyms

not only indicates a certain deafness to linguistic meanings, which would be serious enough, but it has also resulted in a kind of blindness to the realities they correspond to.

Theirs is not, however, a naive or innocent blindness, but has at its base a particular and historically specific conceptual-cum-political reduction:

> Behind the apparent confusion is a firm conviction in whose light all distinctions would be, at best, of minor importance: the conviction that the most crucial political issue is, and always has been, the question of Who rules Whom? Power, strength, force, authority, violence – these are but words to indicate the means by which man rules over man; they are held to be synonyms because they have the same function.

But, she adds, 'It is only after one ceases to reduce public affairs to the business of dominion' – i.e., of 'power over' – 'that the original data in the realm of human affairs will appear, or, rather, reappear, in their authentic diversity.'[44]

According to Arendt, political power is a potentiality or capacity for acting that arises when equals come together. This mode of mutual empowerment is the medium of political action. For politics is acting with words; it is the communicative activity that constitutes and sustains political communities. Such communication is necessarily two-way, requiring that speakers and listeners be engaged in mutually meaningful conversation, debate and dialogue.[45] Through speech we communicate our views and coordinate our activities. It is people's coming together for this purpose that makes power possible and necessary. 'Power,' writes Arendt, 'corresponds to the human ability not just to act but to act in concert. Power is never the property of an individual; it belongs to a group and remains in existence only so long as the group keeps together.' Her point is that groups or communities, acting in concert, have the capacity – the 'power' – to 'empower' their members and/or leaders. So, for example, 'When we say of somebody that he is "in power" we actually refer to his being empowered by a certain number of people to act in their name. The moment the group, from which the power originated . . . disappears, "his power" also vanishes.'[46] 'All political institutions,' she says, 'are manifestations and materializations of power;

they petrify and decay as soon as the living power of the people ceases to uphold them.'[47]

Like the communities out of which it arises, power is communicatively constituted:

> . . . the public realm, . . . because it ultimately resides on action and speech, never altogether loses its potential [i.e., power-generating] character. . . . Power is actualized only where word and deed have not parted company, where words are not empty and deeds not brutal, where words are not used to veil intentions but to disclose realities, and deeds are not used to violate and destroy but to establish relations and create new realities. Power is what keeps the public realm, the potential space of appearance between acting and speaking men, in existence.[48]

Power is no more and no less perishable than the communication community that brings it into being. And if that community conflates the concepts constitutive of its discourse – 'power' and 'violence' amongst them – then its common speech is impoverished and its very existence threatened.

Some of Arendt's critics have found her account of 'power' peculiar, to say the least. Even one as sympathetic as Steven Lukes calls hers 'an interestingly idiosyncratic concept of power'.[49] But when seen from the vantage point of conceptual history, her concept of power, although arguably archaic, is hardly idiosyncratic. Indeed, it harks back to the classical concept of power captured in the Ciceronian maxim, which I quoted earlier (in 4.2, above) and to which she refers repeatedly. Cicero's *potestas in populo*, she translates as, 'without a people or group there is no power.'[50] And it has affinities with Hegel's master-slave dialectic, with Marx's account of proletarian revolution, and with Heidegger's notion of ontological empowerment, all of which point to the kind of power possessed *in potentia* by those who are supposedly powerless.[51]

More recently, a variant of Arendt's communications concept of power can also be found in contemporary Critical Theory and in the programme for a critical social science. Brian Fay, for example, argues that political power is a 'dyadic' or two-way relationship 'rooted in part in the reflections and will of those interacting, both the powerless as well as the powerful'. Because people have the capacity to reflect critically upon their situation, those self-understandings – and the relations of power predicated upon them – are subject to change. Power can, in short, be a relation in which people are not dominated but empowered./The task of a critical social science is to discover the conditions under which the powerless can empower themselves:

> For critical social science, power exists not only when a group is controlled but also when a group comes together, becomes energized, and organizes itself, thereby becoming able to achieve something for itself. Here the paradigm case is not one of command but one of enablement in which a disorganized and unfocused group acquires an identity and a resolve to act in light of its new-found sense of purpose.

Thus, for example, education, understood as a critical practice, 'is in part a process of empowerment in which a group of people who do not understand themselves to be such a group gradually discover that they are and gain the will to act in concert.' A critical social science sees people 'as creatures actively involved in creating and sustaining all their forms of social life, including their relations of power.'[52]

Jürgen Habermas elucidates the communicative concept of power by contrasting Weber's views with those of Arendt. Weber 'defined power as the possibility of forcing one's own will, whatever it may be, on the conduct of others.' But 'Arendt, by contrast, understands power as the capacity to agree in uncoerced communication on some community action.' Although they are alike in 'discuss[ing] power as a potency realized in actions', Habermas notes, 'each relies on a different model of action' (and thus, I would add, on ontologically different models of agency as well).[53] Weber subscribes to a 'teleological model of action in which an individual subject or a group has a set purpose and chooses the means suitable for realizing it.' To the degree that this requires the assent or actions of other human beings, 'power' refers to the means by which their compliance is secured. Power, for Weber, is essentially instrumental or 'manipulative'. Weber's 'teleological model of action,' Habermas contends, 'considers only agents who are oriented toward their own success and not toward agreement.'[54]

Arendt's 'communicative model of action', on the other hand, is predicated upon the idea that 'the basic phenomenon' of political life is not 'the instrumentalizing of another's will for one's own purposes but the formation of a common will in a communication aimed at agreement.' Power arises out of communal deliberation and decision. It therefore 'rests on conviction and hence on that peculiarly coercion-free force with which insights prevail.' In short, 'The communicatively engendered power of common convictions goes back to the fact that the parties are oriented toward agreement and not just toward their own respective success. . . . Power is formed within communicative action; it is a group effect of speech in which agreement is an end in itself for all parties.'[55]

Habermas' recasting of Arendt's analysis of power in the terms of Austinian speech–act theory and of his own counterfactual ideal speech situation need not detain us here. Of greater interest to the critical conceptual historian are Habermas' reasons for believing Arendt's communications concept of power to be in need of updating. The 'few weaknesses' in her concept of power stem, he says, 'from the fact that Arendt remains bound to the historical and conceptual constellation of Aristotelian thought' which, Habermas holds, is anachronistic within the setting supplied by the modern nation-state.[56] Within a progressively 'rationalized' society, 'the elements of strategic action' described by Weber and decried by Arendt 'have increased in scope and importance'. Although Arendt is right to say that political communities and institutions 'live not by violence but by recognition', Habermas nevertheless maintains that 'we cannot exclude the element of strategic action from the concept of the political.' For 'politics' means something different in our time than it did in Aristotle's. Politics is, for us, an activity from which force and violence are not conceptually or categorically excluded. 'Political violence' is no longer an oxymoron but a 'means for acquiring and holding onto power'. And insofar as the strategic 'struggle for political power has . . . been institutionalized in the modern state' – via interest groups, political parties and other organized associations – 'it thereby becomes a normal component of the political system.'[57] Moreover, as critical theorists and as citizens we need to be aware of the ways in which violence is used by some individuals or groups 'to keep other individuals or groups from perceiving their interests'. A concept of power that fails to recognize these developments is inadequate.

Of what use or relevance, then, is the communictions concept of power? It is useful, Habermas maintains, insofar as it supplies a standard or criterion for assessing the legitimacy of political actions and practices. For 'it does not make good sense that someone should be able to generate legitimate power just because he is in a position to keep others from perceiving their interests. Legitimate power arises among those who form common convictions in communication free from coercion.'[58] In Habermas' hands the communications concept of power becomes a counterfactual ideal or standard to which action should aspire, even though it is incapable of being achieved in the modern world. It is, in short, the kind of power present in the ideal speech situation, in which discourse is free from domination and 'the forceless force of the better argument' reigns supreme.[59]

A second and equally fundamental challenge to the heretofore dominant understanding of power comes from metascientific 'realism'.[60] At first a dissident movement within the philosophy of the natural sciences, realism has been amongst the post-positivist challengers to the reigning empiricist orthodoxy. More recently, the discourse of realism has been transferred to the social sciences, where it is altering the meaning of the terms constitutive of its discourse – including 'power'. As a philosophy of social science, realism is a species of 'naturalism'; that is, realists hold that there are no differences in principle between the methods and explanatory practices of the natural sciences and the social sciences. At this abstract and programmatic level realists and empiricists are in agreement. But this increasingly influential philosophy of science holds that the empiricist tradition's understanding of science, and its conception of causal explanation in particular, is radically flawed. Instead of viewing causal relations in contingent Humean terms, realists speak of 'intrinsic natures', 'causal powers' and 'natural necessity.' Thus, for example, one of the causal powers of copper is the power to conduct electricity and one of the causal powers of glass the inability to do so.[61]

The social-scientific realist maintains that human beings have species-specific 'powers' in the social world in much the same sense that copper, glass and other substances do in the natural world. They possess these powers not *qua* individuals but by virtue of occupying certain socially structured roles and being in

certain sorts of socially defined and relatively enduring relationships.[62] A teacher, for example, has the power to teach and
examine students; a policeman the power to direct traffic; a
legislator the power to legislate, and so on. Realism's rejection of
empiricism and its understanding of 'power' provide the
grounding for their critique of behaviouralism's understanding of
power.

Defenders of the realist revision of 'power' maintain that the
'three faces of power' controversy was a tempest in the old
empiricist teapot. Lukes, no less than the proponents of the first
and second faces, remains committed to the ontology and epis-
temology of empiricism. Realists propose, accordingly, to reject
the behaviouralist understanding of power by undermining its
empiricist foundations, and to revise that concept in the light of a
rival philosophy of science. Several points about that exercise in
conceptual revision are worth noting.[63] The first is that power
remains, for the realist, a causal relation; but realism's ontology
and its understanding of causation differ from that of the empiricist tradition. Whereas empiricists were ontological (and methodological) individualists, realists are ontological (and methodological) relationalists.[64] That is, realists hold that power is possessed and exercised not by individuals *qua* individuals but by
people in their capacity as socially situated role-bearers possessing
certain intrinsic characteristics or 'natures'. As Jeffrey Isaac notes,
in speaking of 'the intrinsic natures of social agents', the realist
refers 'not [to] their unique characteristics as individuals, but [to]
their social identities as participants in enduring, socially structured relationships.'[65] Second, causal powers are viewed by
realists as capacities or dispositions to act that are actualized in, but
not exhausted by, their exercise. The possession of such powers is
socially and logically necessary, but their successful exercise is not.
'The possession of these powers in the performance of social
activities,' writes Isaac, 'is necessary to these activities; but the
successful exercise of these powers is contingent.'[66] Thus realists
insist upon distinguishing, as Hume and modern behaviouralists
did not, between the possession and the (successful) exercise of an
agent's power. Third, such social and political power is not
equivalent to or translatable as 'power over' or domination, but as
'power to' – the power to engage in certain sorts of socially

defined practices (teaching, etc.) and to exercise the powers that are constitutive of those practices. And even when it is appropriate to talk about 'power over' – as in the master's power over the slave – such power is nevertheless parasitic upon a socially given 'power to' act in certain ways. Fourth, power is necessary inasmuch as human societies would fall apart without the kind of capacity for coordinated action that we call power. Fifth, for the realist, the concept of interest has no necessary connection with the concept of power. The teacher's possession and exercise of her power, for instance, need not imply any disregard of the student's interests; quite the contrary, in fact. And finally, following from the aforementioned features of realist discourse, power is not a normatively negative concept. Power is not necessarily repressive; it is, rather, a necessary and indispensable feature of social and political life.

This is not to say, however, that the realist understanding of 'power' and its place in social-scientific inquiry is wholly without normative import. On the contrary, as Jeffrey Isaac notes,

> The concept of power . . . figures in contemporary debates regarding class structure, gender relations, the nature of the state, [and] nuclear arms. . . . To locate the sources of power in society is to locate the enablements and constraints that operate on all of us . . . To locate power is to fix moral responsibility, both upon those who exercise power illegitimately and upon those social structures that make this power available.[67]

The upshot is that the realist revision of the concept of power is itself empowering: it enables social agents armed with it to see, and to participate in, the social world in a new way.

A third attempt to 'deconstruct' and revise the concept of power was undertaken by the late Michel Foucault. His understanding of power, as he admits, underwent a radical change. Until 1970 or so, he writes, 'I accepted the traditional conception of power as an essentially judicial mechanism, as that which lays down the law, which prohibits, which refuses, and which has a whole range of negative effects: exclusion, rejection, denial, obstruction, obfuscation, etc. Now I believe that conception to be inadequate.' It was, he says, 'in the course of a concrete experience that I had with prisons . . . [that] convinced me that the question of power needed to be [re]formulated.'[68]

Foucault's reformulation of 'power' (*le pouvoir*) proceeds along the following lines. He begins by suggesting that the 'force model' implicit in the concept of repression – that is, of domination or 'power over' – 'is a wholly negative, narrow, skeletal conception of power . . . which has been curiously widespread.' Far from simply 'carrying the force of a prohibition', power is productive, i.e., it is implicated in the production and reproduction of social practices:

> If power were never anything but repressive, if it never did anything but to say no, do you really think one would be brought to obey it? What makes power hold good, what makes it accepted, is simply the fact that it doesn't only weigh on us as a force that says no, but that it traverses and produces things, it induces pleasure, forms knowledge, produces discourse. It needs to be considered as a productive network which runs through the whole social body.[69]

The crude force model might in some respects have been suitable for characterizing premodern power which tended to be exercised sporadically, overtly and often brutally.[70] But this model hardly suffices to capture and describe the ways in which, and the means by which, modern power is possessed and exercised. The productive power that makes modern society possible is, Foucault insists, a new kind of power, exercised in new ways.

Modern power, Foucault contends, takes the form of 'disciplinary power'. By this, he means not simply the power to punish, but the power to 'transform human beings into subjects' that has been generated by the various 'disciplines' that belong to what we call 'the human sciences,' including medicine, psychiatry, penology, criminology, and the various social sciences. These disciplines have helped to create and maintain 'a society of normalisation,' in part through their specialized discourses employed at socially specific sites – hospitals, asylums, prisons, etc. – and in part through their employment of the 'apparatuses of knowledge (*savoir*)' peculiar to those disciplines and their discourses.[71] The human sciences are, or at any rate purport to be, caring and humane, their practitioners the bearers of a new kind of power which Foucault calls 'confessional' or 'pastoral power.' This is the supposedly solicitous power to extract confessions, to pry into the innermost secrets of the subject, and to persuade the subject to participate in his own subjection.[72]

Historically, this change in the meaning of 'power' was in part made possible by and went hand in hand with new techniques of administration and surveillance:

> from the seventeenth and eighteenth centuries onwards, there was a veritable technological take-off in the productivity of power. . . [A]bove all, there was established at this period what one might call a new 'economy' of power, that is to say procedures which allowed the effects of power to circulate in a manner at once continuous, uninterrupted, adapted and 'individualised' throughout the entire social body. These new techniques are both much more efficient and much less wasteful (less costly economically, less risky in their results, less open to loopholes and resistances), than the techniques previously employed.[73]

Amongst these new techniques was the institutionalization of 'the gaze' (*le regard*), not only in prisons – some of which were actually modelled on Bentham's plan for a Panopticon – but in asylums, hospitals, schools and other sites. Aware that they were under surveillance, patients, inmates and pupils became obliged to watch themselves, to examine and scrutinize their own conduct, and thereby to participate in the process of their own normalization.

Modern power is in Foucault's account allied as never before with knowledge, or rather with discipline-specific 'knowledges' consisting of specialized skills, techniques, schemes of classification, etc. What is thereby created and sustained is a system in which power and knowledge are inseparable – in short, a *régime du savoir* or 'regime of power/knowledge'.[74] This is not, however, a centralized or state-centred regime but consists instead of a highly decentralized array of 'local' discursive practices operating in unsuspected and subtle ways in everyday life to produce 'normal' subjects and, in so doing, to reproduce itself. This sort of 'bio-power' or 'micro-power' penetrates and circulates through the very 'capillaries' of the social body.[75]

Foucault's revised understanding of power is in several respects novel and unique. But it also shares several affinities with the 'communicative' and 'realist' views examined earlier. The following list, though hardly exhaustive, might suggest some points of contact between apparently disparate perspectives. Like the realists – and like Marx, who may be read as a realist of a certain sort[76]

– Foucault's focus is not upon isolated individuals but upon individuals as role-bearers implicated in the production and reproduction of relatively enduring and systematically structured social relations. And like Arendt, Foucault insists that power relations are discursively or communicatively constituted by and between speaking subjects. Thus violence, being mute – or at least not needing speech – must be sharply distinguished from power. Far from being power's 'primitive form, its permanent secret and its last resource', violence works in a very different way. 'A relationship of violence acts upon a body or upon things; it forces, it bends, it breaks on the wheel, it destroys, or it closes the door on all possibilities.' A relation of power, by contrast, 'can only be articulated on the basis of two elements which are each indispensable if it is really to be a power relationship.' The first is 'that "the other" (the one over whom power is exercised) be thoroughly recognized and maintained to the very end as a person who acts', and not as a passive object or lifeless thing – a 'patient' if you like – upon whom others act and who can in turn only react.[77] 'The term "power",' he writes, 'designates relationships among partners,' adding that 'Relationships of communication . . ., by virtue of modifying the field of information between partners, produce effects of power.'[78] The second feature of a power relationship is that it necessarily implies choices and options: 'faced with a relationship of power, a whole field of responses, reactions, results, and possible interventions may open up.'[79]

In a manner reminiscent of but not identical with Arendt's, Foucault links power with the freedom to choose and to act:

> Power is exercised only over free subjects, and only insofar as they are free. By this we mean individual or collective subjects who are faced with a field of possibilities in which several ways of behaving, several reactions and diverse comportments may be realized. Where the determining factors saturate the whole there is no relationship of power; slavery is not a power relationship when man is in chains. (In this case it is a question of a physical relationship of constraint.) Consequently there is no face to face confrontation of power and freedom which is mutually exclusive . . ., but a much more complicated interplay. In this game freedom may well appear as the condition for the exercise of power (at the same time its precondition, since freedom must exist for power to

be exerted, and also its permanent support, since without the possibility of recalcitrance, power would be equivalent to a physical determination). . . . At the heart of the power relationship, and constantly provoking it, are the recalcitrance of the will and the intransigence of freedom.[80]

Insofar as human beings remain free they retain a capacity for acting and thus the power to resist. There is, he adds, 'no relationship of power without the means of escape or possible flight. Every power relationship implies, at least *in potentia*, a strategy of struggle. . . . It would not be possible for power relations to exist without points of insubordination which, by definition, are means of escape.'[81] The task of the theorist, Foucault maintains, is to participate in the politics of everyday life by clarifying the nature of the micro-practices that constitute modern power, thereby disclosing points of possible intervention and resistance and thus helping to empower others to take advantage of them.

Although there appear to be several points of tangency amongst the three aforementioned attempts to reconstruct the concept of power, it would be claiming too much to suggest that they are identical in all essential respects. Even so, some sort of *rapprochement*, if not of synthesis, remains a real possibility. I want to conclude by considering one recent attempt to arrive at a more synoptic view of power.

In formulating his 'theory of structuration' Anthony Giddens finds it necessary to reformulate the concept of power and to do so, moreover, in a way that points to the possibility of a *rapprochement* between different perspectives. Although he does not mention Arendt or refer to any of the realists, he does refer frequently to Habermas' and Foucault's reformulations of 'power'. Moreover, the vocabulary of his theory of structuration suggests some possible affinities with the three perspectives that I have termed the communicative, the realist and the deconstructionist. Giddens emphasizes the central role of power in the constitution of society, and the increasingly important place of social-scientific theories and concepts – including 'power' – in the discourse of reflective social agents. 'The study of power,' he writes, 'cannot be regarded as a second-order consideration in the social sciences. Power cannot be tacked on, as it were, after the more basic concepts of social science have been formulated. There is no more elemental concept than that of power. . . . Power is one of several primary concepts of social science, all clustered around the relations of action and structure. Power is the means of getting things done and, as such, directly implied in human action.'[82]

Conventional social-scientific treatments of power are defective, Giddens claims, insofar as they are ensnared in such obfuscating ontological dichotomies as 'the dualism of subject and object' – and, I would add, of 'agent' and 'patient' – which in turn undergird the idea that power is necessarily a relation of division, disagreement or conflict (whether overt or concealed or only potential). 'A reconstructed theory of power,' Giddens contends, 'would begin from the premise that such views are untenable. Power is not necessarily linked with conflict in the sense of either division of interest or active struggle, and power is not inherently oppressive.' Instead, he continues, 'Power is the capacity to achieve outcomes; whether or not these are connected to purely sectional interests is not germane to its definition.' Giddens, like Foucault and Arendt, rejects the simple force model. 'The development of force or its threat,' he writes, is 'not the type case of the use of power. Blood and fury, the heat of battle, direct confrontation of rival camps – these are not necessarily the historical conjunctures in which the most far-reaching effects of power are either felt or established.'[83]

Giddens – in common with Foucault, Arendt, and metascientific realists, with their emphasis on 'power to' – insists that power, construed as 'the capacity to achieve outcomes . . . is not, as such, an obstacle to freedom or emancipation but is their very medium.'[84] Power is thus constitutive of free action and human energy, understood as the ability to 'act otherwise' or to 'make a difference' by deploying one's socially supplied 'causal powers':

> To be able to 'act otherwise' means being able to intervene in the world, or to refrain from such intervention, with the effect of influencing a specific process or state of affairs. This presumes that to be an agent is to be able to deploy . . . a range of causal powers, including that of influencing those deployed by others. Action depends upon the capacity of the individual to 'make a difference'

to a pre-existing state of affairs or course of events. An agent ceases to be such if he or she loses the capability to 'make a difference,' that is, to exercise some sort of power.[85]

The connection between free agency and power, he adds, is not contingent but conceptual; that is, 'action logically involves power in the sense of transformative capacity. In this sense, the most all-embracing meaning of "power", power is logically prior to subjectivity, to the constitution of the reflexive monitoring of conduct.'[86] Power is in this way necessarily implicated in the constitution of subjects and of society itself.

If I am not greatly mistaken, Giddens' theory of structuration at least points in the direction of a synthesis of the three views discussed earlier, even if it does not quite succeed in achieving it. To be sure, neither Giddens' nor any of the other perspectives sketched here is without difficulties, and certainly none is above criticism.[87] And of course it is as yet too early to tell whether any or all of them might presage a new and quite different understanding of power. But, if nothing else, they are now forcing us to consider anew the meaning of 'power' and its place in political discourse.

5

How Not to Reconstruct Authority

5.1 INTRODUCTION

Why, someone asked several years ago, is authority such a problem?[1] In one version or another, this question has been asked by virtually every modern political thinker. Although their answers differ widely, there does appear to be a widespread consensus that authority is, in the modern world at least, a peculiarly problematic concept. In attempting to shed some new light on this question I plan to proceed as follows. I shall begin by suggesting that the problematic character of 'authority' is less a matter for armchair analysis than for critical historical inquiry. Such an inquiry would show just how that concept came to be understood in different ways as it was embedded in successive conceptual schemes. One of the few political thinkers to have attempted something like this is Hannah Arendt, whose under-standing of what 'authority' (really) is, or was, is rather narrowly tied to one historically specific experience. A more adequate conceptual history would show how 'authority' has been repeatedly reconstructed by being relocated in different conceptual schemes or theories. To write such a history is not my task in this chapter, however. My main focus will instead be upon two relatively recent attempts to reconstruct authority.

These two attempts at conceptual reconstruction I shall, for the sake of simplicity and analytical clarity, present as ideal types. The first is the 'emotivist' view that an authoritative law, policy or command is any one that people feel, for whatever reason, that they ought to obey. The second is the 'epistemocratic' construal in which authority is tied to claims of technical expertise or special-ized knowledge. These two understandings of authority are in the main advanced and defended by modern social scientists – the first by a certain kind of behaviourally oriented political scientist, and the second by the prophets of the coming of a knowledge-based 'post-industrial' society. I shall conclude with some critical reflections upon these newly emergent understandings of authority.

5.2 AUTHORITY AND CONCEPTUAL CHANGE

The line of inquiry staked out in preceding chapters suggests at least one way to begin to address, if not answer, the question with which I began. As I noted in chapter 1, human societies are communicatively constituted. The concepts that make possible particular kinds of communication – and therefore particular kinds of communities, be they religious, moral, political, or even scientific – are characteristically embedded in conceptual schemes, frameworks or theories from which they derive their place and function in a community's discursive constitution and reconstitution. When a scheme is overthrown, outgrown, or otherwise discredited, the concepts constituting it lose their meaning, or retain only a simulacrum of their original meaning. Such, arguably, is the case in much of modern Western society with 'virtue', and more certainly with once-respectable scientific concepts like 'aether' and 'phlogiston'. The same might also be said of 'authority'. Authority, or any other concept for that matter, becomes problematic and therefore philosophically interesting when its value as one of the common coins of communication is called into question.

In attempting to render authority intelligible and meaningful, we might take any one of three tacks. The first is the essentially historical tack of reconstructing the framework within which these concepts originally functioned. The second is the critical move of exposing contradictions and incoherences inherent in contemporary concepts and the practices that they partially constitute.[2] The third tack consists of trying to revive and rehabilitate contested concepts by redefining and relocating them in a more modern, more familiar, and therefore presumably more intelligible framework.[3]

The first and second tacks were taken, and the third criticized, by Hannah Arendt in an essay first entitled 'What Was Authority?'

and later retitled 'What is Authority?' Arendt offered a sensitive reconstruction of an earlier Romano-religious framework in which authority, or *auctoritas*, was not at all peculiar or deserving of philosophical attention. For my present purposes, three features of Arendt's anaylysis are especially noteworthy. The first is that although she did not employ the now-fashionable notion of a conceptual scheme, she did nevertheless stress the importance of recalling the framework in which the concept of authority originally functioned. Secondly, she showed that concepts – in this case 'authority' – have histories and are accordingly incapable of withstanding the ravages of time.[4] Some concepts, indeed, must be spoken of in the past tense. Thus she asked, What *was* authority? and, more startlingly still, she maintained that 'Authority has disappeared from the modern world.'[5] Thirdly, Arendt tellingly criticized several modern attempts to rehabilitate and modernize the concept of authority by functionalizing or operationalizing it.

By the 'functionalizing' of authority Arendt referred to the tendency – once especially evident among some social scientists – to regard authority as essentially equivalent to power, violence, coercion, intimidation, or whatever else might make people obey. Although arguably exaggerated in several respects, Arendt's portrait of the functionally oriented social scientist nevertheless contains, like any caricature, an important grain of truth. 'Their concern is only with functions, and whatever fulfills the same function can, according to this view, be called the same.' Hence 'if violence fulfils the same function as authority – namely, makes people obey – then violence is authority.' 'It is,' she adds, 'as though I had the right to call the heel of my shoe a hammer because I, like most women, use it to drive nails into the wall.'[6]

Her own view, 'based on the conviction of the importance of making distinctions',[7] stands in marked contrast to the social scientist's search for functional equivalence, and in some respects resembles the 'ordinary language' philosopher's penchant for discerning minute distinctions between ostensible synonyms. The main danger in conflating or equating different concepts and in failing to draw fine distinctions is not abstractly philosophical but concretely political. Political communities are communicatively constituted. To the degree that different concepts are muddled, their meanings conflated, and distinctions obliterated or ignored, the political-cum-communicative constitution of that community is endangered. We will, she warns,

> have ceased to live in a common world where the words we have in common possess an unquestionable meaningfulness, so that, short of being condemned to live verbally in an altogether meaningless world, we grant each other the right to retreat into our own worlds of meaning, and demand only that each of us remain consistent within his own private terminology.[8]

A community whose members are incapable of distinguishing between violence and authority will see nothing wrong in attempting to use the former to fulfil the function of the latter. The result will be 'that we shall use violence and pretend to have restored authority.'[9] Nor is this a purely academic matter. For the language of the social scientist – the policy scientist, planner, expert, or manager – is increasingly dominant in what passes for political discourse, debate and discussion. In a kind of conceptual counterpart of Gresham's law, debased language drives out the more valuable currencies of communication. Only by conflating authority and violence can policy makers speak of near-genocidal campaigns as 'pacification programs' and the like.

Arendt is hardly alone in decrying the contemporary deforma-tion of 'authority'. Hans-Georg Gadamer maintains that the Enlightenment's 'prejudice against prejudice' (*Vorurteil*) and 'tradition' results in 'the denigration of authority'. The result is that 'within the Enlightenment the very *concept* of authority becomes deformed. On the basis of its concept of reason and freedom, the concept of authority could be seen as diametrically opposed to reason and freedom: to be, in fact, blind obedience.'[10] And in a similar spirit John Schaar writes:

> I believe that genuine authority is all but lost to us today, and that perhaps we have lost even the concept of authority, so that we cannot know what honorable obedience consists in. This is no small loss, and no amount of liberation will make up for it, because if we do not know what authority is, we cannot know what liberty is either. Perhaps that is why so many people today find themselves as bewildered and unsatisfied after a succession of liberations as they were before.[11]

Despite differences of argument and accent, Arendt, Gadamer and Schaar are agreed that the concept of authority itself has been largely lost to us. They maintain, moreover, that the loss is largely the result of our having inherited the Enlightenment's antinomies – freedom *versus* authority, reason *versus* prejudice, and autonomy *versus* obedience – and that the social sciences, and perhaps political science in particular, have for the most part simply assumed and augmented these antinomies even as they have ignored or banished other distinctions. The result, unsurprisingly, is that social scientists are apt to construe authority as a mixture of blind prejudice and raw power.

But is it possible that Arendt, Gadamer and Schaar be mistaken in claiming that authority has disappeared? *Auctoritas* has indeed vanished, along with the conceptual scheme in which it was located, and 'authority' may well have been changed in successive reformulations. Far from having disappeared from the modern world, is it not simply that 'authority' has assumed newer and distinctly more modern meanings by virtue of its having been redefined and relocated in frameworks that are radically different from the one that Arendt rightly indentified as authority's original home?[12] Without suggesting that all conceptual change is necessarily for the better, we might nevertheless argue that the meaning of 'authority' is no less mutable than the meaning of (say) 'party' or 'power'.

Like any other political concept, 'authority' has its history, and its history is the story of change, of alteration through argumentation and rhetorical restatement. Of the many restatements in the complex and chequered history of 'authority', two are of particular interest to me here. These two construals of 'authority' might best be termed the 'emotivist' and the 'epistemocratic', respectively. The first functionalizes authority; the second rationalizes it by tying it to claims of expertise and specialized knowledge. The former is predicated upon an emotivist view of the meaning of moral and political concepts; the latter assimilates authority to the model of technical expertise.

Before turning to an examination of these attempts to reconstruct authority, a disclaimer: my two models are ideal types that do not yet describe or correspond to or constitute political reality. My question is two-fold. What would the political world look like if we were to construe authority in these ways? And what would it mean for us as agents and citizens to speak of and think about authority in either of these radically new idioms?

5.3   THE EMOTIVIST MODEL

What Arendt called the functionalizing of authority was originally a philosophical stratagem that social scientists and political analysts inherited, willingly though perhaps unwittingly, from a certain sort of philosopher. According to the non-cognitivist or emotivist theory of ethics espoused by logical positivists, the terms of moral and political discourse are not cognitively meaningful but serve only to signal the speaker's feelings. Thus to call something good (or just or beautiful) means merely that one approves of it; to label it bad (unjust, ugly) means that one dislikes or disapproves of it for whatever personal or idiosyncratic reason. When Hobbes, for example, said that 'tyranny' is merely 'monarchy misliked', he advanced an early version of this view.[13] Later and more sophisticated versions of emotivism are to be found in the writings of philosophers like A. J. Ayer and C. L. Stevenson. But the version of emotivism embraced by many modern social scientists tends to be of the earlier and cruder variety. Of course social scientists are apt to deny any affinities with this or that particular school of moral philosophy. But what generally happens when social scientists attempt to ignore philosophical and ethical concerns is that they nevertheless opt unconsciously, and therefore uncritically, for a particular philosophical and ethical perspective. Their attempts to reformulate moral and political concepts, presumably to make them more precise and scientifically servicable, more often result in bad moral philosophy than in good social science.

Lest this seem an overstatement, consider the way in which a distinguished political scientist attempts to define authority. There are at least three reasons for reconsidering David Easton's contribution to the debate about authority. The first is that 'authority' is clearly central to Easton's 'systems' approach to the analysis of political phenomena, an approach that he has since qualified but by no means abandoned. Secondly, all the aforementioned themes are to be found in Easton's analysis of authority. And not least, even as social scientists eschewed Easton's systems approach, their own analyses of authority have often followed his fairly closely.[14]

According to Easton's oft-quoted definition, politics is the activity of authoritatively allocating values. And since 'all social mechanisms are means of allocating values', it follows that politics is differentiated only by virtue of being 'authoritative' in its allocations. Hence 'authority' is conceptually prior to 'politics' itself.[15] A question that has vexed generations of political philosophers – what is authority and how are we to know it when we see it? – Easton answers with despatch. 'Although the literature is replete with discussions about the nature of authority,' he writes, 'the meaning of this term can be resolved quickly for our purposes.'[16] All the muddle of a benighted, philosophical, pre-scientific past is swept away with a simple operational definition: 'A policy is authoritative when the people to whom it is intended to apply or who are affected by it consider that they must or ought to obey it.'[17] Lest this seem a trifle simple, Easton justifies his redefinition 'because it gives to the term a meaning that enables us to determine factually whether a group of people do in practice consider a policy to be authoritative.'[18] The test of whether a policy is or is not authoritative is behavioural – namely, do those at whom it is aimed obey it, or not? The political scientist need only observe the obedience of the citizenry to ascertain that a particular policy is indeed 'authoritative', is promulgated by 'authorities', and thus qualifies as an exercise of 'authority'.

Easton does not deny that authority may have a moral dimension. He wishes merely to point out 'that the grounds upon which a person accepts a policy as authoritative can be distinguished from the actual acceptance of the authority of the policy.'[19] The latter, he adds, 'may flow from a number of sources: moral, traditional or customary, or purely from fear of the consequences.'[20] In other words, the 'moral aspect' of authority, which has to do with the sorts of reasons that people give for obeying (or disobeying) laws or policies, are of no concern to the political scientist *qua* scientist. 'For purposes of . . . political research, whatever the motivations, a policy is clearly authoritative when the feeling prevails that it must or ought to be obeyed.'[21] So far as the correct application of the concept of authority is concerned, the reasons, arguments and justifications offered by those over whom authority is exercised are irrelevant and immaterial. Not reasons for obeying but causes of obedient behaviour; not considered judgements but 'feelings' – these are the stuff of authority according to Easton's criteria.

Several things are striking, not to say strange, about Easton's reconstruction of authority. For one, it becomes simply a synonym for anything that engenders obedience and compliance. This is all the more remarkable when we recall that authority is central to – indeed, constitutive of – Easton's systems-theoretic conception of politics. We are left, then, with a warmed-over Weberian (or perhaps a reheated Hobbesian) view that command and obedience are the poles of political life. Politics thus becomes, in Hobbes' terms, a relation between a powerful or authoritative agent and a passive or powerless patient. Moreover, since authority is operationally reducible to anything that produces obedience, it follows that all obedient behaviour provides proof positive of the presence of authority: where there is obedience – whatever its cause, reason or justification – there also is authority. And if the effect of such compliant behaviour is to 'allocate values', the relationship is necessarily a 'political' one. This might seem unproblematic, until we reflect that the thief who robs me at knife-point is by Easton's lights engaged in 'political' activity. That I obey because he has a knife in my ribs is beside the point; the political scientist is interested in my compliant behaviour, not in my reasons for complying, save for the fact that I do (under the circumstances) feel that his re-allocative 'policy' of robbing people 'must or ought to be obeyed'. And the empirically observable fact that I do obey would suffice to show that the relationship between thief and victim is indeed 'authoritative' and hence 'political'.

Anyone employing Easton's criteria would therefore find it difficult if not impossible to distinguish between robbery and politics, or for that matter between politics and almost any kind of coercive activity. And indeed Easton admits as much. In a long footnote, apparently added as an afterthought, he writes:

My classification of power relationships . . . views the ability to command as one of a number of types. It may be exercised legitimately or illegitimately. If a thief orders you, at the point of a gun, to yield your wallet and you obey him, he has the ability to command you. He therefore can be said to have authority over you even though, because you would challenge its legitimacy, you consider it coercive. . . . I am aware, of course, that this diverges from ordinary usage. Authority is usually applied only to situations in which there is a belief in the legitimacy of the orders or commands. Nevertheless it is more useful to broaden the term to cover all command-obedience relationships, discriminating further in each case by reference to the reasons why the exercise of the power or authority is effective.

'This,' Easton adds, 'is clearly a matter of definition, but it has important theoretical as well as empirical implications.'[22] Indeed it does. But Easton fails to see the even more important *political* implications of his departure from 'ordinary usage'.

Although the scientific and analytical advantages of Easton's notion of 'authority' are nowhere specified, its political conse-quences are clear enough. All regimes wish to claim the mantle of authority. This they can do, according to Easton, if they are able to supply their subjects with reasons to obey. In the discourse of systems theory it matters not a whit what these reasons are. They can rest upon love and respect, or habit and sentiment, or upon fear of arrest, imprisonment, torture and murder. This 'functionalist' conception of authority is explicitly emotivist. For, as Easton stipulates, '*whatever* the motivations, a policy is clearly authori-tative when the *feeling* prevails that it must or ought to be obeyed.'[23] If Easton had not banished 'the state' from the systems vocabulary, one could say that state terrorism, when sufficiently terrifying to be effective, is no less authoritative than the milder measures of a loving parent.

The point is not that Easton in any way condones coercion or illegitimate authority; it is, rather, that his emotivist construal of authority makes the distinction between legitimate and illegiti-mate authority into a subjective one involving 'feelings' of approval or disapproval. Just as Hobbes claimed that 'tyranny' was merely 'monarchy misliked', so Professor Easton implies that illegitimate authority is simply authority misliked. In this respect, at least, Easton is indeed Hobbes' heir.

It is of course true that the tide has long since turned, in some quarters anyway, against extreme behaviouralism in political science. My reason for reexamining this particular episode in the history of the social sciences is not to single out Professor Easton for special censure but to trace the political implications of a certain view of conceptual revision that remains very much alive and readily evident in some attempts to transform contemporary political discourse. I mean only to point out the moral and political deficiencies of emotivism, and of an emotivist account of authority in particular. I turn now to a consideration of a second restatement of 'authority'.

5.4 THE EPISTEMOCRATIC MODEL

We need to begin by drawing a distinction between epistemic and epistemocratic authority. Epistemic authority is that which is ascribed to the possessor of specialized knowledge, skills or expertise.[24] We defer to the physician in medical matters and to the lawyer on legal questions. When we are ill we want to be treated by an authority on the healing arts, and when we face legal difficulties we want to consult an authority on the law. Epistemocratic authority, by contrast, refers to the claim of one class, group or person to rule another by virtue of the former's possessing specialized knowledge not available to the latter. Epistemocratic authority is therefore conceptually parasitic upon epistemic authority. Or, to put it slightly differently, epistemocratic authority attempts to assimilate political authority to the nonpolitical epistemic authority of the technician or expert.

This distinction is related to one that is commonly drawn between one who by virtue of office or position is *in* authority and one who by dint of specialized knowledge or expertise is *an* authority.[25] Thus the president, though an authority on nothing in particular, is nevertheless in authority. And a plumber, though an authority on taps and drains, is nowhere in authority (save, perhaps, in flooded basements). Politically speaking, the distinction between being *in* authority and being *an* authority, far from applying universally, is applicable only within a certain kind of society. In the sort of society in which the distinction marks a real difference, political rule and claims of expertise or epistemic privilege are separable, and the roles of ruler and expert are occupied by different persons and justified on different grounds. Yet this distinction is, in modern bureaucratized societies, increasingly blurred if not conflated altogether. To speak in the Maoist idiom, one might say that in modern societies, communist and noncommunist alike, the Red is increasingly giving way to the Expert, and the amateur deferring to the authority of the professional. More and more, the expert is in authority because he or she is an authority, in medicine, management science, accounting, law, education, or any one of a dozen domains. Our social practices and institutions increasingly exemplify an ideal that is less democratic than technocratic. Or, to coin a neologism, modern societies increasingly resemble epistemocracies ruled by people claiming to possess specialized knowledge and expertise.

Now it might be objected that there is nothing novel or peculiarly modern about these developments. After all, does not the history of political thought harbour an ancient and recurring vision of the good society in which political authority and expertise are inseparable and in which ruler and expert are one and the same person? It is worth rehearsing that claim in order to criticize it.

The *locus classicus* of the epistemocratic vision is ofttimes held to be Plato's *Republic*.[26] There and elsewhere (*The Statesman*, for example) Plato relies repeatedly upon analogies between the art (*techne*) of ruling and other arts, particularly medicine and navigation. The variable, ill-formed opinion (*doxa*) of the citizen, the patient and the passenger is contrasted with the genuine knowledge (*episteme*) of the philosopher-king, the physician and the navigator. Even so, he warned, one's possessing a *techne* or specialized technical knowledge is not tantamount to having true insight into the good. For this and other reasons, the otherwise understandable temptation to designate Plato as the first proponent of epistemocracy is fraught with anomalies and interpretative problems too numerous and difficult to discuss here.[27] One might then be tempted to turn to Hobbes. For it was Hobbes who first claimed to have set political philosophy on a firm scientific footing, and to have based the undivided authority of the Sovereign upon that foundation. But, again, the temptation should be resisted. For nowhere does Hobbes claim that the Sovereign is smarter or in any way more knowledgeable than his subjects. Whatever its other features, Hobbes' ideal common-wealth is no epistemocracy.[28]

In its full-blown form, the epistemocratic ideal may most justly be traced to nineteenth-century positivism, and to Saint-Simon and Comte in particular. Holding that 'domination should be proportionate to enlightenment', Saint-Simon called for the man-agement and coordination of social and economic relations by twenty-one experts.[29] The authority of *les industriels* rests in particular upon the *kind* of knowledge that they purport to possess. Theirs is, above all, a nomological knowledge of the heretofore hidden general laws governing human behaviour. As Comte put it, 'Social phenomena are subject to natural laws, admitting of rational prevision' and, hence, of purposive human intervention, manipulation and control. Rather than controlling their own affairs, the citizenry must henceforth defer to the authority of experts. The 'elite of the human race' can now be trusted to manage the affairs of the whole society. Those outside the elite have no right to engage in the 'mischief' of criticizing those more knowledgable than they. Indeed, 'the critical spirit,' Comte continues, 'is directly contrary to that which ought to reign in scientific politics.'[30]

It is altogether too easy to dismiss these as the mad utopian fantasies of a fevered nineteenth-century imagination. That past is still very much with us. Modern variations on the epistemocratic theme include Lenin's notion of a vanguard party, the behaviour-ist utopia of B. F. Skinner's *Walden II*, and, still more recently, the vision of a coming post-industrial 'knowledge society'.[31]

The only thing wrong with earlier versions of epistemocracy and epistemocratic authority, say the prophets of post-industria-lism, is that they were premature.[32] The sort of knowledge needed to 'steer' (note the Platonic navigational simile) a complex society was not available to anyone in Plato's day, and least of all to philosophers. Nor was such knowledge needed in order to govern a small society like the Greek *polis*. By contrast, the steering of large, bureaucratized, centralized societies requires specialized skills and expert knowledge. Questions about arms control and disarmament, defence expenditures and weapons systems, foreign policy, public assistance programmes, pollution and toxic waste disposal, alternative energy sources, the exploration of space, acid rain, and a hundred others seem more suited for scientists than for citizens. We are therefore understandably tempted to turn to them, not only to advise and guide but to govern us. Already those who are nominally or formally in authority are apt to turn to someone who is an authority on this subject or that. One who is an authority is required to fulfil a function that those in authority are unable to fulfil. The epistemocratic ideal is one in which politicians are replaced by planners and citizens by clients. It is an ideal to which political reality in some respects increasingly corresponds.

That the influence of this new class of epistemocrats is increasing has been noted by enthusiasts and critics alike.[33] Enthusiasts like Daniel Bell and the late Herman Kahn see the emergence of epistemocracy as a hopeful development. Critics like Robert Dahl and Michael Walzer are less sanguine, seeing in this development a danger to democracy.[34] The danger, I want to suggest, is not that we will concede too much authority to experts but that we will come to think of political authority exclusively in terms of expertise. Thus my question is not, 'How much authority should we give to the experts?', but is instead, 'What would the political world look (and be) like if one of the concepts constitutive of political discourse – namely, authority – were to be construed along epistemocratic lines, as advocated by the prophets of post-industrialism?' In sketching the barest outlines of an answer I shall suggest, strange as it may sound, that epistemocracy poses a danger not only to democracy but to political authority itself. Epistemocratic authority is in fact a debased simulacrum of political authority precisely because it is an oxymoron. Let us see why.

In its epistemocratic form, 'authority' in matters moral and political is assimilated to the paradigm of epistemic authority: one is *in* authority because he or she is *an* authority on something. This assimilation assumes that politics and ethics are activities in which there are experts, and that most of us are not now, and perhaps cannot even aspire to be, expert in these matters. To see why and in what respects this epistemocratic contention might be mistaken, we could do worse than consult Aristotle. Although he can scarcely speak to us with the authority that he once possessed, Aristotle did draw some useful distinctions which we ignore at our peril. In Aristotle's distinction, politics is *praxis*, not *poiesis* or *techne*. If politics were a 'technical' rather than a 'practical' activity, it could be left to the experts. But politics is not, in the nature of the case, an exact science admitting of determinate answers about which there can be no dispute or disagreement, but an art – the art of collective deliberation, dialogue and judgement. From the fact that politics is a dialogical activity admitting of differences of opinion and judgement it follows either that in politics and ethics there are no experts or, as Aristotle would have it, that each citizen has expertise sufficient to join the discussion, to listen and learn, to hear and to be heard. Or, to put it another way, politics is not essentially an instrumental or goal-oriented activity undertaken for the sake of some separately identifiable end, but is instead the medium of the moral education of the citizenry.

When the late Carl Friedrich averred that authority involves the 'capacity for reasoned elaboration', he did not go quite far enough in the right direction.[35] For the engineer, scientist, technician, physician – indeed any expert to whom epistemic authority is ascribed – can also supply reasons for arriving at a particular conclusion or recommending one regimen rather than another. But when epistemic authority (being *an* authority) is used as a model or template for analysing political authority (being *in* authority), we misunderstand the essential distinguishing features of the activity of politics and of the place of authority in that practice. The kinds of reasons that are relevant in political deliberation are those internal to that practice and are themselves arrived at in the course of such deliberation. Politics, as Gadamer reminds us, is a matter of practical reason. To turn to experts and the kinds of reasons that they can give, and which we may or may not understand, is to denature politics by viewing it not as *praxis* but as a *techne*. It is this misunderstanding, more than any other, Gadamer contends, that has deformed and debased the concept of authority. And this deformation is due less to ambitious would-be epistemocrats than to disaffected citizens eager to cast off the burdens of citizenship:

> the problem of our society is that the longing of the citizenry for orientation and normative patterns invests the expert with an exaggerated authority. Modern society expects him to provide a substitute for past moral and political orientations. Consequently,

the concept of '*praxis*' which was developed in the last two centuries is an awful deformation of what practice really is. In all the debates of the last century practice was understood as application of science to technical tasks. This is a very inadequate notion. It degrades practical reason to technical control.[36]

This epistemocratic deformation of politics and practical reason, Gadamer continues, 'is the peculiar falsehood of modern consciousness: the idolatry of scientific method and of the anonymous authority of the sciences.' To recognize that 'practical and political reason can only be realized and transmitted dialogically' would be to 'vindicate again the noblest task of the citizen – decision-making according to one's own responsibility – instead of conceding that task to the expert.'[37]

The epistemocratic rejoinder is that this democratic ideal cannot be realized in modern society. The democratic vision of an active, informed and responsible citizenry is naive at best, and dangerous at worst. Ill-informed people are apt to make mistakes that are altogether too costly to risk. Better, then, to leave such matters to experts. To this criticism Dahl's reply is eloquent:

> It is true that a democratic regime runs the risk that the people will make mistakes. But the risk of mistake exists in all regimes in the real world, and the worst blunders of this century have been made by leaders in nondemocratic regimes. Moreover, the opportunity to make mistakes is an opportunity to learn. Just as we reject paternalism in individual decisions because it prevents the development of our moral capacities, so too we should reject guardianship in public affairs because it will stunt the development of the moral capacities of an entire people. At its best, only the democratic vision can offer the hope, which guardianship can never do, that by engaging in governing themselves, all people, and not merely a few, may learn to act as morally responsible human beings.[38]

As a vision of political authority, then, the epistemocratic vision of rule by an elite of experts is deficient for reasons that are above all pedagogical. Were it to become partly constitutive of democratic discourse, the epistemocratic construal of authority would, as I shall argue in chapter 6, undermine civic character.

5.5   CONCLUDING CRITICAL POSTSCRIPT

To transform the concept of authority along either emotivist or epistemocratic lines would require that we dismiss or ignore a number of otherwise crucial distinctions. As regards the former, perhaps the most important of these, as MacIntyre says in another context, 'is the fact that emotivism entails the obliteration of any genuine distinction between manipulative and non-manipulative social relations.'[39] And epistemocratic authority is deficient in conflating the distinctions between epistemic and epistemocratic authority and between being *in* authority and being *an* authority, in both instances by assimilating the former to the latter.

The political import of these developments could hardly be clearer. For as our society becomes increasingly rationalized, the social scientist's studied indifference to these and other distinctions takes on added political importance. As Arendt often noted, to conflate conceptual distinctions is to make our language not more precise but less, thereby impoverishing the very medium through which political communities are constituted and reconstituted.[40] To reconstruct 'authority' is not merely to alter the meaning of the word but to restructure the world in ways both subtle and ominous. Politics is a dialogical activity practised by citizens. Its medium is speech, its form of reason 'practical' in the original meaning of that term. As the concepts constitutive of that speech are not merely changed but corrupted – primarily by being confused with other, nonpolitical concepts and practices – the activity it makes possible is also necessarily impoverished. That some sectors of our society and many modern governments have an interest in impoverishment of this sort seems beyond doubt or dispute. Political and social scientists, in particular, might do well to ask themselves whether they should be aiding and abetting this process, or resisting and criticizing it.

6

The Economic Reconstruction of Democratic Discourse

6.1 INTRODUCTION

My aim in this chapter is not to construct a comprehensive conceptual history of 'democracy' but to consider a particular episode in that history. More specifically, I propose to examine what is sometimes thought to be a distinctively twentieth-century mutation in the meaning of 'democracy'. The change to which I refer has been largely though not exclusively wrought by social scientists, and by economists in particular. This I shall, for short, call the 'economic theory of democracy'.[1] This theory recasts democracy in the idiom of economics, or more specifically of neoclassical economic theory and the more recent 'rational choice' research programme predicated upon it.[2] Here I want to look closely and critically at this emergent understanding of democracy and the new meanings it assigns to citizenship, to participation and voting, and even to 'politics' itself. To sharpen my focus, I want to contrast the economic theory of democracy with another, which I shall call the 'educative theory'. According to the latter (which is sometimes called the 'participatory' or 'self-development' view), civic participation is not a public means to an essentially private end but a mode of instruction and a constitutive feature of one's moral and political development. Instead of treating these two competing views as theories in the full-fledged sense of the term, I propose to consider them as different discourses or moral languages out of which the concepts of politics, democracy and citizenship are constituted, or rather, in the case of the rational choice research programme, radically reconstituted. I shall suggest that so much of importance is lost when we try to translate from the educative idiom into the economic one, that we should seriously question the wisdom of even making the attempt (which, I argue, fails in any event). Even so, I conclude that something valuable may be learned from reflecting critically upon the attempt.

My route to this conclusion is a rather circuitous one. I begin by briefly reiterating several key features of the constitutive or expressivist view of language, including the claim that any discourse delimits if it does not determine the kinds of characters we have or are, or aspire to be. Similarly, competing democratic discourses delimit in different ways the self-understandings and thereby the character of democratic citizens. On the one side, the discourse of the economic theory of democracy constitutes citizens as self-interested rational actors bent on maximizing their own utility. On the other side, by contrast, the educative theory sees citizens as repeatedly resituating and redefining themselves in relation to their ever-expanding horizons and changing self-understandings. I then go on to examine the way in which these two democratic discourses are conventionally situated in relation to one another. The economic theory is usually viewed as the more modern of the two, and indeed as an advance over the outmoded and idealistic educative theory. This conventional view, I argue, is mistaken inasmuch as it rests upon a bad piece of conceptual history. After attempting to identify and rectify the historical mistake, I go on to argue that the discourse of the economic theory of democracy is, in the final analysis, an incoherent *civic* discourse.

Before beginning I should say that my target in this chapter is not the theoretical discourse of economics or social-choice theory. Their value as theoretical disciplines is not in question. My intent is to discover what happens when their theoretical discourse spills over into, informs, and eventually transforms the language of political agents themselves. The simplifying assumptions that are enabling and empowering in the one discourse become disabling and disempowering in the other.

6.2 LANGUAGE, AGENCY AND CHARACTER

A political theory offers, among other things, a moral language or lexicon in which to describe and appraise political phenomena. To the degree that it is beholden to the classical idea of *theoria*, or vision, a theory offers a new angle of vision, a new way of seeing – and of being in – the political world. For this language not only permits one to redescribe and reappraise this world, but to reconstitute the relationships comprising it. This is possible because political theories – including ostensibly scientific ones – have a feature that is wholly absent from theories in the natural sciences. This feature, often referred to as 'reflexivity', is unique to theories whose objects are self-interpreting subjects.[3] These subjects are also capable of learning new ways of thinking about and interpreting the meanings of their lives, their roles and the situations in which they must act. 'As social actors come to accept theoretical accounts of social phenomena,' Donald Moon notes, 'these accounts will become part of the social world itself, altering, in unpredictable ways, the very institutions and practices that had originally been described.'[4] As agents come to speak, to think and to act in its terms, the theory not only informs but transforms their practices.

It is for precisely this reason that the shambles in which democratic theory nowadays finds itself is, or should be, a source of some concern to democrats. Political theories, including theories of democracy, are modes of self-understanding; to the degree that these modes are disordered, confused or otherwise impaired, so too must be our practices. It is for that reason and in that spirit that I propose to look closely and critically at the economic theory of democracy, which I take to be symptomatic of the grave disorder of democratic theory in the West.[5] My aim here is to discover how two kinds of democratic discourse might inform and transform the theories, the practices – and indeed the characters – of those who subscribe to them.

Like any other political theory, a theory of democracy supplies a civic lexicon, a moral language that shapes and sustains the characters of those who speak in and on its terms. This it does in at least two ways. First, as we speak, so we are. Our language expresses the kinds of characters we are, or aspire to be. As James Boyd White puts it, 'in important ways we become the languages that we use,' for 'the languages we speak, and the cultural practices they at once reflect and make possible, mark or form our minds by habituating them to certain forms of attention, certain ways of seeing and conceiving of oneself and of the world.'[6] No language or lexicon – be it that of the law or computer programming or economics – is morally neutral; each enables or encourages or constrains speakers to think and act in certain ways and not in others. The argumentative and rhetorical resources of my language mark the limits of the moral world in which I think and act. Different discourses create and sustain different kinds of characters with different understandings of human agency and action.

This, in turn, leads us to a second consideration. All political theories, including theories of democracy, either envision or presuppose agents of a certain type. Typically, these agents have certain kinds of powers and limitations, are at home in specific sorts of settings, and are capable of forming certain kinds of intentions. They are, in short, characters of a more or less readily identifiable type. 'Characters,' says Alasdair MacIntyre, 'are, so to speak, the moral representatives of their culture and they are so because of the way in which moral and metaphysical ideas and theories assume through them an embodied existence in the social world. Characters are the masks worn by moral philosophies.'[7] A particular moral or political theory might thus be viewed as a systematic articulation of that idealized agent's own self-understanding, including his understanding of the aim or purpose of political life itself.[8]

The point at which I am driving was perhaps made most clearly by Hegel. In *The Philosophy of Right* Hegel contrasts two ideal-typical social structures and the kinds of characters to be found in each. 'Civil society' (*bürgerliche Gesellschaft*) is inhabited by rational egoists, each competing against all the others to maximize his or her share of scarce resources. Civil society is the sphere of 'universal egoism' in which agents are traders bent on maximizing their advantage in a competitive market environment. The 'state', by contrast, is the sphere of 'universal altruism'. It is a community of citizens, collectively seeking to realize the public good or common interest as determined in the course of rational deliberation and reflection. The citizen and the state emerge, indeed, out of a process of reflection whereby rational egoists come to acknowledge and appreciate the depth and degree of their interdependence, not merely in an economic but in a more profound political and social sense. The nature of their interdependence determines not only what but who they are, individually and collectively.[9]

Yet there are, as Hegel well knew, numerous barriers in civil society to the kind of critical self-reflection that would be required to turn traders and competitors into citizens. In this respect, at least, Hegel, although no democrat, has proved to be a prescient prophet. For, as Alan Ryan remarks, 'there is visible in the political thought of the past century and a half a division of opinion over the point or the goals of political and social life in general', and nowhere is this split more visible than in the contrasting accounts supplied by the economic or 'market' view and the alternative to be found in the 'participant' or 'self-developmental' account.[10] Each, in effect, envisions agents of different character-types.

Consider first the character created and much admired by economists and game theorists, the rational actor. He is by definition one who views himself and his actions – and other people and their actions – through the lenses of a particular discourse, which one might term the Discourse of Exchange. Within the terms of this discourse, it would be irrational, not to say immoral and unintelligible, for an actor to give up something without receiving in return something of equal or greater value. All expenditures or 'costs' must be balanced against expected gains or 'benefits'. In short, the agent featured in the economic theory of democracy has had his character discursively formed in and by and for civil society. He is an egoist and a calculator; his character has been created for that purpose and for no other. When this agent comes to play the part of citizen he has nothing new to learn. Although he may of course acquire new 'information' and sharpen his skills *qua* calculator, he is not expected to change his character or to become a different sort of person as a result of his having engaged in civic activities. Political participation is accordingly viewed as a 'cost' from which he, as a rational calculator and utility maximizer, expects to receive a benefit of equal or greater value.

Like any character, the rational actor speaks in a particular idiom or language. What is most notable about the rational actor's language is that certain concepts – of 'civic virtue', say, or 'corruption' – are wholly absent, while others, such as 'citizen-ship', are transformed almost beyond recognition. Thus the older language of democratic citizenship becomes unintelligible, the meaningless babble of madmen and fools. The language that shapes and lends legitimacy to the rational actor's character is the discourse of commerce and commodification, of barter and exchange, of profits and losses, of utility and disutility. Lest you doubt it, you need only consult one of the classics of the 'economic' theory of democracy.

One of the not inconsiderable virtues of Anthony Downs' *An Economic Theory of Democracy* is the boldness with which concepts that are normally employed in (and are indeed constitutive of) economic discourse are systematically substituted for the concepts constitutive of democratic political discourse. Such substitution is especially evident in the redescription of even the most prosaic political act. For example, in redescribing the simple act of voting in the idiom of neoclassical economic theory, Downs writes that 'voting is [not] a costless act. . . because every act takes time. In fact, time is the principal cost of voting: time to register, to discover what parties are running, to deliberate, to go to the polls, and to mark the ballot. Since time is a scarce resource, voting is inherently costly.' Thus 'rational abstention' is naturally to be expected of an agent whose costs outweigh expected returns.[11] For such an agent the point of political life, as of all pursuits, is to maximize expected utility. From this perspective, then, the role of citizen is indistinguishable from – indeed it is identical with – those of competitor and consumer, buyer and seller. Political parties and leaders are 'entrepreneurs' competing with one another for the votes of 'consumers' who will 'spend' their votes (and bear the 'costs' of voting) for those whom they believe will best serve their interests. Whatever the role or activity, the agent's character – the agent-as-trader – remains the same.

A moral language and a character of very different kind is sketched by 'educative' theorists of democracy. The character of the citizen is not fully formed from the outset. He does, to be sure, have certain powers or potentialities, including that of knowing and acting upon his own narrow self-interest. But of all his powers, one predominates: the power to learn, to change his views – including his view of what constitutes his interest *qua* citizen – and therefore to become a different sort of person. In the course of playing his part he has, at least potentially, the capacity to transcend his original standpoint and to survey the scene – and his place in it – from a loftier vantage point. As Sheldon Wolin remarks, the role of citizen is unlike any other:

> the specialized roles assigned the individual, or adopted by him, are not a full substitute for citizenship because citizenship provides what other roles cannot, namely an integrative experience which brings together the multiple role-activities of the contemporary person and demands that the separate roles be surveyed from a more general point of view. . . . [P]olitical theory must once again be viewed as that form of knowledge which deals with what is general and integrative to men, a life of common involvements.[12]

Yet it is only too obvious that much of what passes for political theory – and particularly the 'economic' theory of democracy – not only does nothing of the sort, but rather renders the very idea of restoring and enriching citizenship largely chimerical, not to say irrational and unintelligible.

If contemporary democratic discourse is to regain some measure of coherence we need, I believe, to retrace our steps over 'abandoned stages of reflection' in order to see how we got into this predicament and how we might yet get out of it.[13] It is just here that critical conceptual history can be of some help. More specifically, a study of the way in which the concept of democracy has been transformed by social scientists (and by economists in particular) reveals that the conceptual transformation was made possible, in part, by a piece of bad conceptual history. To expose those errors, and to reconstruct a better alternative account, may take us some way toward the transformation and revitalization of democratic discourse.

6.3   A MODERN MYTH

To some considerable degree, Joseph Schumpeter's sketchy conceptual history of 'democracy' underpins and legitimizes the economic theory of democracy defended by Downs. 'Schumpeter's profound analysis of democracy,' says Downs, 'forms the inspiration and foundation for our whole thesis, and our debt and gratitude to him are great indeed.'[14] But because Downs and other economic theorists have been content to get their history from Schumpeter, they have made three interconnected mistakes. Firstly, they have muddled both the chronology and the contexts in which the two theories appeared. Secondly, in so doing they have denied their true philosophical paternity. Finally, and not least, they have exaggerated their own originality. It is worth trying to untangle that tale, if only because it functions as a modern myth which contributes to and serves to legitimize the widely held belief that the economic theory not only suceeds but supersedes and improves upon the educative theory.

The widely shared but mistaken view that the economic theory of democracy is more modern than the educative view stems, I suspect, from Schumpeter's influential narrative about the move from a 'classical' moralistic theory of democracy to a more realistic and enlightened 'economic' theory. The 'classical' theory of democracy, as described (or perhaps one should say invented) by Schumpeter, supposes that there is a unique and univocal 'common good' which can be discovered by public-spirited voters and implemented by their representatives. The 'classical doctrine' of democracy holds

that there exists a Common Good, the obvious beacon light of policy, which is always simple to define and which every normal person can be made to see by means of rational argument. There is hence no excuse for not seeing it and in fact no explanation for the presence of people who do not see it except ignorance – which can be removed – stupidity and anti-social interest. Moreover, this common good implies definite answers to all questions so that every social fact and every measure taken . . . can unequivocally be classed as 'good' or 'bad'. All people having therefore to agree, in principle at least, there is also a Common Will of the people (= will of all reasonable individuals) that is exactly coterminous with the common good or interest or welfare or happiness. . . . Thus every member of the community, conscious of that goal, knowing his or her mind, discerning what is good and what is bad, takes part, actively and responsibly, in furthering the former and fighting the latter and all the members taken together control their public affairs.[15]

As to who, exactly, ever subscribed to this remarkably muddled and simplistic view of democracy and the common good, Schumpeter is strangely silent, save to say that it is an 'eighteenth-century' view propounded by unnamed 'utilitarian rationalists'. But, as his more historically minded critics have shown, there is good reason for Schumpeter's silence on this score. He does not cite specific thinkers and texts, because he cannot: they do not exist. The 'classical doctrine' of democracy, says Carole Pateman, is 'a myth' concocted of a motley amalgam of incommensurable views drawn from, or more often imputed to, thinkers of very different orientations.[16] The late John Plamenatz was blunter still. Schumpeter's 'attack [on] what he called "the classical theory of democracy",' wrote Plamenatz, 'is ignorant and inept' and 'entirely misconceived, for no writer on democracy has ever subscribed to it in the sense he defines. In attacking it, he attacks, not a dead horse, but one that was never alive, at least not in the stable of democratic theory.'[17]

Why then bother to criticize Schumpeter's attack upon a doctrine of his own devising? That attack, says Plamenatz, 'is worth discussing only because it has been taken seriously', if only by some ahistorically minded social scientists. 'I suspect,' Plamenatz continues, 'that not a few American political scientists, immersed in their studies of political behaviour in the largest of the Western democracies, gladly took [Schumpeter's] word for it that the theories of the past, which they were too busy to read, were so unrealistic as not to be worth reading.'[18] It is surely ironic that supposedly hard-headed social scientists should have swallowed Schumpeter's mythic construct whole, without a hint of intellectual indigestion and even with gratitude.

Plamenatz's point, and mine, is that their having swallowed Schumpeter's myth is no mere academic mistake on which nothing important hangs. On the contrary, bad conceptual history makes for inept and politically pernicious conceptual transformations. And these in turn delimit if they do not determine the limits of our language and our common world. Nowhere are these limitations more evident than in contemporary attempts to supply an 'economic' redefinition of democracy and democratic citizenship.

In order to see how this process works, we would need to note in some detail how Schumpeter gets his facts wrong and how he misunderstands or misinterprets those that he gets right. Such a detailed inquiry being beyond the bounds of the present chapter, let me mention only one of the many misunderstandings that mar Schumpeter's influential story of the passage from the 'classical' to the 'economic' theory of democracy.

Consider Schumpter's claim that 'utilitarian rationalists' subscribed to the notion of a unique and nondivisible Common Good that is at the heart of the 'classical' theory. Here even his critics (Plamenatz excepted) have been insufficiently critical. Pateman is surely too generous in conceding that 'Bentham and James Mill provide examples of writers from whose theories one could extract something which bears a family resemblance to Schumpeter's definition of the "classical" theory.'[19] In fact, neither Bentham nor James Mill believed that there was a nondivisible common good waiting to be discovered by selfless citizens; there was only 'the greatest happiness of the greatest number' which could in turn be discovered and acted upon only if each citizen honestly and accurately registered his or her view about which of the available alternatives would best serve his or her individual interest in happiness.

Schumpeter's claim that his economic theory of democracy provides a hard-headed and realistic alternative to the moralistic classical theory cannot withstand close critical scrutiny. Schumpeter, Downs and other economic theorists subscribe to a particular moral philosophy whose core assumptions include self-interestedness, the perpetual scarcity of valued goods (especially wealth and power), competition, etc., and in which the weighing of costs and benefits is central. That moral philosophy is of course utilitarianism. Far from squaring with Schumpeter's caricature of the 'classical doctrine' of democracy, the Benthamite or Utilitarian view not only corresponds quite closely with but is indeed the forerunner of the prototype for the 'economic' view sketched by Schumpeter and defended in greater detail by Downs.

The connection can perhaps be most clearly delineated by examining James Mill's *Essay on Government* (1820). Mill, like Schumpeter and Downs, begins by accepting the postulates of scarcity and self-interest. Chief amongst the resources that men wish to protect are their power and their property. This being true of all men, it is perforce true of office-holders, whether they be

hereditary monarchs or duly elected representatives. Unless somehow constrained, a representative will act in his own interest
rather than in the interests of his constituents. One might think
that this would point to the desirability of direct democracy, but
the elder Mill argues otherwise. Direct democracy, he says in
what sounds like an anticipatory paraphrase of Downs, would
take too much time away from the essential economic activity of
earning one's livelihood. Direct democracy being economically
inefficient, representative government must be so arranged as to
make the interests of the representative in being reelected coin-
cident with the voters' interest in protecting their property – and,
in doing so, 'spending' as little time and effort as possible.
Therefore, says Mill, he has in good deductive fashion 'demon-
strated' the necessity of frequent elections, short terms in office,
and other means by which constituents can check their representatives' natural tendency to serve their own rather than their
constituents' interests.[20]

The Utilitarian defence of democracy rests upon the argument
that, of all the available alternatives, representative democracy
best serves the end of protecting the property and other interests
of individuals. Everyone being the best judge of his own interests,
and each being inclined to ride roughshod over the interests of
others when it is to his advantage to do so, each citizen should
have a say in who should represent his interests.

6.4   THE EDUCATIVE DEFENCE OF DEMOCRACY

It was precisely against the Utilitarian defence of democracy that
John Stuart Mill directed several of the central arguments in
Considerations on Representative Government (1861). The Utilitarian
view that representative democracy is to be recommended because
it affords the best possible protection to private interests, the
younger Mill maintains, is of secondary importance.[21] Indeed it
pales into insignificance when compared with what we might call
Mill's educative argument for increased participation. In Mill's
view the most morally compelling argument for democracy is that
it increases the citizen's sense of civic competence and responsibility:

The food of feeling is action. . . . Let a person have nothing to do for his country, and he will not care for it. . . . Leaving things to the Government, like leaving them to Providence, is synonymous with caring nothing about them, and accepting the results, when disagreeable, as visitations of Nature.[22]

'Passive characters' unaccustomed to action are, he adds, apt to take account only of their own narrowly private interests and concerns. '[T]he intelligence and sentiments of the whole people,' he says, 'are given up to the material interests, and, when these are provided for, to the amusement and ornamentation of private life.'[23]

It is important to note that there is, according to the Utilitarian and/or economic account, nothing to be said against those whose concerns are wholly self-centred. On the contrary, they are the rational actors *par excellence* without whom a utilitarian polity could not exist, much less function with any degree of efficiency. Yet to the degree that these paragons of rationality pursue only their own essentially economic interests they are, in Mill's view, morally deficient. This is not to say, however, that Mill is opposed to the idea that we have interests which we may quite legitimately pursue through various channels, including the political. His point is instead that we reveal and express our characters by the kinds of interests we have and choose to pursue. The problem with a crude version of Utilitarianism – and, we might add, of the Schumpeterian and Downsian versions of the economic theory of democracy – is that the kinds of characters it envisions, or rather requires, are stunted and self-centred ones who take too narrow a view of what their interests are (and indeed of the very selves who have those interests). The 'interest-philosophy of the Bentham school', as Mill says elsewhere, construes the concept of interest in an unduly constricted way, so that it means, in the main, 'material, or worldly interests'.[24] Claiming to take people as they are, the Benthamites equate interests with what economists today call revealed preferences. But what people really reveal in stating and pursuing their respective preferences, Mill suggests, is the kinds of characters they have, and are, or aspire to be.

Debates about 'the ideally best polity', Mill insists, are not only about particular forms of government or institutions or laws. In the end they turn on 'a still more fundamental [question], namely, which of two common types of character, for the general good of humanity, it is more desirable should predominate – the active, or the passive type; that which struggles against evils, or that which endures them; that which bends to circumstances, or that which endeavours to make circumstances bend to itself.'[25] Participatory democracy provides the training ground for characters of the former type: 'the passive type of character is favoured by the government of one or a few, and the active self-helping type by that of the Many.'[26] The 'action' which is 'the food of feeling', as Mill remarks in his review of Tocqueville's *Democracy in America*, 'can only be learned in action.' Just as 'we do not learn to read or write . . . by being merely told how to do it, but by doing it,' so, says Mill, we learn to be democratic citizens and active characters by actually engaging in political activities.[27]

Unlike his father and Bentham – and subsequently Schumpeter and Downs – Mill insists that the infrequent act of voting for a distant candidate is, from a moral or political point of view, a pretty paltry substitute for active citizenship. More frequent and regular avenues must be found or created, if politically active characters are to be moulded and made fit for citizenship. The likelihood that 'Englishmen of the lower middle class' will 'be placed on juries' and elected to 'serve [in] parish offices' affords a rudimentary civic education for some. 'Still more salutary,' says Mill, 'is the moral part of the instruction afforded by the participation of the private citizen, if even rarely, in public functions.'

> He is called upon, while so engaged, to weigh interests not his own; to be guided, in case of conflicting claims, by another rule than his private partialities; to apply, at every turn, principles and maxims which have for their reason of existence the common good. . . . He is made to feel himself one of the public, and whatever is for their benefit to be for his benefit.[28]

And, in what might almost be read as an anticipatory rebuke to Schumpeter and Downs, Mill adds:

> Where this school of public spirit does not exist, scarcely any sense is entertained that private persons . . . owe any duties to society, except to obey the laws and submit to the government. There is no unselfish sentiment of identification with the public. Every thought

or feeling, either of interest or of duty, is absorbed in the individual and in the family. The man never thinks of any collective interest, or any objects to be pursued jointly with others, but only in competition with them, and in some measure at their expense. A neighbour . . . is therefore only a rival. Thus even private morality suffers, while public is actually extinct. Were this the universal and only possible state of things, the utmost aspirations of the lawgiver or the moralist could only stretch to make the bulk of the community a flock of sheep innocently nibbling the grass side by side.[29]

An almost perfect picture of modern consumer society, surely.

6.5   ECONOMIC DISCOURSE AND DEMOCRATIC THEORY

It is of course precisely the language of economics – the discourse of consumption, production, profit-maximizing, political 'competition' and 'entrepreneurship', and the rest – that constitutes the civic lexicon of the economic theory of democracy. The *beau idéal* of the economic theory is nothing less than Mill's passive character actively searching after his own 'material, or worldly interest'. The language of moral development, of character, of education cannot even begin to be translated into the vocabulary of this theory and can accordingly only be received as so much static or noise in the otherwise clear channel of civil society. That theory, or rather various versions of it, have as their ancestors the very perspective that Mill meant to criticize. If their characters are of the 'active' type, citizens are not just voters, and voters are not simply consumers; citizenship is not equivalent to consumership. Yet it is just this doubtful equivalence that the economic theory of democracy insists upon asserting.

Such assertions are not of course purely logical or technical ones, nor are they morally neutral. They are, on the contrary, rhetorical stratagems serving political purposes. It may be instructive to examine, if only in passing, a number of rhetorical stratagems employed in economic discourse. For, as Donald McCloskey and James Boyd White have recently pointed out, economics is in no small part persuasive speech. That discipline's increasingly technical and formal character tends to discourage or disable critics who are not economists, even as it lends an aura of scientific legitimacy to those who speak in its idiom.[30] But, more than that, economic discourse is bound to have a certain appeal in the kind of competitive market society in which we live. Within that society economics constitutes an imperialistic discourse which, depending upon one's point of view, either threatens or promises to supplant or at any rate radically reconstitute other discursive modes.[31] Economic analogies and metaphors abound, not only in technical journals but in everyday speech (the reader is invited to supply his or her own examples). Some of these may, on occasion, prove illuminating; but they are never innocent or decorative or 'merely' metaphorical. For metaphors, as Max Black and Mary Hesse have noted, constitute a 'secondary linguistic system' initially intended to illuminate or extend the range of a 'primary linguistic system'. But, if successful, the secondary system soon supplants the primary one, and we come to speak exclusively in its terms.[32] And not only to speak, but – since in politics we act with words – to act as well.

The metaphors in which those ostensibly antimetaphorical thinkers Bentham and James Mill – not to mention Schumpeter and his successors – recommend we recast our thoughts and actions are those of the competitive market, of production and consumption, profit and loss. In Schumpeter's variant of economic discourse democracy becomes a 'method' for 'choosing leaders', whereby citizens act as 'consumers' choosing between 'competitors' who are in turn entrepreneurs vying for their vote by putting together appealing packages or products. 'The democratic method,' says Schumpeter, 'is that institutional arrangement for arriving at political decisions in which individuals acquire the power to decide by means of a competitive struggle for the people's vote.'[33] The 'primary function of the electorate,' he continues, 'is to produce a government.'[34] Government requires 'leadership', and 'acceptance of leadership is the true function of the electorate's vote.'[35] The citizen of a democracy is free in precisely the same sense in which the consumer in a competitive market society is free. The 'kind of competition for leadership which . . . define[s] democracy' is 'free competition for a free vote.' Thus 'the concept of competition in the economic sphere' is the one with which democratic political competition 'may be usefully compared'.[36]

Political theories having a reflexive dimension, it comes as no surprise that such analogies and comparisons are already being reflected in, and are increasingly constitutive of, our own self-understandings of what it means to be a citizen in a consumer society more civil and economic than political and democratic.[37] The onus of argument begins to shift perceptibly as democratic discourse is subordinated to, and transformed into, economic discourse. This is of course nothing new. James Mill, no less than Schumpeter, criticized direct democracy on economic grounds of expense and efficiency. Moreover, as Mancur Olson has argued, democratic citizens have a well-demonstrated penchant for meddling with the machinery of the market, which necessarily precipitates the economic decline of democratic nations.[38] Even worse, says Samuel Huntington, the 'democratic distemper' leads citizens to entertain naive and unrealistically high aspirations and expectations about the possibility of arriving at political solutions to what are essentially economic questions better left to technicians and experts.[39]

Such criticisms should come as no surprise since, as we saw in the preceding chapter, a palpable tension has long existed between epistemocratic and democratic discourses. And yet, as the discourse of democracy itself becomes bifurcated, and as the 'economic' variant becomes hegemonic, this particular tension is reduced if not eliminated altogether. Democracy is implicitly redefined so that it is either compatible with or is a species of epistemocracy: voting is left to citizens and governing to the experts. Another, and at first sight more surprising, outcome of this process of conceptual transformation is that democracy is nowadays not only criticized but defended in economic terms. As one economist has recently written, democracy is defensible not because it affords the best moral and civic education for the citizenry but because it 'makes economic sense'.[40] That democracy is both attacked and defended in 'economic' terms suggests that the discourse of economics is now in the ascendant and, correlatively, that the concept of democracy itself is undergoing (if it has not already undergone) a profound transformation.

6.6   A POLITICAL PARADOX

Yet the mode of civic self-understanding recommended by the economic theory of democracy proves, upon closer examination, to be a peculiarly problematic one. Indeed it may, to adapt a phrase from Alasdair MacIntyre, be so contradictory as to be incapable of political embodiment.[41] To see why this may be so, one need look no farther than the so-called paradox of voting, which has so far defied resolution.

Briefly, the by now familiar paradox arises in the following way. A rational actor, according to Downs, acts solely from considerations of expected utility. Whatever he does, he does because he expects to gain something from it. From this it follows that he will 'spend' the time and energy it takes to vote only if he expects to make a return on his investment. But in an election in which many votes are cast, the probability that his single vote will make any appreciable difference to the outcome is so small as to be negligible. Because voting does not 'pay', rational voters will abstain from voting and democracy dies on the vine.

Downs claimed the credit for making this troubling discovery, which, as he rightly noted, follows from his own premises.[42] But his predilection for ignoring the past leads him to claim credit for a discovery that he was by no means the first to make. A century and a half earlier Hegel noted that the narrowly self-interested inhabitants of civil society would have no good reason to vote: 'Popular suffrage, . . . especially in large states, leads inevitably to electoral indifference, since the casting of a single vote is of no significance where there is a multitude of electors. Even if a voting qualification is highly valued and esteemed by those who are entitled to it, they still do not enter the polling booth. Thus the result of [popular suffrage in civil society] is more likely to be the opposite of what was intended'.[43] The paradox arises for the first time – as Hegel notes but Downs does not – in a particular historical epoch, with the rise of a civil society populated by self-interested individuals bent on maximizing their personal gain. Hegel takes that paradox to be among the many contradictions that will, when reflected upon, lead to the transformation of people's consciousness and thereby to the transformation of competitive civil society, with its relations of universal egoism, into the state in which citizens relate to one another on the basis of those common interests that they, *qua* citizens, all share. Hegel, in short, sees the discovery of this contradiction as an opportunity for the kind of critical reflection that transforms competitive egoists into cooperative and public-spirited citizens.

Not so Downs. The concepts of critical reflection and political education form no part of his discourse. For him the contradiction is a theoretical one requiring a technical or theoretical solution available (and of interest) to academic social scientists. A rational individual, he suggests, would be willing to pay the cost of voting, even if he gained nothing save the satisfaction derived from 'do[ing] his share in providing long-run benefits' for himself and others, by helping to maintain the democratic system.[44] But then, as Downs' critics were quick to point out, the solution is no solution at all, inasmuch as it is utterly inconsistent with the very premises of the utility-maximizing model of political participation. As Brian Barry noted,

'Doing his share' is a concept foreign to the kind of 'economic' rationality with which Downs is working. It requires our citizen to reason that since the benefits he gets depend on the efforts of others, he should contribute too. This may be good ethics, but it is not consistent with the assumptions of the model, which require the citizen to compute the advantage that accrues to him from his doing x rather than y; not the advantage that would accrue to him from himself and others doing x rather than y, unless, of course his doing it is a necessary and sufficient condition of others doing it.[45]

And, as I have noted elsewhere,[46] Downs' 'adjustment' is not only *ad hoc* but it calls into question one of the core assumptions of the rational choice research programme, namely, that a rational agent will not 'pay' for something if he can get it for nothing. Given that he prefers candidate (or policy) A to B, and that many people prefer one or the other and will vote accordingly, then the probability that his voting for A will result in A's victory is miniscule. And so long as there are any 'costs' incurred in voting, he will not vote. Moreover, if his candidate wins, he can enjoy the fruits of victory without having to pay for them; he can, as it were, ride for free (hence the so-called 'free rider' problem). But when we extend this logic to the long-term rewards accruing to himself and others from maintaining the democratic system, one has to admit, as Downs does, that 'he will actually get this reward [too], even if he himself does not vote.'[47] He would therefore be irrational if he did vote. To argue otherwise, as Downs nevertheless does, is to reject the rational choice programme's core tenets of self-interestedness and instrumental rationality.

Rejecting Downs' introduction of other-regarding or altruistic motives into the calculus of voting, William Riker and Peter Ordeshook attempted to resolve the paradox of voting in terms that they took to be consistent with the core assumptions of the rational choice programme. A rational individual does stand to benefit from voting, they maintain, even if those benefits be non-material 'rewards' or psychological 'satisfactions' stemming from 'affirming allegiance to the political system', 'affirming a partisan preference', and even 'compliance with the ethic of voting'.[48] Yet this attempt to resolve the paradox is every bit as *ad hoc* as Downs'. As Barry quite rightly remarks:

> Now it may well be true that much voting can be accounted for in this way, and one can of course formally fit it into an 'economic' framework by saying that people get certain 'rewards' from voting. But this is purely formal. And it forces us to ask what really is the point and value of the whole 'economic' approach. It is no trick to restate all behaviour in terms of 'rewards' and 'costs'; it may for some purposes be a useful conceptual device, but it does not in itself provide anything more than a set of empty boxes waiting to be filled. . . . Insofar as it includes voting as a purely expressive act, not undertaken with any expectation of changing the state of the world, it fails to fit the minimum requirements of the means–end model of rational behaviour.[49]

These failed attempts to resolve the paradox of voting were soon followed by others. One of the more ingenious of these was proposed by John Ferejohn and Morris Fiorina. Rational choice theorists, they argued, took a wrong turn in 'equating the notion of rational behaviour with the rule of maximizing expected utility'. Instead of assuming that rational voters would be expected-utility maximizers, we should assume that they are maximum-regret minimizers. That is, instead of seeking to maximize gains, they minimize their maximum loss or greatest possible 'regret'. Ferejohn and Fiorina's 'minimax regretter' votes, not because he expects to increase significantly the probablility that his candidate will win, but because he seeks to avoid what he regards as the worst possible outcome, namely, his candidate's losing by a single vote. In contrast to the expected-utility maximizer,

> The minimax regret decision maker uses a simpler rule. He imagines himself in each possible future state of the world and looks at how much in error each of his available actions could be, given that state. Then he chooses that action whose maximum error over the states of nature is least. If asked why he voted, a minimax regret decision maker might reply, 'My God, what if I didn't vote and my preferred candidate lost by one vote? I'd feel like killing myself.' Notice that for the expected-utility maximizer the probability of such an event is very important, whereas for the minimax regret decision maker the mere logical possibility of such an event is enough.[50]

If one assumes that voters are minimax regretters rather than expected-utility maximizers, it is rational for them to vote. Thus, claim Ferejohn and Fiorina, the voting paradox is solved, or perhaps dissolved, and in a way that is entirely consistent with the core assumptions of the rational choice programme.

The Ferejohn-Fiorina 'solution' has not wanted for critics, however. Some contended that theirs was a pseudo-solution[51] and others that it is not in any event applicable to voting decisions,[52] at least by 'ethical voters'.[53] One critic pointed out that the solution can be purchased only at the price of producing further and equally insoluble paradoxes.[54] Ferejohn and Fiorina's reply[55] having failed to satisfy their critics, the consensus now appears to be that the paradox of voting is not only unsolved but is quite possibly insoluble.

Much as academic social scientists might lament this state of affairs, the issue is not in the final analysis an academic one. Far from being an abstract academic conundrum, the so-called paradox of voting amounts to a genuine civic contradiction. For to the degree that we came to understand ourselves and our relations with others in the terms supplied by the economic theory of democracy, we would necessarily be divided and contradictory creatures. We could give no rationally adequate, or even intelligible, account of ourselves as active and concerned citizens.[56] We would, in short, be unable to account for our adherence to democracy, even – or, rather, especially – if we subscribe to latter-day versions of the very protectionist arguments that are supposed to appeal to us as self-interested individuals. To follow out the logic of the protectionist argument is to see that the economic theory is, for all its show of analytic rigour, incoherent and incapable of serving as a source of self-understanding for democrats. The attempt to translate the language of active citizenship into the idiom of consumership results in a deeply incoherent account of democratic citizenship.

As I noted in my introductory chapter, the exposure and criticism of contradictions is one of the key sources of conceptual change. But it may also serve a preventive purpose by precluding some proposed changes from taking a firm hold in the first place. This, I think, is what happens, or can happen, in the case of the economic theory of democracy. Once exposed to critical scrutiny, its all too obvious contradictions keep it from claiming the allegiance of reflective democratic citizens. This particular conceptual transformation turns out, upon closer inspection, to be rationally resistable.

There is in all this a certain irony. For to explore and critically reflect upon the radical deficiencies of the economic theory, with its studied obliviousness to the educative argument, is itself a splendid source of civic education.

7

Justice between Generations

7.1 INTRODUCTION

One might be tempted to suppose that the phenomenon of conceptual change, once recognized and acknowledged, will at most shape the way in which we write the history of moral philosophy and political theory, leaving untouched more pressing questions of moral conduct and public policy. My purpose in this concluding chapter is to suggest that this supposition is illusory and that the temptation should, accordingly, be resisted. If I am right, to recognize that the concepts constitutive of political practices are themselves historically mutable not only affects the way in which we write the history of those practices; it also affects all who participate in them. To illustrate this otherwise obscure claim I shall dwell at some length upon a question of considerable interest not only to contemporary moral and political philosophers but to concerned citizens as well. What might it mean to say that one generation has (or alternatively does not have) a duty to act justly toward future generations? To ask this question in light of our preceding inquiries into the phenomenon of conceptual change yields several counterintuitive conclusions.

Insofar as the present chapter is about avoiding temptation it inevitably has about it the air of a sermon. And since every sermon must have its text, I take mine from Chekhov. Reflecting rather morosely upon the relations between present and future generations, Vershinin, in Chekhov's *The Three Sisters*, remarks:

> The things that seem great, significant, and very important to us now will no more seem to be important with time. It's certainly an interesting fact that we cannot possibly know today what in the future will be considered great and important or just pitiful and ridiculous. . . . It is quite likely that our present life, to which

we are so reconciled, will in time appear to be odd, uncomfortable, stupid, not particularly clean and, perhaps, even immoral.[1]

Not only unclean and immoral but, because moral and political concepts have historically mutable meanings, quite conceivably *unjust*. It is this possibility, and its implications for our thinking about intergenerational justice, that I propose to explore here.

Simplifying somewhat, there are at present two ways of thinking about justice between generations. The first is the view that future people have all the rights accorded to presently existing individuals, including the right to be treated justly. Where justice is concerned, temporal distance constitutes no morally relevant difference between individuals. From the fact that future generations do not (yet) exist it does not follow that they have no rights, nor that we have no obligation to respect those rights. From the fact that we are in a position to help or to harm them, but not vice versa, it does not follow that we owe them nothing or that we may do as we please in the present without paying heed to possible far-distant future consequences.

Proponents of the second view claim, by contrast, that 'intergenerational justice' is an oxymoron. They maintain that we can act justly only toward individuals and not toward abstract entities such as generations; that only actually existing individuals can be the bearers of rights; and that since the individuals comprising future generations do not (yet) exist, we are under no obligation to treat them justly or to respect their rights (since, strictly speaking, they have none to respect). Moreover, members of one generation are in no position to know or to predict the preferences, preference-orderings, tastes, talents, interests and inclinations of individuals belonging to later generations, and more especially to those far distant in time. We are, accordingly, obliged only to act justly toward presently existing individuals, since they alone have rights (including the right to be treated justly) and interests about which we can actually know. The moral import and political implications of these opposing views have, over the last decade or so, been spelled out in a series of important essays.[2]

My aim here is to dissent from both views. Against the former I shall argue that the very idea of intergenerational justice, however admirable or attuned to our intuitions, is itself incoherent, though not for any of the reasons advanced by defenders of the latter view. And against the latter I shall argue that their policy of benign neglect is unwarranted.

My argument in the present chapter unfolds in the following way. I begin by noting that the concepts constitutive of moral and political discourse have historically mutable meanings. 'Justice' is just such a concept. The meaning of justice – not only what the word means but what it means to act justly, the criteria used to identify and appraise (un)just actions, etc. – changes from one age and generation to another. Plato's understanding of justice, for example, is not ours. And that is not (only) because he was speaking of *diké* and we of 'justice' but because our concepts are made meaningful and intelligible by virtue of being embedded in conceptual schemes, frameworks or theories that are themselves subject to criticism, revision or outright replacement, in light of alternative theories. The direction and destination(s) of conceptual change and theoretical innovation are, moreover, inherently unpredictable. Because we cannot know what men and women in distant generations will mean by 'justice', we cannot know what they will regard as just and unjust. If their understanding of justice differs markedly from ours, and if we have no way of knowing what that understanding will be, then we are in no position to act toward them in ways that we would both recognize as just. One generation can act justly toward another only if they share the same (or at any rate similar or commensurable) conceptions of justice. The more distant the generations, the greater the likelihood that their moral concepts and ours will be at least partially or even perhaps wholly incommensurable.[3] Thus a generation of people sharing (say) a Platonic conception of justice would be in no position, logically speaking, to act justly toward those of a later distant generation whose understanding of justice, and indeed whose entire moral-conceptual framework, differs from theirs in fundamental respects. The upshot of my several arguments, if successful, is that the very idea of intergenerational justice is incoherent. I close by suggesting what does – and more importantly what does *not* – follow from this distressingly counterintuitive conclusion.

7.2 NATURE, CONVENTION AND HISTORY

In one sense my subject is as old as the classical debate about *physis* and *nomos*, nature and convention. The Sophists of the fifth century claimed that conceptions of justice are relative to the customs and conventions of different cultures and societies. Their nemesis Plato, by contrast, claimed that the concept of justice (*diké*) has a single, true and timeless meaning, namely the one supplied by Socrates in Book I of *The Republic*: justice consists in each person's doing that for which he or she is naturally suited. And Aristotle, ever the mediator, attempts to synthesize these two views:

> There are two forms of justice, the natural and the conventional. It is natural when it has the same validity everywhere and is unaffected by any view we may take about the justice of it. It is conventional when there is no original reason why it should take one form rather than another and the rule it imposes is reached by agreement, after which it holds good. . . . Some philosophers are of the opinion that justice is conventional in all its branches, arguing that a law of nature admits of no variation and operates in exactly the same way everywhere – thus fire *burns* here and in Persia – while rules of justice keep changing before our eyes. . . . It is not obvious what rules of justice are natural, and what are legal and conventional, in cases where variation is possible. . . .

Even so, Aristotle adds, 'it remains true that there is such a thing as natural, as well as conventional, justice.'[4]

The details of Aristotle's analysis of natural and conventional justice need not concern us here.[5] Of greater immediate interest is the way in which he frames the issue. By posing it as a question about cross-cultural differences – i.e., about the conventions of justice obtaining in different countries and cultures *versus* those that are universally shared – Aristotle avoids the vexing *historical* questions about justice between distant generations. The plane on which he raises the issue is synchronic, so to speak, rather then diachronic or historical. Aristotle is able to answer the question to his satisfaction, I suggest, because he did not frame it in historical terms.[6] The import of this difference is obvious. We can have available to us an account of the conventions and conceptions of justice obtaining in other cultures and can therefore communicate with them, and they with us, regarding our respective standards of justice and fairness. Of course such communication need not imply agreement, only mutual understanding and the possibility of partial agreement.[7] We are therefore in a position, in principle at least, to attempt to act toward our contemporaries in other cultures in ways that they will recognize as just.

What is true of the differences (conceptual and conventional) between contemporaneous cultures is not true, however, of differences and disagreements between distant generations. For between the latter there is no possibility of two-way communication; earlier generations can communicate with later ones, but not vice versa. Later generations can accordingly know the customs, convictions, concepts and conventions of their ancestors, but their ancestors can know nothing of theirs. Time's arrow points relentlessly and irreversibly forward. Nor is it possible, even in principle, to predict radical conceptual change.[8] From this it follows that no one in an earlier generation can predict radical changes in the meaning of 'justice', or indeed any other concept constitutive of the moral beliefs and behaviour of their distant descendants. Nor can we predict (or preclude) the emergence of novel theories of justice upon whose basis our descendants will judge not only their own actions, policies and practices, but ours. One good reason for studying the history of ethical and political thought is that it enables us to see this very vividly. Or at least it does so if the historian writes real histories instead of ahistorical 'text-book' tales of conceptual continuity or ersatz traditions.[9] As Alasdair MacIntyre remarks,

> it would be a fatal mistake to write as if, in the history of moral philosophy, there had been one single task of analyzing the concept of, for example, justice, to the performance of which Plato, Hobbes, and Bentham all set themselves. . . . It does not of course follow that what Plato says about δικαιοσύνη and what Hobbes or Bentham says about *justice* are totally irrelevant to one another. There are continuities as well as breaks in the history of moral concepts. Just here lies the complexity of the history.[10]

Herein lies also the difficulty facing the historically situated moral or political agent, considered not only as actor but as critic and judge. It is precisely because of conceptual change and theoretical innovation that practices and institutions deemed just in one generation can and characteristically will be judged to be unjust in later generations. As we shall see, such radical conceptual change renders the very idea of intergenerational justice incoherent and any claim to have formulated a timelessly true theory of justice indefensible.

At this point a critic might raise two objections. The first is that I am remiss in failing to follow Rawls' lead in drawing a distinction between the (timeless, transhistorical) *concept* of justice and the various (historically variable) *conceptions* of justice.[11] Conceptions of justice come and go, but the concept of justice endures. Thus there is a transhistorical core of the concept of justice that is somehow immune to the ravages of history and to which these various conceptions are somehow connected. Different conceptions of justice are alike in sharing one or more features of the core meaning of the concept.[12] It is presumably this core concept that an adequate theory of justice is a theory *of*. Secondly, there need be no insuperable difficulties raised by the idea of intergenerational justice. We need only stipulate that the systematic ignorance of rational and self-interested people choosing principles of justice behind the Veil of Ignorance would include their being unaware of the particular generation to which they belong. The principles that they would then presumably choose would be timeless and not subject to historical change or revision.[13] Hence, my critic might conclude, we need not worry about any special problems posed by one generation's attempting to act justly toward another. Justice between generations need be no more problematic, in principle, than justice within a single generation.

This is of course to miss the main point. The drawing of a distinction between concept and conception, and the stratagem of having rational egoists choosing timeless principles of justice behind a hypothetical veil of ignorance, does not solve the historical problem I have raised; it simply precludes it from arising by assuming without argument that every generation of choosers would mean more or less the same thing by 'justice'. This ahistorical assumption is quite clearly unwarranted. In order to choose a principle of justice, some understanding of that concept must be available to us. But the understanding of justice that is available to us need not be the same one available to our ancestors, nor, for that matter, to future speakers of our language (and, more certainly still, to speakers of languages that do not yet exist). Virtually all of our concepts are historically mutable ones whose meanings change over time. 'Justice' is no less mutable than other concepts in our moral and political vocabulary. It is a safe bet that Aristotle, asked to formulate principles of justice from the vantage point of the original position, would not arrive at anything resembling Rawls' two principles, or indeed at any ones that a modern liberal would recognize as principles of justice.[14] Clearly, 'justice' isn't what it used to be. Nor are our present-day understandings of justice likely to last forever. Contemporary theorists of justice might do well to heed the Kierkegaardian warning sounded in my opening chapter. 'Concepts, like individuals,' Kierkegaard wrote, 'have their histories, and are just as incapable of withstanding the ravages of time as are individuals.'[15]

Yet, surprisingly, most contemporary theorists continue to think about justice as though Kierkegaard had never lived (or rather, perhaps, as though Plato had never died). They continue to theorize as though there were no history of conceptual change, or as though that history had somehow come to an end in the modern age. Only by adopting this ahistorical attitude is it possible to think that one is taking 'the perspective of eternity' and is thereby theorizing *sub specie aeternitatis* about justice within and between all generations, past, present and future.[16] One might almost say about modern theorists of justice what Marx said about the political economists of his day: while they acknowledge that there has been history it is now, so to speak, safely confined to the past and incapable of contaminating the present.[17] But what is true of the past is no less true of the present. The present is forever slipping into the past. If history teaches us anything, it is that the concepts constitutive of our moral frameworks, political theories and social practices are no exception to the rule that nothing human lasts forever.

No less mutable than our concepts and theories of justice are the theories of the good, however 'thin', upon which they are predicated. Plato's and Aristotle's conceptions of the good are markedly different from St. Augustine's, and all are in their turn different from Machiavelli's, Hobbes' and Marx's contrasting conceptions. And our distant descendants – if we have any – are likely to subscribe to still other, as yet unimagined (indeed unimaginable) views of the good. This possibility, nay probability, cannot simply be stipulated out of existence or assumed away. We cannot, for example, follow Galston's 'stipulat[ion] . . . that we know nothing about the composition of remote future generations except that they will be composed of beings very much like ourselves, with the same mix of claims and similar conceptions of the human good.'[18] Such a stipulation seems unwarranted because it is almost certainly false. Indeed, I suspect that its converse is closer to the mark: we can know very little about remote future generations, save that they will probably be composed of beings quite unlike ourselves and with a different mix of claims and dissimilar conceptions of the human good.

My contention, if correct, has two important implications. The first is by now fairly obvious: there can be no timelessly true or valid theory of justice.[19] But this entails a second, nonobvious, and heretofore unnoticed implication: if there is no transhistorically true theory of justice there can be no well-warranted theory of intergenerational justice either. (The domino theory, though false in foreign affairs, is nevertheless quite true in moral and political philosophy.) If, as philosophers as different as Michael Oakeshott and Charles Taylor are agreed, our moral and political theories – including theories of justice – are more or less systematic articulations of the presuppositions and justifications of historically parochial practices, aims and aspirations,[20] it follows that the intuitively appealing idea that one generation has a duty to act justly toward distant future generations is itself incoherent. No theory of justice can, accordingly, be a theory of *intergenerational* justice, where the generations in question are distant ones whose members subscribe to radically different theories of justice. In order for an earlier generation to act toward a later one in ways which both can agree are just, they must share the same, or at any rate similar or commensurable, conceptions of justice. Between adjacent or overlapping generations this ordinarily poses no problem, since conceptual change tends to be gradual and two-way communication remains a real possibility. But matters are very different as regards relations between distant generations.

Between distant generations yawns the chasm of conceptual discontinuity and theoretical incommensurability.

7.3 THE SPECTRE OF RELATIVISM

Although the argument I am advancing is admittedly relativistic, its implications are, *contra* Karl Popper, neither nihilistic nor irrationalist. 'One of the most disturbing features of intellectual life at the present time,' Popper writes,

> is the way in which irrationalism is so widely advocated, and irrationalist doctrines taken for granted. In my view one of the main components of modern irrationalism is relativism (the doctrine that truth is relative to our intellectual background or framework: that it may change from one framework to another), and in particular, the doctrine of the impossibility of mutual understanding between different cultures, generations, or historical periods.[21]

The key word here is 'mutual': that there can be no *mutual* understanding between different (distant) generations or historical periods is not, *pace* Popper, a 'doctrine' to which one may choose to subscribe or not, but an inescapable fact of historical existence. Historical understanding is necessarily not mutual but exclusive and one-way, so to speak, in two different directions: we can understand our predecessors but they cannot understand us; and they can in some sense communicate with us (through texts and other artifacts), but we cannot communicate with them. Thus the idea of a dialogue or 'conversation between the generations' is, at best, a metaphor, and a rather mixed one at that.[22] Barring the invention of some sort of time-machine, two-way communication is impossible. But even if we could travel backward and forward through time, we would doubtless find – as Mark Twain's Connecticut Yankee did – that communication with our distant ancestors is exceedingly difficult, if not impossible. For we speak different moral languages and live in different moral worlds. The world of Odysseus, of the *polis*, of King Arthur's Court, is not our world; our moral concepts are not theirs, nor are their theories ours.[23] And while we can with some difficulty reconstruct and at least partially comprehend their concepts, conventions and practices, they were of necessity in no position to predict ours. From this it follows that they could not have acted toward us in ways that we would recognize as just, even if they had wanted to do so. For their understanding of justice is not ours, nor is ours theirs. Such conceptual discontinuity renders the idea of inter-generational justice incoherent.

By way of illustration consider two cases. Let us suppose that the Greeks of Plato's day had wished to act toward all future generations, including our own, in ways that they and we would agree are just. It is immediately obvious that they could not have done so, inasmuch as our understanding of justice differs from theirs in ways that they could neither know nor predict. An attentive critic would, I suspect, find at least two flaws in this illustration. It might be objected, firstly, that Attic Greek and English are two different natural languages, and that *diké* does not mean 'justice', the common practice of translators notwithstanding. In a very real sense the Greeks did not and could not know what justice is, what is just, etc., even though they did know what *diké* was and what was *dikaios*. Our different understandings of 'justice' (sic) are not, strictly speaking, the consequence of conceptual change; they are simply different concepts in different languages. Although sceptical about arguments of this sort, I can accept this one without undermining my main point.

Of greater moment, perhaps, is a second apparent flaw. It is exceedingly difficult even to imagine the sorts of things that anyone living more than two thousand years ago could do to or for us that we would, or conceivably could, recognize as (un)just. One would even, I think, be hard pressed to say that the wanton destruction of works of art, of temples and texts – the burning of the great library at Alexandria in 47 B.C. being amongst the most horrible of many instances – in any way constitutes acts of injustice perpetrated against those now living. These acts of destruction were and are most unfortunate, to be sure, and we are no doubt the poorer for the absence of the things that were destroyed. Yet, much as we might now want these things and lament their loss, our being denied them is not, by our lights, an act of *injustice*, inasmuch as we can claim no *right* to have and to enjoy them.[24] Much the same can also be said of the enjoyments and benefits that we derive from that portion of our classical heritage that has so far escaped destruction. That these works of art, literature and philosophy were bequeathed to us, was not an act of justice on our Greek forbears' part but, at most, an act of generosity – a gift, if you like – which neither their understanding of justice nor ours could conceivably require them to perform. The giving of a gift may be an act of generosity or of charity or of mercy, but cannot, by our lights, be an act of *justice*.

If the Greek example seems in some respects unsatisfactory and inconclusive, consider a second, half-historical, half-hypothetical case. According to our moral intuitions and modern sensibilities, the institution of slavery is a veritable paradigm of injustice. This view, and indeed the understanding of justice upon which it is based, was not however shared by our Southern slave-owning ancestors of a few generations back. Indeed, as Bertram Wyatt-Brown has shown, slavery was widely viewed in the antebellum South as a normal, natural and eminently just institution. Their regarding slavery in this favourable light was due less to psycho-pathology than to the fact that Southerners subscribed to a moral code markedly different from ours. As Wyatt-Brown remarks,

> Southern whites believed (as most people do) that they conducted their lives by the highest ethical standards. They thought that they had made peace with God's natural order. Above all else, white Southerners adhered to a moral code that may be summarized as the rule of honor. Today we would not define as an ethical scheme a code of morality that could legitimate injustice – racial or class. Yet so it was defined in the Old South. The sources of that ethic lay deep in mythology, literature, history, and civilisation. It long preceded the slave system in America. Since the earliest times, honor was inseparable from hierarchy and entitlement, defense of family blood and community needs. All these exigencies required the rejection of the lowly, the alien, and the shamed. Such unhappy creatures belonged outside the circle of honor. Fate had so decreed.[25]

The Southern theory of justice (if I may call it that) was, in a word, functionalist; for it held that each race, class and sex had different but complementary natural functions to perform, and that justice consisted in each fulfilling its respective function. (That this theory should in some respects resemble Plato's is not altogether surprising, since both belonged to societies whose economies were based largely upon slave labour.) According to this functionalist framework, white men were by nature masculine and masterful, white women frail and feminine, and blacks stupid and slavish. The paradigm of the just society was the plantation, with its settled hierarchy of rules, roles and relations. To fail to fill one's appointed place, much less to upset or to attempt to overthrow that order, would be to act unjustly.[26]

Against this backdrop the activities of the Abolitionists and of rebellious slaves were, not surprisingly, viewed as patently unjust and unnatural attempts to subvert, indeed to invert, the natural order of things. Slave revolts, like the one led by Nat Turner in Virginia in 1831, were viewed with particular horror. Such revolts were treated not as ordinary criminal offences but as extraordinary offences against the religion of honour and hierarchy.[27] Regarded as revolts against justice itself, slave insurrections were suppressed with unsurpassed ferocity. Justice required that such revolts be not only punished but, if possible, prevented. To act justly toward future generations is to act in ways that will secure their safety, preserve their way of life, and perpetuate the institution of slavery. To prevent or even to preclude the possibility of future slave revolts would therefore be viewed as eminently just – particularly in a culture not only committed to the continuation of slavery but bound by a code of honour to tradition, to venerating ancestors, and to treating distant descendants as one would treat contemporaries. The way of life prescribed by this moral code, which strikes modern liberal individualists as so peculiarly perverse, had its own sharp coherence.[28] It is just this code that is embodied, for example, in the behaviour of Charles Malleson in Faulkner's *Intruder in the Dust*. Past, present and future are, according to this code, indistinguishable. 'It's all *now*, you see', says Malleson. 'Yesterday won't be over until tomorrow and tomorrow began ten thousand years ago.'[29] If it were possible to prevent future slave revolts, the direction of one's duty would therefore be quite clear.

For all the foregoing there is ample historical evidence. Let us suppose – finally and counterfactually – that our slave-owning Southern ancestors had had available to them certain biomedical technologies, including an ability to alter the genetic constitution of individuals and all their descendants. Believing that future generations would benefit from, and regard as just, the prevention of all future slave rebellions, our ancestors alter irreversibly the genetic make-up of slaves so as to make them and their descendants docile and intellectually incapable of rebelling against their masters. Satisfied that they have acted justly *vis-à-vis* future generations, including ours, our ancestors believe that they have done their duty and can die with clear consciences.

What our ancestors could neither know nor predict was that our understanding of justice would differ radically from theirs and that we would, in consequence, view the institution of slavery as immoral and their actions as appallingly unjust. They sincerely believed themselves to be acting justly toward their descendants; we regard them as having behaved unjustly toward their slaves and, even now, toward our black contemporaries, their children, and their children's children for all generations to come. Unable to correct the condition of our black contemporaries, we curse our forefathers for their short-sightedness, their meanness, their injustice.[30]

If nothing else, this admittedly extreme (and, happily, hypothetical) illustration suggests how and why the idea of intergenerational justice is incoherent. This conclusion seems to me as unavoidable as it is uncomfortable. At all events we have no way of knowing whether well-meant actions and policies in the present will be adjudged just or unjust by future generations. We act, unavoidably, into an unknown future. It is entirely possible – and over the long haul likely – that our present practices, policies, institutions and way of life will strike members of future generations as barbaric and unjust. Having quite a different understanding of justice, our children's great-grandchildren are more likely to curse our injustice (as they see it) than to praise our farsightedness. However well-meaning, however just by our lights, however solicitous we may be of their welfare, we act without any guarantee of their gratitude.

7.4 TWO ALTERNATIVE ACCOUNTS

Much the same conclusion has been reached by others, albeit by different routes. Among these, the arguments advanced by Martin

Golding and Michael Walzer are particularly noteworthy.[31] Although neither makes his case in terms of conceptual change, their arguments and mine lead in the same general direction if not to identical conclusions.

Unlike many contemporary theorists of justice – Rawls most notably and Ronald Dworkin most recently[32] – Golding and Walzer are alike in maintaining that our moral principles and standards, including our standards of justice, are local standards, applicable only in particular moral communities. Playing Protagoras to Rawls' and Dworkin's Plato, they contend that determining what is (un)just is not a matter of applying universally valid and agreed upon principles but of consulting these historically and culturally specific community standards. What is deemed to be just in one community will not necessarily be recognized as such in another. Moral communities are differentiated one from another by virtue of their members' sharing quite different and communally specific social meanings and self-understandings.

Moral communities exist not only contemporaneously across cultures, but historically within a culture. Social meanings, self-understandings and standards shift over time, even within an identifiably continuous culture. These shifting standards include criteria of justice and conceptions of the good. Hence, as Golding notes, generations can either be tied together or untied according to whether they share recognizably similar standards and self-understandings. Only insofar as they do can one generation be said to have obligations to another. Conversely, of course, obligations cease when we cross (historically defined) communal boundaries.[33] There is, according to Golding, reason to doubt whether members of far-distant future generations can actually be said to belong to our moral community. For they 'comprise the community of the future, a community with which we cannot expect to share a common life'. It therefore follows that 'the more remote the members of this [future] community are, the more problematic our obligations to them become. That they are members of our moral community is highly doubtful, for we probably do not know what to desire for them.' Thus, Golding concludes, 'the more distant the generation, . . . the less likely it is that we have an obligation to promote its good,' or indeed to treat its members justly.[34]

Golding's argument can be construed as an intergenerational variation on a theme by Michael Walzer. In *Obligations* Walzer argues that obligation is proportional to intimacy and that our most binding duties derive from our membership in, and our attachments and loyalties to, those local communities with which we are most intimately affiliated.[35] Unlike Golding, Walzer in *Obligations* says little about justice and nothing at all about intergenerational justice or obligations to future generations. Walzer's more recent *Spheres of Justice*, however, deals indirectly but suggestively with these matters, and in a manner entirely consistent with his earlier argument.

In *Spheres of Justice* Walzer focuses upon the shared social meanings conferred upon the goods distributed by and among the members of historically and culturally specific communities. This slant results, unsurprisingly, in a distinctly relativist construal of 'justice'. 'Justice,' Walzer writes, 'is relative to social meanings.' A particular society 'is just if its substantive life is lived in a certain way – that is, in a way faithful to the shared understandings of its members.'[36] More radically still, he suggests that 'there are no external or universal principles [of justice]. . . . Every substantive account of distributive justice is a local account.'[37] Knowing what is just and how to act justly thus becomes, in Geertz's phrase, a matter of 'local knowledge'.[38] To act justly is in this view to respect boundaries between the different 'spheres' of social life within a community, and to honour the differences between differently constituted communities. 'To override those [shared] understandings is (always) to act unjustly.'[39] Justice thus becomes a matter of 'boundary maintenance' and tyranny tantamount to 'trespass'.[40]

Yet such trespasses do occur. Far from being fixed and frozen, the 'boundaries' between 'spheres' are regularly violated and periodically redrawn. History is in large part the story of such 'shifts in social meaning'. No one, Walzer remarks, can predict future boundary shifts: 'We can't anticipate the deeper changes in consciousness, not in our own community and certainly not in any other. The social world will one day look different from the way it does today, and distributive justice will take on a different character than it has for us. Eternal vigilance is no guarantee of eternity.'[41]

Walzer stops short of tracing out the implications of this Chekhovian insight. Had he done so he might, I think, have argued as follows. Understandings of justice are not only geographically and culturally local; they are historically local as well. In other words, understandings of justice are relative not only to place but to time. Since we are powerless to predict changes in future understandings of what is and is not just, we are in no position to act justly toward those living in the far distant future. And yet act we must. We cannot avoid acting in ways that impinge, for better or for worse, upon the consciousness of generations yet unborn. Political action in the present shapes, often unintentionally and sometimes irreversibly, the setting in which future generations think about justice and act (un)justly. 'Politics present,' Walzer writes, 'is the product of politics past. It establishes an unavoidable setting for the consideration of distributive justice.'[42] So also, one might add, policies future is the product of politics present. We have no way of knowing whether, or to what extent, well-meant actions and politics in the present will be adjudged just or unjust by future generations. We act, unavoidably, into an unknown future. It is entirely possible – and over the long term likely – that our present practices, policies, institutions and way of life will strike members of future generations as barbaric and unjust. Having a very different understanding of justice, our children's great-grandchildren are more likely to curse our injustice (as they see it) than to praise us for our far-sightedness, much less our love of justice.

There remains a curious lacuna in Walzer's argument. Although he recognizes that shared social meanings – including the meaning of 'justice' itself – change over time, he fails to note *how* meanings change and major boundary shifts occur. Presumably they occur as a result of repeated and persistent trespass. The ironic upshot is that new and unforeseen understandings of 'justice' are wrought by earlier injustices, or at any rate by acts deemed unjust by older standards. This would not surprise Hume or Marx, and still less Nietzsche, who viewed present moral standards as so much fossilized violence. By painting a curiously apolitical picture of conceptual change, Walzer understates the extent to which conceptual changes come about as a result of real grievances conceived and articulated by real agents bent not only upon invoking but upon changing their society's standards of justice.

Yet, despite my minor disagreements with Walzer and Golding, we are in the main agreed that understandings of justice are culturally and historically variable and that the idea of intergenerational justice is in consequence wellnigh incoherent. If the arguments advanced in support of this claim are relativistic, does it follow that the conclusions to which they lead are necessarily nihilistic ones? I for one do not believe this to be the case.

7.5 A NON-NIHILISTIC CONCLUSION

If to this point my argument appears to be a rather melancholy one, I do not mean it to be so. There is method in my melancholy. I have constructed the strongest possible relativist case for three reasons. The first is to suggest that there can be no timeless or transhistorical theory of justice, or indeed of any other concept whose meaning is historically mutable. The second, following from the first, is that the very idea of intergenerational justice is incoherent. My third and most important purpose in advancing this radically relativistic argument is to show what does *not* follow from it. From the fact that distant generations are unlikely to share our concept of justice, it does not follow – *pace* Golding – that we are thereby absolved of any responsibility to attempt to act justly toward them. It is a philosophical truism that ought implies can; we cannot be morally required or obliged to do what we are, despite our best efforts, unable to do. This truism applies to thoughts no less than to actions (the latter being, of course, partially constituted by the former). We can have no moral obligation to think thoughts or to perform actions for which we do not (yet) possess – and cannot predict the emergence of – the required concepts or moral language. I have argued that we are unable to predict theoretical and conceptual changes, including changes in the meaning of 'justice'.

At least two further conclusions follow from my argument. The first is that we have no obligation to act towards our distant descendants in ways that *they* will recognize as just but that our own theory or framework forbids us from seeing as just. But the more crucial second point is this: from the fact that we are unable to treat them justly by *their* lights it does *not* follow that we need not worry about their welfare. Still less does it follow that we are entitled to treat future generations in ways that are unfair or unjust by *our* lights. We ought only do what we can do; and all that we can do is to try to treat them justly, given our standards and our understanding of justice. And this we have so far clearly failed to do.

All tales must have a moral, and mine is this: as political theorists, as moral agents, and as citizens, we cannot transcend our own history. Our moral and political theories – including our theories of justice – are located in history and are incapable of withstanding its ravages. Perhaps Hegel, that most historically minded of philosophers, put it best:

> Whatever happens, every individual is a child of his time; so philosophy too is its own time apprehended in thoughts. It is just as absurd to fancy that a philosophy can transcend its contemporary world as it is to fancy that an individual can overleap his own age, jump over Rhodes. If his theory really goes beyond the world as it is and builds an ideal one as it ought to be, that world exists indeed, but only in his opinions, an unsubstantial element where anything you please may, in fancy, be built.[43]

All hope of theorizing *sub specie aeternitatis* about justice, or anything else, is therefore chimerical. We are historical creatures who can only think and theorize – and act – with concepts whose meanings are as mutable as we are mortal.

Notes

CHAPTER 1 POLITICAL ARGUMENT AND CONCEPTUAL CHANGE

1 See James Boyd White, *When Words Lose Their Meaning: Constitutions and Reconstitutions of Language, Character, and Community* (Chicago: University of Chicago Press, 1984).
2 Mihail Lermontov, *A Hero of Our Time*, trans. Vladimir Nabokov (New York: Anchor Books, 1958), p. 2.
3 Honoré de Balzac, 'Louis Lambert', *La Comédie Humaine*, in *Oeuvres Complètes* (Paris: Alexandre Houssiaux, 1863), p. 111.
4 Heinrich Böll, *The Lost Honor of Katharina Blum* (New York: McGraw-Hill, 1975). Compare Peter Berger, 'On the Obsolescence of the Concept of Honor', in *Revisions*, ed. Alasdair MacIntyre and Stanley Hauerwas (Notre Dame, Ind.: University of Notre Dame Press, 1983), pp. 172–81.
5 Thomas Mann, *The Magic Mountain*, trans. H.T. Lowe-Porter (New York: Knopf, 1966), p. 101.
6 George Orwell, *1984* (New York: New American Library, 1981), p. 46.
7 The phrase comes from the title of John Florio's Italian-English dictionary, *A Worlde of Wordes* (London, 1598). Like Balzac's Louis Lambert, Florio likens the investigation of language to the explorer's discovery of new worlds.
8 John Locke, *An Essay Concerning Human Understanding*, ed. J.W. Yolton (London: Oxford University Press, 1961), I, Bk. III, sec. 1.
9 See R. G. Collingwood, *An Essay on Metaphysics* (Oxford: Clarendon Press, 1962), chapter 5.
10 Quoted in Frederic Jameson, *The Prison-House of Language* (Princeton, N.J.: Princeton University Press, 1972), p. i.
11 Søren Kierkegaard, *The Concept of Irony*, trans. L. M. Capel (London: Collins, 1966), p. 47.
12 See *The Linguistic Turn*, ed. Richard Rorty (Chicago: University of Chicago Press, 1967).

13 See, *inter alia*, David Miller, 'Linguistic Philosophy and Political Theory', in *The Nature of Political Theory*, ed. David Miller and Larry Siedentop (Oxford: Clarendon Press, 1983), pp. 35–51; and William E. Connolly, *The Terms of Political Discourse*, 2nd edn. (Princeton, N.J.: Princeton University Press, 1983), chapters 1, 5 and 6.

14 Ludwig Wittgenstein, *Culture and Value*, trans. Peter Winch (Oxford: Blackwell, 1980), 78e.

15 J. L. Austin, *Philosophical Papers*, 2nd edn. (Oxford: Clarendon Press, 1970), p. 201.

16 Ibid., p. 182; but compare p. 185. The charge that ordinary language analysis is inherently conservative has been levelled by several critics. See, *inter alia*, Ernest Gellner, *Words and Things* (Boston: Beacon Press, 1959), p. 256f; Herbert Marcuse, *One-Dimensional Man* (Boston: Beacon Press, 1964), chapter 7; and the more sophisticated criticisms in Keith Graham, *J.L. Austin: A Critique of Ordinary Language Philosophy* (Hassocks: Harvester Press, 1977), pp. 37–9, 46–52, 262–4, 266 n.4. For a defence of ordinary language against this charge, see Alan Wertheimer, 'Is Ordinary Language Analysis Conservative?', *Political Theory*, 4 (November 1976), pp. 405–22.

17 Karl Marx, *The Poverty of Philosophy* (New York: International Publishers, 1963), p. 121.

18 See, *inter alia*, Alasdair MacIntyre, *A Short History of Ethics* (New York: Macmillan, 1966); J. G. A. Pocock, *Politics, Language, and Time* (New York: Atheneum, 1973), esp. chapter 1, and 'The Concept of a Language and the *Métier d'historien*: Some Considerations on Practice', in *The Languages of Political Theory in Early Modern Europe*, ed. Anthony Pagden (Cambridge: Cambridge University Press, 1987); Quentin Skinner, 'Language and Political Change', in *Political Innovation and Conceptual Change*, ed. Terence Ball, James Farr and Russell L. Hanson (Cambridge: Cambridge University Press, 1988), chapter 1; and James Farr, 'Understanding Conceptual Change Politically', in *Political Innovation and Conceptual Change*, chapter 2, followed by fourteen conceptual histories by various authors.

19 See Stephen E. Toulmin, 'From Logical Analysis to Conceptual History', in *The Legacy of Logical Positivism*, ed. Peter Achinstein and Stephen F. Barker (Baltimore, Md.: Johns Hopkins University Press, 1969), pp. 25–53, and *Human Understanding* (Oxford: Clarendon Press, 1972), vol. I, chapter 1, 'The Problem of Conceptual Change'.

20 This appears to have been the view taken by Michel Foucault in his 1969 essay, 'What Is an Author?' reprinted in *Language, Counter-Memory, Practice*, ed. Donald F. Bouchard (Ithaca, N.Y.: Cornell University Press, 1977), pp. 113–38. The difficulty, if not the

impossibility, of sustaining such a view is recognized by Foucault in the opening paragraphs of his 'The Order of Discourse' (1970), reprinted in *Language and Politics*, ed. Michael Shapiro (New York: New York University Press, 1984), chapter 7.

21 Diane Macdonell, *Theories of Discourse* (Oxford: Blackwell, 1985), p. 51.
22 Quentin Skinner, 'On Performing and Explaining Linguistic Actions', *Philosophical Quarterly*, 21 (1971), pp. 1–21; and 'Some Problems in the Analysis of Political Thought and Action', *Political Theory*, 2 (1974), pp. 277–303.
23 Louis Althusser, *Lenin and Philosophy and Other Essays*, trans. Ben Brewster (London: New Left Books, 1971), p. 24. Also quoted approvingly by Michel Pêcheux, *Language, Semantics and Ideology: Stating the Obvious*, trans. Harbans Nagpal (London: Macmillan, 1982), p. 153; and Macdonell, *Theories of Discourse*, p. 51.
24 Reinhart Koselleck, *Futures Past: On the Semantics of Historical Time*, trans. Keith Tribe (Cambridge, Mass.: M.I.T. Press, 1985), p. 74.
25 Ibid., p. 77.
26 *Geschichtliche Grundbegriffe. Historisches Lexikon zur Politisch-Sozialer Sprache in Deutschland*, ed. Otto Brunner, Werner Conze and Reinhart Koselleck, 5 vols to date (Stuttgart: Klett-Cotta, 1972–); *Handbuch politisch-sozialer Grundbegriffe in Frankreich*, 1680–1820, ed. Rolf Reichardt and Eberhard Schmitt, 2 vols to date (Munich: Oldenbourg Verlag, 1985–). A 'historical dictionary' of less 'political' and more narrowly 'philosophical' concepts is the *Historisches Wörterbuch der Philosophie*, ed. Joachim Ritter and Karlfried Grunder, 6 vols to date (Basel and Stuttgart: Schwabe, 1971–). See also the very useful overviews by Melvin Richter, 'Conceptual History [*Begriffsgeschichte*] and Political Theory', *Political Theory*, 14 (1986), pp. 604–37; and 'The History of Concepts and the History of Ideas', *Journal of the History of Ideas*, 48 (April-June 1987), pp. 247–63.
27 White, *When Words Lose Their Meaning*, p. 193.
28 See Pocock, 'The Concept of a Language'.
29 Martin Heidegger, *The Piety of Thinking* (Bloomington, Ind.: Indiana University Press, 1976), p. 28.
30 George Eliot, *Middlemarch* (Harmondsworth: Penguin, 1965), Bk I, ch. 10, p. 111.
31 James Boyd White, 'Economics and Law: Two Cultures in Tension', *Tennessee Law Review*, 54 (Winter, 1987), pp. 161–202, at p. 166.
32 Karl Marx, 'The Eighteenth Brumaire of Louis Bonaparte', in *Karl Marx: Selected Writings*, ed. David McLellan (Oxford: Oxford University Press, 1977), p. 300.

33   Bertrand de Jouvenel, *Sovereignty: An Inquiry into the Public Good*, trans. J. F. Huntington (Chicago: University of Chicago Press, 1957), p. 304.

34   Jürgen Habermas, *Knowledge and Human Interests*, trans. Jeremy J. Shapiro (London: Heinemann, 1972), p. 314; and *Communication and the Evolution of Society*, trans. Thomas McCarthy (Boston: Beacon Press, 1979), chapter 1.

35   Hobbes is perhaps the preeminent exponent of this view. See Terence Ball, 'Hobbes' Linguistic Turn', *Polity*, 18 (Summer, 1985), pp. 739–60.

36   W. B. Gallie, 'Essentially Contested Concepts', *Proceedings of the Aristotelian Society*, 56 (1955–6). See, further, Alasdair MacIntyre, 'The Essential Contestability of Some Social Concepts', *Ethics*, 84 (1973), pp. 1–9; and Connolly, *The Terms of Political Discourse*, chapter 1.

37   John Gray, 'On the Essential Contestability of Some Social and Political Concepts', *Political Theory*, 5 (1977), pp. 331–48; and 'Political Power, Social Theory, and Essential Contestability', in *The Nature of Political Theory*, ed. Miller and Siedentop, pp. 75–101.

38   One might even, in some instances, wish to invoke one or another scientific 'research tradition'. See Larry Laudan, *Progress and Its Problems* (Berkeley and Los Angeles: University of California Press, 1977). On research traditions in the social sciences, and political science in particular, see Terence Ball, 'Is There Progress in Political Science?', in *Idioms of Inquiry: Critique and Renewal in Political Science* (Albany, N.Y.: State University of New York Press, 1987), chapter 1.

39   This is the tack taken by James Boyd White in 'Thinking About Our Language', *Yale Law Journal*, 96 (July 1987), pp. 1960–83, at pp. 1965–6.

40   I borrow the example from Quentin Skinner, 'Language and Political Change', in *Political Innovation and Conceptual Change*, chapter 1.

41   See Richard Dagger, 'Rights', in ibid., chapter 14.

42   *Vide* Quentin Skinner, 'The State', in ibid., chapter 5.

43   See John Dunn, 'Revolution', in ibid., chapter 16.

44   See Mark Goldie, 'Ideology', in ibid., chapter 13.

45   *Vide* Mary G. Dietz, 'Patriotism', in ibid., chapter 8.

46   See James Farr, 'Understanding Conceptual Change Politically', in ibid., chapter 2; and 'Historical Concepts in Political Science: The Case of "Revolution"', *American Journal of Political Science*, 26 (November 1982), pp. 688–708.

47   Alasdair MacIntyre, *A Short History of Ethics*, pp. 2–3.

48 See, e.g., Quentin Skinner, 'The Idea of Negative Liberty: Philo-
sophical and Historical Perspectives,' in *Philosophy in History*, ed.
Richard Rorty, J. B. Schneewind, and Quentin Skinner (Cambridge:
Cambridge University Press, 1984), ch. 9.

CHAPTER 2 THE PREHISTORY OF PARTY

1 J. A. W. Gunn, ed., *Factions No More: Attitudes to Party in Government
and Opposition in Eighteenth Century England* (Frank Cass, London:
1972), p. 1.
2 Indispensable collections of original sources include *English Party
Politics*, ed. Alan Beattie (London: Weidenfeld and Nicholson, 1970),
2 vols; and Gunn, *Factions No More*. Useful surveys are also to be
found in Caroline Robbins, '"Discordant Parties": A Study of the
Acceptance of Parties by Englishmen', *Political Science Quarterly*, 73
(December, 1958), pp. 505–29; Richard Hofstadter, *The Idea of a Party
System* (Berkeley and Los Angeles: University of California Press,
1970); Giovanni Sartori, *Parties and Party Systems* (Cambridge:
Cambridge University Press, 1976), 2 vols.; and Klaus Von Beyme,
'Partei, Faktion', in *Geschichtliche Grundbegriffe: Historisches Lexikon
juridisch-sozialen Sprache in Deutschland*, ed. Otto Brunner, Werner
Conze and Reinhart Kosellek (Stuttgart: Klett-Cotta, 1978), vol. 4.
3 Harvey Mansfield, Jr., *Statesmanship and Party Government: A Study of
Burke and Bolingbroke* (Chicago: University of Chicago Press, 1965),
p. 2. A similar tack is taken by Hofstadter, *The Idea of a Party System*,
pp. 4, 39.
4 The following account is adapted from Quentin Skinner, *The
Foundations of Modern Political Thought* (Cambridge: Cambridge
University Press, 1978), 2 vols, Preface to vol. I.
5 Ibid., pp. xii–xiii.
6 Isaiah Berlin, 'Does Political Theory Still Exist?', in his *Concepts and
Categories* (New York: Viking Press, 1979), p. 154.
7 George Armstrong Kelly, 'Mortal Man, Immortal Society? Political
Metaphors in Eighteenth-Century France,' *Political Theory*, 14 (February, 1986), pp. 5–29, at p. 9.
8 See Diane Macdonell, *Theories of Discourse: An Introduction* (Oxford:
Blackwell, 1986); and George Lakoff and Mark Johnson, *Metaphors
We Live By* (Chicago: University of Chicago Press, 1980).
9 A. H. M. Jones, *Athenian Democracy* (Oxford: Blackwell, 1957), pp.

166 *Notes*

130–1. Perhaps the closest modern counterparts to such political groupings would be the 'parties' formed by and around such charismatic leaders as the late Juan Peron and Charles De Gaulle.

10 F. E. Adcock, *Roman Political Ideas and Practice* (Ann Arbor: University of Michigan Press, 1959), pp. 60–2.

11 Dante, *Inferno*, Canto IV, lines 130–1.

12 Thomas Aquinas, *Selected Political Writings*, ed. A. P. D'Entreves (Oxford: Blackwell, 1965), pp. 189–93.

13 See Skinner, *Foundations*, I, pp. 53–65.

14 Marsiglio of Padua, *The Defender of the Peace*, trans. Alan Gewirth (New York: Harper Torchbooks, 1967), pp. 83–4.

15 See J. G. A. Pocock, *The Machiavellian Moment* (Princeton, N.J.: Princeton University Press, 1975), pp. 261–3.

16 Francesco Guicciardini, *Ricordi* (New York: S. F. Vanni, 1949), pp. 2–3.

17 Niccolo Machiavelli, *Istorie Fiorentine*, in *Opere Complete* (Florence: Alcide Parenti, 1843), p. 149.

18 Machiavelli, *Discorsi*, in ibid., p. 261.

19 Pocock, *Machiavellian Moment*, p. 252, n. 71.

20 Machiavelli, *Opere Complete*, pp. 265–6.

21 Ibid., p. 394.

22 An altogether different account of Machiavelli's views on party and sect is given by Harvey Mansfield, Jr., 'Party and Sect in Machiavelli's Florentine Histories', in *Machiavelli and the Nature of Political Thought*, ed. Martin Fleisher (New York: Atheneum, 1972), and is ably criticized by Mark Phillips and J. A. W. Gunn in ibid., pp. 267–81.

23 Thomas Hobbes, *Leviathan*, ed. C. B. Macpherson (Harmondsworth: Penguin, 1968), ch. 29 *passim*.

24 Hobbes, *De Cive*, in *Man and Citizen*, ed. Bernard Gert (Garden City, N.Y.: Anchor Books, 1972), p. 255.

25 Hobbes, *Behemoth*, in *English Works*, ed. William Molesworth (London: John Bohn, 1839), vol. 6, p. 316.

26 George Sabine, Introduction to *Works of Gerrard Winstanley*, ed. Sabine (Ithaca, N.Y.: Cornell University Press, 1941), p. 5.

27 H. N. Brailsford, *The Levellers and the English Revolution*, ed. Christopher Hill (Stanford, Calif.: Stanford University Press, 1961), p. 317.

28 John Winthrop, 'A Model of Christian Charity', in *Puritan Political Ideas, 1558–1794*, ed. Edmund S. Morgan (Indianapolis, Ind.: Bobbs-Merrill, 1965), p. 90.

29 Ibid., p. 84.

30 The 'contractual' picture of the origins of the state is, of course, very

old. A rudimentary version of social contract theory was advanced by Sophists like Lycophon and was put into the mouth of Glaucon in Plato's *Republic* (358e – 362; cf. *Laws* 683c – 694). This contractual view is introduced, however, only in order to be refuted. Likewise Aristotle denies that the polis is an artificial or temporary alliance (*koinonia symmachia*) resting upon the prior agreement of the contracting parties and dissolvable at will (*Politics* 1280 b 10). Cicero makes much the same point (*De re publica*, I, 25; III, 13). That this anti-contractarian orthodoxy met with no successful challenge until the seventeenth century might be explained less in terms of the perceived inadequacy of Aristotelian arguments than in the breakdown of bodily or organic imagery that underlay and served to sustain those arguments.

31 Although it could be mistaken for one, with predictably amusing results. The following story is told about a Soviet diplomat newly arrived in Washington, D.C. Making reservations at a fashionable Washington restaurant, he was asked how many people were in his party, whereupon the surprised diplomat replied, 'Seventeen million'.

32 *Vide* Beattie, *English Party Politics*, I, p. 5.

33 John Locke, *Second Treatise*, in *Two Treatises of Government*, ed. Peter Laslett (Cambridge: Cambridge University Press, 1963), § 158.

34 Ibid., § 171.

35 Gunn, *Factions No More*, p. 44.

36 See Caroline Robbins, *The Eighteenth Century Commonwealthman* (New York: Atheneum, 1968), *passim*.

37 Beattie, *English Party Politics*, I, pp. 19–20.

38 Gunn, *Factions No More*, p. 54.

39 Robert Molesworth, *Account of Denmark* (London: T. Goodwin, 1694), pp. 25–51.

40 Walter Moyle, 'An Essay on the Roman Government', in *Works* (London, 1726), vol. I, p. 112.

41 Henry Fielding (?), *The Freeholder's Alarm to His Brethren* (London, 1734), p. 8.

42 John Toland, *The State-Anatomy of Great Britain* (London, 1716), p. 18.

43 Gunn, *Factions No More*, pp. 82–3.

44 Hofstadter, *The Idea of a Party System*, p. 18.

45 Bolingbroke, *The Idea of a Patriot King* (London, 1749), p. 62.

46 Henry St. John, 1st Viscount Bolingbroke, *A Dissertation Upon Parties*, originally published in 1735; reprinted in *Works* (London, 1841), vol. II, p. 48.

47 Bolingbroke, *The Idea of a Patriot King* p. 47.
48 David Hume, *Essays Moral, Political, and Literary*, ed. Eugene Miller (Indianapolis, Ind.: Liberty Press, 1985), pp. 56, 59.
49 Ibid., p. 63.
50 Ibid., p. 60.
51 Ibid., p. 465.
52 On this much, at least, Hume agreed with Bolingbroke. See Wolfgang Jäger, *Politische Partei und Parlementarische Opposition: eine Studie zum Politischenen Denken von Lord Bolingbroke und David Hume* (Berlin: Duncker & Humboldt, 1971).
53 Samuel Johnson, *Dictionary of the English Language* (London, 1755).
54 For insightful inquiries into the rhetorical structure of Burke's arguments, see James T. Boulton, *The Language of Politics in the Age of Wilkes and Burke* (London: Routledge & Kegan Paul, 1963), ch. 5; and Christopher Reid, *Edmund Burke and the Practice of Political Writing* (Dublin: Gill and Macmillan, 1985), *passim*.
55 Burke's master, the Marquis of Rockingham, articulated very succinctly the then new connection between the older concept of 'part' and the modern 'party' dedicated to particular political principles and committed to playing the part of a loyal opposition. 'We and *only we* of all the parts now in Opposition,' he said in 1769, 'are so on principle.' Quoted in Archibald Foord, *His Majesty's Opposition, 1714–1830* (Oxford: Clarendon Press, 1964), p. 315.
56 Edmund Burke, *Works* (London: C. and J. Rivington, 1826), II, p. 220.
57 Ibid., p. 329.
58 Ibid., p. 330.
59 Ibid., p. 335.
60 Quoted in Hofstadter, *The Idea of a Party System*, pp. 2 and 3, n. 1.
61 See John R. Howe, Jr., *The Changing Political Thought of John Adams* (Princeton, N.J.: Princeton University Press, 1966), ch. 7.
62 James Madison, *Federalist 10*, in *The Federalist Papers*, ed. Garry Wills (New York: Bantam Books, 1982), pp. 43–4.
63 Madison, 'Parties' (1972), in *The Papers of James Madison*, ed. Robert A. Rutland *et al.* (Charlottesville, Virginia: University Press of Virginia, 1983), vol. 14, pp. 197–8.
64 Madison, 'A Candid State of Parties,' in ibid., pp. 371–2.
65 Jefferson to Madison, 29 June 1792, in ibid., p. 333.
66 Hofstadter, *The Idea of a Party System*, p. 123.
67 Ibid., p. 153, n. 28.
68 Ibid., p. 2; Lance Banning, *The Jeffersonian Persuasion: Evolution of a Party Ideology* (Ithaca, N.Y.: Cornell University Press, 1978), p. 162.

Chapter 3   Reconstituting Republican Discourse

Abbreviations:

FP *The Federalist Papers*, ed. Garry Wills (New York: Bantam Books, 1982).
CAF *The Complete Anti-Federalist*, ed. Herbert J. Storing (Chicago: University of Chicago Press, 1981), 7 vols.
AF *The Anti-Federalist*, abridged 1-vol. edition of *CAF*, ed. Murray Dry (Chicago: University of Chicago Press, 1985).
WMQ *William and Mary Quarterly*

1 The literature is vast and growing. The thesis of a Lockean-liberal American founding, propounded by Louis Hartz in the mid-1950s and discredited by Bernard Bailyn, Gerald Stourzh, Gordon S. Wood, J. G. A. Pocock, Lance Banning and other proponents of a 'republian synthesis' in the late 1960s and 1970s, has been revived of late by Joyce Appleby, Isaac Kramnick and John Patrick Diggins. Douglas Adair's claim that the American founding owes a large debt to Hume and other thinkers of the Scottish Enlightenment has recently been revived and defended by Garry Wills and disputed by Ronald Hamowy. See, *inter alia*, Louis Hartz, *The Liberal Tradition in America* (New York: Harcourt Brace, 1955); Bernard Bailyn, *Ideological Origins of the American Revolution* (Cambridge, Mass.: Harvard University Press, 1967), ch. 2; Gordon S. Wood, *The Creation of the American Republic, 1776–1787* (Chapel Hill, N.C.: University of North Carolina Press, 1969), chs. 1–3; Gerald Stourzh, *Alexander Hamilton and the Idea of Republican Government* (Stanford, Calif.: Stanford University Press, 1970), chs. 1–3; J. G. A. Pocock, 'Machiavelli, Harrington, and English Political Ideologies in the Eighteenth Century', *WMQ*, 3rd series, XXII (1965) and *The Machiavellian Moment: Florentine Political Thought and the Atlantic Republican Tradition* (Princeton, N.J.: Princeton University Press, 1975), ch. 15; Lance Banning, *The Jeffersonian Persuasion: Evolution of a Party Ideology* (Ithaca, N.Y.: Cornell University Press, 1978) and 'Jeffersonian Ideology Revisited: Liberal and Classic Ideas in the New American Republic', *WMQ*, 3rd series, XLIII (January 1986), pp. 3–19; and the useful overviews and assessments by Robert E. Shalhope, 'Toward a Republican Synthesis: The Emergence of an Understanding of Republicanism in American Historiography',

WMQ, 3rd series, XXIX (January 1972), pp. 49–80, and 'Republicanism and Early American Historiography', *WMQ*, 3rd series, XXXIX (April 1982), pp. 334–56; and Jean Yarbrough, 'Republicanism Reconsidered: Some Thoughts on the Foundation and Preservation of the American Republic', *Review of Politics*, 41 (January 1979), pp. 61–95. This emerging republican synthesis has come under attack by, *inter alia*, Isaac Karmnick, 'Republican Revisionism Revisited', *American Historical Review*, 87 (1982), pp. 629–64; and Joyce Appleby, 'Republicanism and Ideology', *American Quarterly*, 37 (1985), pp. 461–73, and 'Republicanism in Old and New Contexts', *WMQ*, 3rd series, XLIII (January 1986), pp. 20–34. The thesis of a Humean-Scottish founding has been advanced and defended by Douglass Adair, *Fame and the Founding Fathers*, ed. Trevor Colbourn (New York: Norton, 1974) and by Garry Wills, *Inventing America: Jefferson's Declaration of Independence* (Garden City, N.Y.: Doubleday, 1978) and *Explaining America: The Federalist* (Garden City, N.Y.: Doubleday, 1981); and criticized by Ronald Hamowy, 'Jefferson and the Scottish Enlightenment: A Critique of Garry Wills' *Inventing America*', *WMQ*, 3rd series, XXXVI (1979), pp. 503–23. Recent reconsiderations include Richard C. Sinopoli, 'Liberalism, Republicanism and the Constitution', *Polity*, 19 (Spring 1987), pp. 331–52; and Lance Banning, 'Some Second Thoughts on "Virtue" and the Course of Revolutionary Thinking', in *Conceptual Change and the Constitution*, ed. Terence Ball and J. G. A. Pocock (Lawrence, Kansas: University Press of Kansas, 1988), ch. 10.

2 Keith Thomas, 'Politics as Language', a review of J. G. A. Pocock's *Virtue, Commerce and History*, in the *New York Review of Books*, 27 February 1986, p. 39.

3 Of course, not all Antifederalists spoke with one voice. For a discussion of their differences, see James H. Hutson, 'Country, Court, and Constitution: Antifederalism and the Historians', *WMQ*, 3rd series, XXXVIII (1981), pp. 337–68.

4 Cicero, *De Re Publica*, Bk. I, sec. 15; English trans. *On the Commonwealth*, G. H. Sabine and S. B. Smith (Indianapolis, Ind.: Bobbs-Merrill, 1929), p. 129.

5 Augustine, *Epist.* 138. 10; quoted in ibid., pp. 129–30.

6 See Quentin Skinner, *The Foundations of Modern Political Thought* (Cambridge: Cambridge University Press, 1978), 2 vols., I, pp. 144–52.

7 Cf. Felix Gilbert, 'Bernardo Rucellai and the Orti Oricellari: A Study on the Origin of Modern Political Thought', *Journal of the Warburg and Courtauld Institutes*, 12 (1949), pp. 101–31.

Notes 171

8 *Vide* Skinner, *Foundations*, I, 6; and Pocock, *Machiavellian Moment*.
9 This theme is developed by Bruce James Smith, *Politics and Remembrance: Republican Themes in Machiavelli, Burke and Tocqueville* (Princeton, N.J.: Princeton University Press, 1985), ch. 2.
10 Machiavelli, *Discourses*, in *The Prince and the Discourses*, ed. Max Lerner (New York: Modern Library, 1950), Bk. I *passim*; Bk. III, ch. 1.
11 *Oceana*, in *The Political Works of James Harrington* (Cambridge: Cambridge University Press, 1977), pp. 155 ff.
12 See, *inter alia*, Caroline Robbins, *The Eighteenth Century Commonwealthman* (New York: Atheneum, 1968); *Two English Republican Tracts*, ed. Caroline Robbins (Cambridge: Cambridge University Press, 1969); Pocock, *Machiavellian Moment*, chs. 14 and 15; *The English Libertarian Heritage*, ed. David L. Jacobson (Indianapolis, Ind.: Bobbs-Merrill, 1965).
13 Montesquieu, *Spirit of the Laws*, trans. Thomas Nugent (New York: Hafner, 1948), p. 8.
14 Ibid., pp. 15–17.
15 Ibid., pp. 8–9.
16 Ibid., pp. 40–2.
17 Ibid., p. 120.
18 Ibid., pp. 126–7.
19 See Paul M. Spurlin, *Montesquieu in America* (Baton Rouge, LA: Louisiana State University Press, 1940), *passim*.
20 Forrest McDonald, *Novus Ordo Seclorum* (Lawrence, KS: University Press of Kansas, 1986), pp. 80–1.
21 See Wood, *Creation of the American Republic*, ch. 2; Willi Paul Adams, *The First American Constitutions: Republican Ideology and the Making of the State Constitutions in the Revolutionary Era*, trans. Rita and Robert Kimber (Chapel Hill: University of North Carolina Press, 1980), ch. 4, and 'Republicanism in Political Rhetoric before 1776', *Political Science Quarterly*, 85 (1970), pp. 397–421.
22 See Zera S. Fink, *The Classical Republicans* (Evanston, Ill.: Northwestern University Press, 1945); Caroline Robbins, *The Eighteenth Century Commonwealthman* (New York: Atheneum, 1968; first publ. 1959); Bailyn, *Ideological Origins*; Wood, *Creation*, chs. 1–3; Pocock, *Machiavellian Moment*, ch. 15; Banning, *Jeffersonian Persuasion*, chs. 1–3; Michael Leinesch, 'In Defence of the Antifederalists', *History of Political Thought*, IV (February 1983), pp. 65–87; W. P. Adams, *The First American Constitutions*.
23 The degree to which Shays' Rebellion can be accounted a cause of, or at least a reasonable pretext for, the calling of the Philadelphia

convention is disputed by historians. The orthodox view – that it was the condition *sine qua non* for the Philadelphia meeting – is defended by Robert A. Feer, 'Shays' Rebellion and the Constitution: A Study in Causation', *New England Quarterly*, XLII (1969), pp. 388–410, and disputed by Gordon S. Wood, 'Interests and Disinterestedness in the Making of the Constitution', in *Beyond Confederation: Origins of the Constitution and American National Identity*, ed. Richard Beeman, Stephen Botein and Edward C. Carter III (Chapel Hill: University of North Carolina Press, 1987), pp. 69–109, at p. 73. It was, Wood insists, 'good old American popular politics, . . . especially as practiced in the state legislatures, that lay behind the founders' sense of crisis.' No doubt; but it bears mentioning that Shays' Rebellion is the only contemporary political event decried by name in *The Federalist* (*FP* 6, p. 23).

24 Wood, *Creation*, pp. 608–9. Cf. also Michael Kammen, *Spheres of Liberty: Changing Perceptions of Liberty in American Culture* (Madison: University of Wisconsin Press, 1986).

25 Herbert J. Storing, *What the Anti-Federalists Were For, CAF*, vol. 1, p. 3.

26 See Russell L. Hanson, *The Democratic Imagination in America: Conversations With Our Past* (Princeton, N.J.: Princeton University Press, 1985), pp. 58, 64–83; and Banning, *Jeffersonian Persuasion*, p. 106.

27 *CAF* 2.8.72; *AF*, pp. 67–8.

28 *FP* 73, p. 374.

29 *CAF* 2.9.11; *AF*, p. 113. Brutus' attack appeared on 18 October 1787 and was almost certainly on Madison's mind as he drafted *FP* 10. See next note.

30 An earlier version of the argument for an extended republic had been rehearsed previously at the Philadelphia convention, and sharpened subsequently in private correspondence. See, e.g., Madison to Jefferson, 24 October 1787, in *The Origins of the American Constitution: A Documentary History*, ed. Michael Kammen (New York: Penguin Books, 1986), esp. p. 71.

31 *FP* 9, pp. 37–8.

32 David Hume, 'Of Civil Liberty', *Essays Moral, Political, and Literary*, ed. Eugene F. Miller (Indianapolis, Ind.: Liberty Classics, 1985), pp. 87–8.

33 *FP* 9, p. 38.

34 *FP* 9, p. 39.

35 *FP* 9, p. 39.

36 *FP* 9, p. 42.

37 *FP* 10, p. 46.
38 *Contra* Charles Beard, Jackson Turner Maine and Gordon S. Wood, who with respectively increasing degrees of sophistication make the Antifederalists into agrarian democrats-cum-populists. *Contra* also Storing's assertion that 'The Anti-Federalists are liberals – reluctant and traditional, indeed – in the decisive sense that they see the end of government as the security of individual liberty, not the promotion of virtue or the fostering of some organic common good.' *CAF* 1, p. 83, n. 7.
39 *CAF* 2.9.12; *AF*, p. 113.
40 *CAF* 2.9.13–14; *AF*, p. 114.
41 *CAF* 2.9.36; *AF*, pp. 122–3.
42 Hanna Fenichel Pitkin, *The Concept of Representation* (Berkeley and Los Angeles: University of California Press, 1967), ch. 7.
43 The *locus classicus* of the 'independence' view is Burke's 'Letter to the Sheriffs of Bristol' (1777) in *Edmund Burke: Selected Writings and Speeches*, ed. Peter J. Stanlis (Garden City, N.Y.: Anchor Books, 1963), pp. 186–208. Publius' source appears, however, to be Hume, 'Of the First Principles of Government', *Essays*, pp. 32–6; cf. also 'Of the Independency of Parliament', ibid., pp. 42–6. See, further, Frederick G. Whelan, *Order and Artifice in Hume's Political Philosophy* (Princeton, N.J.: Princeton University Press, 1985), p. 352; and Wills, *Explaining America*, chs. 27 and 28.
44 *CAF* 2.9.44; *AF*, p. 126.
45 *CAF* 2.9.42; *AF*, pp. 123–5; emphasis added. Cf. the similar strictures adduced by the Federal Farmer, *CAF* 2.8.97–100; *AF*, pp. 74–8. Also see Banning, *Jeffersonian Persuasion*, p. 108.
46 *CAF* 2.9.42; *AF*, p. 125.
47 *CAF* 2.9.42; *AF*, p. 125.
48 *CAF* 2.9.42; *AF*, p. 126.
49 *CAF* 2.9.42; *AF*, p. 126.
50 See the works of Willi Paul Adams cited in n. 21, above.
51 To put the matter in dichotomous terms – 'republican' *vs.* 'democrat' – is to adopt the Madisonian distinction that was by no means widely shared, even by Madison's fellow Federalists. John Adams, for one, maintained that 'Mr. Madison's . . . distinction between a republic and a democracy, cannot be justified. A democracy is really a republic as an oak is a tree, or a temple a building.' Quoted in Stourzh, *Alexander Hamilton*, p. 55. See also Hanson, *Democratic Imagination*, pp. 85–8.
52 *FP* 10, p. 47.
53 *FP* 36, pp. 167–8.

54 See again, *infra*, ch. 2; and J. Peter Euben, 'Corruption', in *Political Innovation and Conceptual Change*, ed. Terence Ball, James Farr and Russell L. Hanson (Cambridge: Cambridge University Press, 1988), ch. 11.

55 Although, as Pocock notes, America during the colonial and confederation period 'constituted a Country without a Court' (*Machiavellian Moment*, p. 509). That, of course, is just the way the Antifederalists hoped to keep it, even as they feared that the new Constitution sought to serve the interests of an emerging commercial or Court party. See, further, John Murrin, 'The Great Inversion, or Court versus Country: A Comparison of the Revolution Settlements in England (1688–1721) and America (1776–1816)', in *Three British Revolutions: 1641, 1688, 1776*, ed. J. G. A. Pocock (Princeton, N.J.: Princeton University Press, 1980), pp. 368–453; and Hutson, 'Country, Court, and Constitution'.

56 *CAF* 2.9.47; *AF*, pp. 128–9.

57 *CAF* 2.9.46; *AF*, p. 128.

58 See Wood, *Creation*, chs. 4–6; Leinesch, 'In Defence of the Antifederalists'; and Adams, *The First American Constitutions*, ch. 4.

59 *CAF* 2.9.42–3; *AF*, p. 126.

60 *CAF* 2.9.33; *AF*, p. 122.

61 *CAF* 2.9.36; *AF*, pp. 122–3.

62 *CAF* 2.9.33; *AF*, p. 122.

63 *FP* 84, p. 438.

64 *FP* 84, p. 436.

65 CAF, 6.7.8.

66 *FP* 84, pp. 436–7.

67 *FP* 51, pp. 262–3.

68 Hume, 'Of the Independency of Parliament', *Essays*, p. 42.

69 *FP* 14, p. 66. Madison later concedes, however, that 'what immediately strikes us' in the idea of an extended republic is its 'novelty' (*FP* 37, p. 177).

70 *FP* 14, p. 63.

71 *FP* 14, pp. 66–7.

72 See, e.g., John DeWitt, 'To the Free Citizens of the Commonwealth of Massachusetts', *CAF* 4.3.7.

73 Machiavelli, *Discourses*, Bk. I, ch. 11; Rousseau, *Social Contract*, Bk. II, ch. 7. Both maintain that the 'translation problem' may be resolved by the legislator's reliance upon the religious idiom of divinely ordained laws and revealed truths.

74 *FP* 37, pp. 179–80.

75 *FP* 1, p. 5.

76 *FP* 10, p. 49.
77 *FP* 39, p. 189.
78 *FP* 39, p. 190.
79 See Ludwig Wittgenstein, *Philosophical Investigations*, trans. G. E. M. Anscombe (Oxford: Blackwell, 1967), paras. 66–70.
80 See W. B. Gallie, 'Essentially Contested Concepts', *Proceedings of the Aristotelian Society*, vol. 56 (1955–6), and the subsequent qualifications and modifications introduced by Hanson, *Democratic Imagination*, ch. 1, and William E. Connolly, *The Terms of Political Discourse*, 2nd edn. (Princeton, N.J.: Princeton University Press, 1983), ch. 1.
81 *FP* 39, p. 190.
82 *FP* 39, p. 190.
83 *FP* 39, p. 191.
84 John Toland, *The State-Anatomy of Great Britain* (London, 1716), p. 18.

CHAPTER 4   THE CHANGING FACE OF POWER

1 Steven Lukes, *Power: A Radical View* (London: Macmillan, 1974), p. 9; William E. Connolly, *The Terms of Political Discourse*, 2nd edn. (Princeton, N.J.: Princeton University Press, 1983), ch. 1.
2 See Hannah Arendt, *The Human Condition* (Chicago: University of Chicago Press, 1958), pp. 200–5; and her 'On Violence', in *Crisis of the Republic* (New York: Harcourt Brace Jovanovich, 1972), especially pp. 139–46.
3 Anthony Giddens, *The Constitution of Society* (Berkeley and Los Angeles: University of California Press, 1984), pp. 246–62.
4 John Donne, 'An Anatomie of the World: The First Anniversary' (1612) in *Donne: Selected Poems*, ed. Andrews Wanning (New York: Dell, 1962), pp. 112–13. See further, E. A. Burtt, *The Metaphysical Foundations of Modern Science*, revised edn. (New York: Humanities Press, 1952); and Alexandre Koyré, *From the Closed World to the Infinite Universe* (Baltimore, Md.: The Johns Hopkins Press, 1957).
5 Thomas Hobbes, *De Corpore*, in *English Works*, ed. Sir William Molesworth (London: John Bohn, 1839), vol. 1, ch. 10.
6 Some of these desires may be described as biologically grounded drives, but not all. Politically, the most significant – because most dangerous – desires are those that derive from human discourse and

communication, including the desires induced by reading the republican philosophers of antiquity. See Terence Ball, 'Hobbes' Linguistic Turn', *Polity*, 18 (Summer 1985), pp. 739–60, at pp. 752–5; and ch. 2, above, sec. 2.3.

7 Hobbes, *Leviathan*, ed. C. B. Macpherson (Harmondsworth: Penguin, 1968), Bk. I, ch. 10.

8 Ibid., Bk. I, ch. 11.

9 John Locke, *An Essay Concerning Human Understanding*, 2 vols. (London: J. M. Dent & Sons, 1961), Vol. I, Bk. II, ch. 6, sec. 8, p. 101.

10 Ibid., Vol. I, Bk. II, ch. 21, sec. 4, pp. 194–5.

11 Ibid., Vol. I, Bk. II, ch. 21, sec. 9, p. 197.

12 It bears mentioning that when Locke in the *Second Treatise* talks about the varieties of power – paternal and political or civil power in particular – this Newtonian reworking of 'power' is not much in evidence. See *Two Treatises of Government*, ed. Peter Laslett (Cambridge: Cambridge University Press, 1960), chs 7, 11–13, and 15, where Locke speaks of role-specific 'powers'. When the legislature acts contrary to its trust, moreover, its power 'devolve[s] into the hands of those that gave it,' namely the people (ch. 13, p. 149). This is Locke's version of Cicero's *potestas in populo*.

13 David Hume, *Enquiry Concerning Human Understanding*, ed. L. A. Selby-Bigge (Oxford: Clarendon Press, 1962), sec. VII, part II, s 60, n. 1, p. 77.

14 Hume, *A Treatise of Human Nature* (New York: Everyman's Library, n.d.), p. 169.

15 Max Weber, *Economy and Society*, ed. Guenther Roth and Claus Wittich (New York: Bedminster Press, 1968), vol. I, p. 53.

16 Harold D. Lasswell and Abraham Kaplan, *Power and Society* (New Haven: Yale University Press, 1950), p. xiv.

17 See, *inter alia*, Felix E. Oppenheim, *Dimensions of Freedom* (New York: St. Martin's Press, 1961), p. 91; V. O. Key, *Politics, Parties and Pressure Groups*, fifth edn. (New York: Crowell, 1964), pp. 2–3; Hans J. Morgenthau, *Politics Among Nations*, third edn. (New York: Knopf, 1965), pp. 4–5; Herbert Simon, *Models of Man* (New York: Wiley & Sons, 1957), p. 4.

18 See Terence Ball, 'Models of Power: Past and Present', *Journal of the History of the Behavioral Sciences*, 11 (July 1975), pp. 211–12.

19 On 'the rule of metaphor', see Fred Dallmayr, *Language and Politics* (Notre Dame, Ind.: University of Notre Dame Press, 1984), ch. 6.

20 The facial simile is suggested by Peter Bachrach and Morton S. Baratz, 'The Two Faces of Power', *American Political Science Review*, 56 (1962), pp. 947–52, and the spatial simile by Lukes, *Power*.

21 Simon, *Models of Man*, p. 5.

22 See, *inter alia*, Robert Dahl, 'The Concept of Power', *Behavioral Science*, 2 (July 1957), pp. 201–15, at p. 202; 'Cause and Effect in the Study of Politics', in *Cause and Effect*, ed. Daniel Lerner (New York: Free Press, 1965), pp. 75–98, esp. p. 88; 'Power', *International Encyclopedia of the Social Sciences*, ed. David L. Sills (New York: Macmillan-Free Press, 1968), Vol. XII, pp. 405–15, at p. 410; James G. March, 'An Introduction to the Theory and Measurement of Influence', *American Political Science Review*, 49 (June 1955), pp. 431–51, at p. 437; Oppenheim, *Dimensions of Freedom*, pp. 40–1; Andrew S. McFarland, *Power and Leadership in Pluralist Systems* (Stanford, Calif.: Stanford University Press, 1969), p. 3.

23 Dahl, *Modern Political Analysis* (Englewood Cliffs, N.J.: Prentice-Hall, 1963), p. 41.

24 Recall George Eliot's remark about metaphor, quoted in ch. 1, above.

25 Dahl, for instance, suggests that power, influence, rule, authority – and *potestas* and *auctoritas* – are 'synonyms': 'The Concept of Power', p. 201.

26 Simon, *Models of Man*, p. 7.

27 See, *inter alia*, Dahl, 'The Concept of Power', p. 204; McFarland, *Power and Leadership*, p. 10; Dorwin Cartwright, *Studies in Social Power* (Ann Arbor: University of Michigan Press, 1959), p. 7.

28 See n. 11, above.

29 See, e.g., Dahl, 'The Concept of Power', p. 202.

30 Again see, *inter alia*, Dahl, 'The Concept of Power', p. 204; William Riker, 'Some Ambiguities in the Notion of Power', *American Political Science Review*, 58 (June 1964), pp. 341–9; McFarland, *Power and Leadership*, p. 9.

31 For further discussion and a critique of the aforementioned series of claims, see Terence Ball, 'Power, Causation and Explanation,' *Polity*, 8 (Winter 1975), pp. 189–214.

32 Bachrach and Baratz, 'Two Faces of Power'; and the elaboration of their views in 'Decisions and Nondecisions: An Analytical Framework', *American Political Science Review*, 57 (1963), pp. 641–51, and *Power and Poverty* (New York: Oxford University Press, 1970), Part I.

33 Lukes, *Power*, p. 26.

34 Ibid., pp. 34–5.

35 Lukes, 'Power and Authority', in *A History of Sociological Analysis*, ed. Tom Bottomore and Robert Nisbet (New York: Basic Books, 1978), p. 669.

36 Lukes, *Power*, ch. 6.

37 *Vide* John Gaventa, *Power and Powerlessness: Quiescence and Rebellion in an Appalachian Valley* (Urbana, Ill.: University of Illinois Press, 1980).

38 These criticisms are made by Felix E. Oppenheim, *Political Concepts: A Reconstruction* (Chicago: University of Chicago Press, 1981), p. 51. They are anticipated, if not countered satisfactorily, by Lukes, *Power*, pp. 32–3.

39 David West, 'Power and Formation: New Foundations for a Radical Concept of Power,' *Inquiry*, 30 (March 1987), 137–54.

40 John Gray, 'Political Power, Social Theory, and Essential Contestability', in *The Nature of Political Theory*, ed. David Miller and Larry Siedentop (Oxford: Clarendon Press, 1983), pp. 75–101, esp. pp. 94–101.

41 See, e.g., the discussion of 'power' in Nancy C. M. Hartsock, *Money, Sex and Power* (London: Longman, 1983), ch. 9.

42 For an attempt to link a typology of 'persuasive communications' or speech-acts with 'power', 'influence', and other concepts, see Ball, 'Power, Causation and Explanation', pp. 211–12.

43 Peter Winch, 'The Idea of a Social Science', in *Rationality*, ed. Bryan R. Wilson (Oxford: Blackwell, 1970), pp. 9–10.

44 Arendt, 'On Violence', pp. 142–3.

45 Arendt, *Human Condition*, pp. 200–5.

46 Arendt, 'On Violence', p. 143.

47 Ibid., p. 140.

48 Arendt, *Human Condition*, p. 200.

49 Lukes, *Power*, pp. 59, 28–31.

50 Arendt, 'On Violence', p. 143.

51 For an explication of Hegel's 'master-slave dialectic', see Terence Ball, 'Two Concepts of Coercion', *Theory and Society*, 8 (January 1978), pp. 97–112. On the affinities between Heidegger's and Arendt's understandings of 'power', see Fred Dallmayr, *Polis and Praxis* (Cambridge, Mass.: M.I.T. Press, 1985), ch. 3.

52 Brian Fay, *Critical Social Science* (Ithaca, N.Y.: Cornell University Press, 1986), p. 130.

53 Jürgen Habermas, 'Hannah Arendt: On the Concept of Power', in *Philosophical-Political Profiles*, trans. Frederick G. Lawrence (Cambridge, Mass.: M.I.T. Press, 1983), pp. 178–89, at p. 173.

54 Ibid., p. 174.

55 Ibid., p. 175.

56 Ibid., p. 176.

57 Ibid., p. 183.

58 Ibid.

59 Habermas, 'Warheitstheorien', in *Wirklichkeit und Reflexion* (Pfullingen: Neske, 1973), p. 239.

60 The 'realism' to which I refer here should not be confused with

two other species of realism. I do not refer to political realism of the Realpolitik variety espoused by Henry Kissinger and other 'realists'. Nor do I refer to the view, defended by some philosophers of science, that scientific theories represent ever-closer approximations to reality. The sort of metascientific realist to whom I refer may, but need not, be a realist of the latter sort.

61   See Rom Harré, 'Powers', *British Journal for the Philosophy of Science*, 21 (1970), pp. 81–101; and Harré and E. H. Madden, *Causal Powers* (Totowa: Rowman and Littlefield, 1975). For an early attempt to link the realists' non-Humean view of causation with alternative ways of thinking about political power, see Ball, 'Power, Causation and Explanation', esp. pp. 209, 213–14; and 'Two Concepts of Coercion'. For a more systematic and sophisticated treatment, see Jeffrey C. Isaac, *Power and Marxist Theory: A Realist View* (Ithaca, N.Y.: Cornell University Press, 1987), particularly Part I.

62   See Russell Keat and John Urry, *Social Theory as Science* (London: Routledge & Kegan Paul, 1975); Roy Bhaskar, *A Realist Theory of Science* (Atlantic Highlands, N.J.: Humanities Press, 1978); Peter T. Manicas, 'On the Concept of Social Structure', *Journal for the Theory of Social Behaviour*, 10 (1980), pp. 65–82; and *A History and Philosophy of the Social Sciences* (Oxford: Blackwell, 1987).

63   The following points are adapted and summarized from Isaac, *Power and Marxist Theory*, chs 2 and 3, and 'After Empiricism: The Realist Alternative', in *Idioms of Inquiry*, ed. Terence Ball (Albany, N.Y.: State University of New York Press, 1987), ch. 8.

64   One need not, however, be a realist in order to be a relationalist. On ontological relationalism, see Ball, 'Two Concepts of Coercion'.

65   Jeffrey C. Isaac, 'Beyond the Three Faces of Power: A Realist Critique,' *Polity*, 20 (Fall 1987), pp. 4–31, at p. 22.

66   Ibid.

67   Isaac, *Power and Marxist Theory*, p. 5.

68   Michel Foucault, *Power/Knowledge*, ed. Colin Gordon (New York: Pantheon, 1980), pp. 183–4. Further observations on power as exercised in specific social settings are to be found in his *Discipline and Punish: The Birth of the Prison*, trans. Alan Sheridan (New York: Random House, 1979); *The History of Sexuality*, trans. Robert Hurley, vol. I (New York: Random House, 1978); and 'Space, Knowledge, and Power', in *The Foucault Reader*, ed. Paul Rabinow (New York: Pantheon, 1984), pp. 239–56.

69   Foucault, *Power/Knowledge*, p. 119.

70   This point is made in a particularly graphic and grisly way in the opening scene (for it is indeed that, rather than a conventional

180 *Notes*

introduction) of *Discipline and Punish*.

71 Foucault, 'The Subject and Power', Afterword to Hubert L. Dreyfus and Paul Rabinow, *Michel Foucault: Beyond Structuralism and Hermeneutics*, 2nd edn. (Chicago: University of Chicago Press, 1983), p. 208; *Power/Knowledge*, p. 106.
72 Foucault, 'The Subject and Power', pp. 213–16.
73 Foucault, *Power/Knowledge*, p. 119.
74 Foucault, 'The Subject and Power', p. 212.
75 Foucault, *Power/Knowledge*, esp. chs 3 and 9.
76 See James Farr, 'Marx's Laws', *Political Studies*, 34 (Spring 1986), pp. 202–22; and Isaac, *Power and Marxist Theory*, ch. 4.
77 Foucault, 'The Subject and Power', p. 218.
78 Ibid.
79 Ibid., p. 220.
80 Ibid., p. 222.
81 Ibid., p. 225.
82 Giddens, *Constitution of Society*, p. 283.
83 Ibid., p. 257.
84 Ibid.
85 Ibid., p. 14.
86 Ibid., p. 15.
87 This is particularly true of Foucault's work on power. See Nancy Fraser, 'Foucault on Modern Power: Empirical Insights and Normative Confusions', *Praxis International*, 1 (October 1981), pp. 272–87.

CHAPTER 5   HOW NOT TO RECONSTRUCT AUTHORITY

1 Richard Tuck, 'Why Is Authority Such a Problem?', in *Philosophy, Politics, and Society*, fourth series, ed. Peter Laslett, W. G. Runciman and Quentin Skinner (Oxford: Blackwell, 1972), pp. 194–207. For further details on authority's problematic character see, *inter alia*, Yves R. Simon, *A General Theory of Authority* (Notre Dame, Ind.: University of Notre Dame Press, 1962), ch. 1; Carl J. Friedrich, *Tradition and Authority* (New York: Praeger, 1972), Part III; Steven Lukes, 'Power and Authority', in *A History of Sociological Analysis*, ed. Tom Bottomore and Robert Nisbet (New York: Basic Books, 1978), pp. 633–76; and Richard E. Flathman, *The Practice of Political Authority* (Chicago: University of Chicago Press, 1980), *passim*.
2 To borrow Foucault's terminology, these first two approaches might

The struggle to describe
how broad, abstract, pivotal
questions (eg. forms of community, sources
of responsibility) _are_ worked out (temp.
resolved through practical conduct in uses
of language ... then go on to inquire
what we might "learn" from these
resolution ...

be termed the archaeological and the genealogical, respectively. Their complementarity is emphasized in William E. Connolly, *The Terms of Political Discourse*, 2nd edn. (Princeton, N.J.: Princeton University Press, 1983), pp. 231–43.

3 One of the best examples of this third approach is Felix E. Oppenheim, *Political Concepts: A Reconstruction* (Chicago: University of Chicago Press, 1981). Unfortunately, Oppenheim considers 'authority' only in passing (pp. 22–3).

4 See n. 12, below.

5 Hannah Arendt, 'What Was Authority?', in *Nomos I: Authority*, ed. Carl J. Friedrich (Cambridge, Mass.: Harvard University Press, 1958), pp. 81–112, at p. 81. Subsequent references are to the revised version, 'What Is Authority?', in *Between Past and Future*, expanded edn. (New York: Viking Press, 1968), pp. 91–141.

6 Arendt, 'What Is Authority?', p. 102.

7 Ibid., p. 95.

8 Ibid., p. 96.

9 Ibid., p. 103.

10 Hans-Georg Gadamer, *Truth and Method*, trans. Garrett Barden and John Cumming (New York: Crossroad Publishers, 1984), p. 248.

11 John H. Schaar, *Legitimacy in the Modern State* (New Brunswick, N.J.: Transaction Books, 1981), p. 2.

12 Although 'concepts, like individuals, have their histories, and are just as incapable of withstanding the ravages of time', they nevertheless 'retain a kind of homesickness for the scenes of their childhood'. Søren Kierkegaard, *The Concept of Irony*, trans. L. M. Capel (London: Collins, 1966), p. 47. If I read her aright, Arendt's analysis of 'authority' addresses that sense of homesickness by reconstructing several salient features of that concept's childhood. The exercise is not, however, sentimental or reactionary but critical and restorative.

13 Thomas Hobbes, *Leviathan*, ed. C. B. Macpherson (Harmondsworth: Penguin, 1968), II, ch. 19, pp. 239–40. I have argued elsewhere that Hobbes' complaint about the state of nature is precisely that it is a condition in which something like the emotivist theory of meaning is true, and that this itself supplies a good (if not a sufficient) reason for leaving that natural state. See my 'Hobbes's Linguistic Turn', *Polity*, 18 (Summer 1985), pp. 739–60, at pp. 757–9.

14 See, e.g., David Easton, 'The Perception of Authority and Political Change', in *Nomos I: Authority*, pp. 170–96, and 'The Political System Besieged by the State', *Political Theory*, 9 (August 1981), pp. 303–25. Compare, *inter alia*, Harry Eckstein and Ted Robert Gurr, *Patterns of Authority* (New York: Wiley, 1975); and Oran R. Young, *Compliance*

182 *Notes*

15 David Easton, *The Political System* (Chicago: University of Chicago Press, 1981; first publ. 1953), pp. 129–34. Cf. also his *A Systems Analysis of Political Life* (Chicago: University of Chicago Press, 1979; first publ. 1965), pp. 21–33, 207–11.

16 Easton, *The Political System*, p. 132.

17 Ibid.

18 Ibid.

19 Ibid.; and the elaboration in *A Systems Analysis of Political Life*, pp. 205–9.

20 Easton, *The Political System*, p. 132.

21 Ibid., p. 133. Compare Easton, 'The Perception of Authority and Political Change', pp. 179–82 and 185.

22 Easton, *A Systems Analysis of Political Life*, p. 208, n. 9.

23 Ibid., p. 133.

24 For an explication and defence of the notion of 'epistemic authority', see Richard T. DeGeorge, *The Nature and Limits of Authority* (Lawrence, Kans.: University Press of Kansas, 1985), ch. 3.

25 See, e.g., Richard S. Peters, 'Authority', and Richard B. Friedman, 'On the Concept of Authority in Political Philosophy', both in *Concepts in Social and Political Philosophy*, ed. Richard E. Flathman (New York: Macmillan, 1973), pp. 150–3 and 139–46, respectively; and Flathman, *The Practice of Political Authority*, pp. 16–19.

26 For a recent discussion, see Robert Dahl, *Controlling Nuclear Weapons: Democracy vs. Guardianship* (Syracuse, N.Y.: Syracuse University Press, 1985), chs 2 and 3. Dahl's suggestive and illuminating study is slightly marred by his failure to distinguish between Platonic 'guardianship' and the later notions of 'technocracy' and 'meritocracy', the latter after Michael Young's splendid satire, *The Rise of the Meritocracy* (London: Thames and Hudson, 1958). Although clearly related, both, I believe, can be further distinguished from what I call epistemocracy.

27 For a suggestive beginning, see Mary P. Nichols, 'The Republic's Two Alternatives: Philosopher-Kings and Socrates', *Political Theory*, 12 (May 1984), pp. 252–74.

28 It is instead, I believe, a linguistically constituted commonwealth. See my 'Hobbes' Linguistic Turn'.

29 Henri Comte de Saint-Simon, *Social Organization, the Science of Man, and Other Writings*, trans. and ed. Felix Markham (New York: Harper Torchbooks, 1964), p. 77.

30 Auguste Comte, in *Auguste Comte and Positivism: The Essential*

Writings, ed. Gertrud Lenzer (New York: Harper Torchbooks, 1975), pp. 223, 57, 54.

31   Cf. William Barrett, *The Illusion of Technique* (Garden City, N.Y.: Anchor Books, 1978).

32   My main source for what follows is Daniel Bell, *The Coming of Post-Industrial Society* (New York: Basic Books, 1976), esp. ch. 6.

33   See, e.g., *The Authority of Experts*, ed. Thomas L. Haskell (Bloomington, Ind.: Indiana University Press, 1984).

34   Cf. Dahl, *Controlling Nuclear Weapons*, ch. 1; and Michael Walzer, *Radical Principles* (New York: Basic Books, 1980), ch. 14.

35   Carl J. Friedrich, 'Authority, Reason, and Discretion,' *Nomos I: Authority*, pp. 28–48, at p. 35 f.; and his later elaborations in *Man and His Government* (New York: McGraw-Hill, 1963), pp. 213–33; 'The Relation of Political Theory to Anthropology', *American Political Science Review*, 62 (June 1968), pp. 536–45; and *Tradition and Authority*, ch. 10. Gadamer reaches much the same conclusion, albeit by a rather different route: *Truth and Method*, pp. 248–9.

36   Gadamer, 'Hermeneutics and Social Science', *Cultural Hermeneutics*, 2 (1975), pp. 307–16, at p. 312. See, further, Gadamer, *Reason in the Age of Science*, trans. F. G. Lawrence (Cambridge, Mass.: MIT Press, 1981), pp. 69–87. For a historical sketch of the radical changes wrought in the concept of *praxis*, see Nicholas Lobkowicz, 'On the History of Theory and Praxis', in *Political Theory and Praxis: New Perspectives*, ed. Terence Ball (Minneapolis: University of Minnesota Press, 1977), pp. 13–27.

37   Gadamer, 'Hermeneutics and Social Science', p. 316.

38   Dahl, *Controlling Nuclear Weapons*, p. 51.

39   Alasdair MacIntyre, *After Virtue* (Notre Dame, Ind.: University of Notre Dame Press, 1981), p. 22.

40   See Arendt, 'On Violence', in *Crises of the Republic* (New York: Harcourt Brace Jovanovich, 1972), esp. pp. 142–4; and the powerful title essay in Schaar, *Legitimacy in the Modern State*.

CHAPTER 6   THE ECONOMIC RECONSTRUCTION OF DEMOCRATIC DISCOURSE

1   What I call the economic theory of democracy should not be confused with 'economic democracy', i.e., the doctrine that questions about economic arrangements, practices, policies and institu-

184   *Notes*

tions should be decided democratically rather than by ostensibly impersonal market forces.

2   *Vide* Terence Ball, 'Is There Progress in Political Science,?' in *Idioms of Inquiry: Critique and Renewal in Political Science*, ed. Ball (Albany, N.Y.: State University of New York Press, 1987), ch. 1.

3   See Charles Taylor, 'Self-Interpreting Animals', *Philosophical Papers*, 2 vols. (Cambridge: Cambridge University Press, 1985), I, ch. 2.

4   J. Donald Moon, 'Political Science and Political Choice: Opacity, Freedom, and Knowledge', in *Idioms of Inquiry*, ed. Ball, p. 239.

5   The criticism does not necessarily apply to dissident democratic thinkers in Eastern Europe. See, *inter alia*, Adam Michnik, *Letters From Prison and Other Essays*, trans. Maya Latynski (Berkeley and Los Angeles: University of California Press, 1985).

6   James Boyd White, 'Economics and Law: Two Cultures in Tension', *Tennessee Law Review*, 54 (Winter 1987), pp. 161–202, at p. 166. My thinking about economics as a language or species of discourse has been both clarified and influenced by White's remarkable essay.

7   Alasdair MacIntyre, *After Virtue* (Notre Dame, Ind.: University of Notre Dame Press, 1981), p. 27.

8   See Charles Taylor, 'Social Theory as Practice', *Philosophical Papers*, II, ch. 3; and Alasdair MacIntyre, 'The Indispensability of Political Theory', in *The Nature of Political Theory*, eds. David Miller and Larry Siedentop (Oxford: Clarendon Press, 1983), ch. 1.

9   G. W. F. Hegel, *Philosophy of Right*, trans. T. M. Knox (New York: Oxford University Press, 1967). Cf. also Shlomo Avineri, *Hegel's Theory of the Modern State* (Cambridge: Cambridge University Press, 1972), ch. 7.

10 Alan Ryan, 'Two Concepts of Politics and Democracy: James and John Stuart Mill', in *Machiavelli and the Nature of Political Thought*, ed. Martin Fleisher (New York: Atheneum, 1972), p. 78.

11 Anthony Downs, *An Economic Theory of Democracy* (New York: Harper & Row, 1957), p. 265. I have, in choosing to look at Downs' book, confined my attention to one particular, historically specific moment in a still-evolving research tradition. Downs' assumptions – and most especially the self-interest axiom – have been challenged from within that tradition by some economists and social choice theorists, including Amartya Sen. See Sen's papers on social choice theory, especially 'Rational Fools', in *Choice, Welfare and Measurement* (Cambridge, Mass.: M.I.T. Press, 1987). See also Howard Margolis, *Selfishness, Altruism, and Rationality* (Cambridge: Cambridge University Press, 1982).

12 Sheldon S. Wolin, *Politics and Vision* (Boston: Little, Brown, 1960), p. 434.

13 The phrase is from Jürgen Habermas, *Knowledge and Human Interests*, trans. Jeremy J. Shapiro (Boston: Beacon Press, 1971), p. vii.

14 Downs, *An Economic Theory*, p. 29, n. 11.

15 Joseph A. Schumpeter, *Capitalism, Socialism, and Democracy*, 3rd edn. (New York: Harper & Row, 1962; first publ. 1942), p. 250.

16 Carole Pateman, *Participation and Democratic Theory* (Cambridge: Cambridge University Press, 1970), p. 17.

17 John Plamenatz, *Democracy and Illusion* (London: Longman, 1973), p. 96.

18 Ibid., pp. 96, 99.

19 Pateman, *Participation*, p. 18. She does go on to say, rightly enough, that 'Neither [James] Mill nor Bentham shared quite the view of the electorate imputed to them by Schumpeter' (p. 19).

20 See James Mill, *An Essay on Government* (Indianapolis; Bobbs-Merrill, n.d.), esp. pp. 48–61.

21 The following account owes much to Dennis F. Thompson, *John Stuart Mill and Representative Government* (Princeton, N.J.: Princeton University Press, 1976), ch. 1, esp. pp. 36–45.

22 John Stuart Mill, *Representative Government*, in *Utilitarianism, Liberty, and Representative Government* (New York: Everyman's Library, 1951), p. 274.

23 Ibid., pp. 274–5.

24 J. S. Mill, *System of Logic* (London: Longman, Green & Co., 1906), Bk. VI, sec. 3, pp. 580–1.

25 Mill, *Representative Government*, p. 283.

26 Ibid., p. 288.

27 Quoted in Thompson, *John Stuart Mill*, p. 45.

28 Mill, *Representative Government*, p. 281.

29 Ibid., p. 291.

30 See Donald N. McCloskey, *The Rhetoric of Economics* (Madison, Wis.: University of Wisconsin Press, 1985); and White, 'Economics and the Law'. More historical analyses of the emergence of economic discourse may be found in Louis Dumont, *From Mandeville to Marx: The Genesis and Triumph of Economic Ideology* (Chicago: University of Chicago Press, 1977); and Milton L. Myers, *The Soul of Modern Economic Man* (Chicago: University of Chicago Press, 1983).

31 See the aptly titled *Economic Imperialism: The Economic Method Applied Outside the Field of Economics*, ed. Gerard Radnitzky and Peter Bernholz (New York: Paragon House, 1987).

32 See Max Black, *Models and Metaphors* (Ithaca, N.Y.: Cornell University Press, 1965), pp. 25–47; and Mary B. Hesse, *Models and*

Analogies in Science (Notre Dame, Ind.: University of Notre Dame Press, 1966), pp. 157–77. Marx makes much the same point in 'The Eighteenth Brumaire': '. . . a beginner who has learnt a new language always translates it back into his mother tongue, but he has assimilated the spirit of the new language and can freely express himself in it only when he finds his way in it without recalling the old and forgets his native tongue in the use of the new.' *Karl Marx: Selected Writings*, ed. David McLellan (Oxford: Oxford University Press, 1977), p. 300.

33 Schumpeter, *Capitalism, Socialism, and Democracy*, p. 269.

34 Ibid., p. 272.

35 Ibid., p. 273.

36 Ibid., p. 271.

37 See Russell L. Hanson, *The Democratic Imagination in America: Conversations With Our Past* (Princeton, N.J.: Princeton University Press, 1985), ch. 8, 'Democratic Consumerism'.

38 Mancur Olson, *The Rise and Decline of Nations* (New Haven, Conn.: Yale University Press, 1983), *passim*.

39 Samuel P. Huntington, 'The United States', in Michel Crozier, Samuel P. Huntington and Joji Watanuki, *The Crisis of Democracy: Report on the Governability of Democracies to the Trilateral Commission* (New York: New York University Press, 1975) ch. 3, esp. pp. 102–15.

40 Robert B. Reich, 'Why Democracy Makes Economic Sense', a review of Olsen's *Rise and Decline of Nations*, in *The New Republic*, 189 (19 December 1983), pp. 25–32.

41 MacIntyre, *After Virtue*, ch. 3.

42 See Downs, *Economic Theory*, ch. 14.

43 Hegel, *Philosophy of Right*, pp. 202–3. An even earlier version of the paradox is to be found in Rousseau's *Contrat Social* (1762), Bk. III, ch. 1.

44 Downs, *An Economic Theory*, p. 270.

45 Brian Barry, *Sociologists, Economists and Democracy* (London: Collier-Macmillan, 1970), p. 20.

46 See Ball, 'Is There Progress in Political Science?', pp. 29–33.

47 Downs, *Economic Theory*, p. 270.

48 William H. Riker and Peter C. Ordeshook, 'A Theory of the Calculus of Voting', *American Political Science Review*, March 1968, pp. 25–42, at p. 28.

49 Barry, *Sociologists, Economists and Democracy*, p. 15.

50 John A. Ferejohn and Morris P. Fiorina, 'The Paradox of Not Voting: A Decision Theoretic Analysis', *American Political Science*

987

Review, 69 (September 1974), pp. 525–36, at p. 535.

51 Stephen V. Stephens, 'The Paradox of Not Voting: A Comment,' in ibid., pp. 914–15.

52 Lawrence S. Mayer and I. J. Good, 'Is Minimax Regret Applicable to Voting Decisions?', in ibid., pp. 916–17.

53 R. E. Goodin and K. W. S. Roberts, 'The Ethical Voter', in ibid., p. 918.

54 Nathaniel Beck, 'The Paradox of Minimax Regret', in ibid., p. 918.

55 Ferejohn and Fiorina, 'Closeness Counts Only in Horseshoes and Dancing', in ibid., pp. 920–5.

56 Such a defence would doubtless require an alternative account of political rationality. For a promising start in this direction, see Stephen L. Elkin, 'Economic and Political Rationality', Polity, 19 (1987), pp. 100–30. See also Lawrence A. Scaff and Helen M. Ingram, 'Politics, Policy, and Public Choice: A Critique and a Proposal', Polity, 19 (Summer, 1987), pp. 613–36; John R. Dryzek, 'Complexity and Rationality in Political Life', Political Studies, 35 (September 1987), pp. 424–42.

CHAPTER 7 JUSTICE BETWEEN GENERATIONS

1 Anton Chekhov, Three Sisters, in Four Plays, trans. David Magarshack (New York: Hill & Wang, 1969), Act I, p. 126.

2 See, inter alia, the essays collected in Ernest Partridge, ed., Responsibilities to Future Generations (Buffalo, N.Y.: Prometheus, 1981) and in R. I. Sikora and Brian Barry, eds, Obligations to Future Generations (Philadelphia: Temple University Press, 1978). For a concise overview of the central issues, see Annette Baier, 'For the Sake of Future Generations', in Earthbound: New Introductory Essays in Environmental Ethics, ed. Tom Regan (New York: Random House, 1984), ch. 7. For a radical re-posing of the questions, see Derek Parfit, Reasons and Persons (Oxford: Clarendon Press, 1984), Part IV.

3 By 'incommensurable' I do not mean 'utterly untranslatable'. As Donald Davidson has shown, it is impossible to make sense of the idea that predicates wholly intelligible in one conceptual scheme may be utterly unintelligible in another: 'On the Very Idea of a Conceptual Scheme', in Michael Krausz and Jack W. Meiland, eds, Relativism: Cognitive and Moral (Notre Dame, Ind.: University of Notre Dame Press, 1982), pp. 68–80. To paraphrase Richard Rorty, what I mean by incommensurable is: unable to be brought under a set of rules which will tell us how rational agreement can be reached or what

would settle the issue on every point where statements seem to conflict. See Rorty, *Philosophy and the Mirror of Nature* (Princeton, N.J.: Princeton University Press, 1979), p. 316.

4 Aristotle, *Nichomachean Ethics*, Bk. V, ch. 7.

5 For an illuminating interpretation, see Renford Bambrough, 'Aristotle on Justice: A Paradigm of Philosophy', in Bambrough, ed., *New Essays on Plato and Aristotle* (London: Routledge & Kegan Paul, 1965), pp. 159–74.

6 I am not, of course, suggesting that he should or even that he could have done so. His was not an historically minded age. Aristotle and his contemporaries took it for granted that there would be conceptual continuity and commensurability across the generations. 'Historical consciousness', understood as 'a full awareness of the historicity of everything present and the [historical] relativity of all opinions', is uniquely 'the privilege of modern man': Hans-Georg Gadamer, 'The Problem of Historical Consciousness', in Paul Rabinow and William M. Sullivan, eds, *Interpretive Social Science* (Berkeley and Los Angeles: University of California Press, 1979), p. 110. For a lucid account of the origins of this relatively recent development in the history of human thought, see Patrick Gardiner, 'German Philosophy and the Rise of Relativism', *The Monist*, 64 (1982), pp. 138–54.

7 The idea that we learn from the clash of opposing frameworks is a theme uniting thinkers as different as Gadamer, Geertz, Winch and Popper. See Gadamer, 'The Problem of Historical Consciousness', esp. pp. 151–2; Clifford Geertz, 'From the Native's Point of View', in Rabinow and Sullivan, *Interpretive Social Science*, ch. 6; Peter Winch, 'Understanding a Primitive Society', in *Rationality*, ed. Brian R. Wilson (Oxford: Blackwell, 1970); and Karl Popper, 'The Myth of the Framework', in *The Abdication of Philosophy*, ed. Eugene Freeman (LaSalle, Ill.: Open Court, 1976). For an overview and synthesis, see Richard J. Bernstein, *Beyond Objectivism and Relativism* (Philadelphia: University of Pennsylvania Press, 1983), Part III.

8 See Karl Popper, *The Poverty of Historicism* (New York: Harper Torchbooks, 1964), pp. vi–viii; and James Farr, 'Historical Concepts in Political Science: The Case of "Revolution"', *American Journal of Political Science* 26 (November 1982), p. 704.

9 See Thomas S. Kuhn, *The Structure of Scientific Revolutions*, 2nd edn. (Chicago, Ill.: University of Chicago Press, 1972), ch. 1; and John G. Gunnell, *Political Theory: Tradition and Interpretation* (Cambridge, Mass.: Winthrop Publisher, 1979), ch. 4.

10 Alasdair MacIntyre, *A Short History of Ethics* (London: Macmillan, 1965), p. 2.

11 John Rawls, *A Theory of Justice* (Cambridge, Mass.: Harvard University Press, 1971), p. 5.

12 The idea that different conceptions of justice, or indeed any moral or political concept, must somehow share certain features or make reference to a universal conceptual core rests upon a residual Platonic prejudice still in need of exorcizing. Wittgenstein's notion of 'family resemblances' may be as apposite in the case of 'justice' as in that of games: to call something 'just' is not to allude to some set of features that all just actions have in common, but to call attention to certain family resemblances among those actions, practices and institutions so characterized in historically specific communities. To see just how varied these characterizations can be, compare Rawls' (or Robert Nozick's) theory of justice with those explicited in, *inter alia*, Eric A. Havelock, *The Greek Concept of Justice* (Cambridge, Mass.: Harvard University Press, 1978) and Majid Khadduri, *The Islamic Conception of Justice* (Baltimore, Md.: Johns Hopkins University Press, 1984).

13 Rawls, *A Theory of Justice*, pp. 137, 284–93. For a critique and partial revision of Rawls' account, see D. Clayton Hubin, 'Justice and Future Generations', *Philosophy and Public Affairs*, 6 (Fall 1976), pp. 70–83. If my argument holds water, however, Hubin's modified version will not suffice either, inasmuch as he, like Rawls, wholly ignores the phenomenon of conceptual change and the problems it poses for any theory of *intergenerational* justice.

14 Indeed, for the distinctly unRawlsian inhabitants of 'traditional' societies, the very idea of choosing without knowing one's role, status or social identity – man or woman, child or elder, citizen or alien, freeman or slave – would be wellnigh unintelligible. This can be seen, for example, in their unwillingness, or perhaps inability, to participate in sociological thought-experiments involving role-playing. See David Riesman's Introduction to Daniel Lerner, *The Passing of Traditional Society* (New York: The Free Press, 1958), p. 3.

15 Søren Kierkegaard, *The Concept of Irony*, trans. L. M. Capel (London: Collins, 1966), p. 47. Compare Nietzsche's remarks on conceptual change in *The Genealogy of Morals*, trans. Francis Golffing (Garden City, N.Y.: Anchor Books, 1956), pp. 212–13.

16 Rawls, *A Theory of Justice*, p. 587.

17 Karl Marx, *The Poverty of Philosophy* (New York: International Publishers, 1983), pp. 120–1.

18 William A. Galston, *Justice and the Human Good* (Chicago: University of Chicago Press, 1980), p. 252.

19 As Rawls himself appears to concede in his Dewey Lectures, 'Kantian Constructivism in Moral Theory', *Journal of Philosophy*, 77 (Septem-

ber 1980), esp. pp. 518–19. Unfortunately Rawls fails to notice how this historicist emendation radically undercuts, if it does not obliterate outright, his account of intergenerational justice. The present chapter is, in effect, an attempt to make good that omission.

20 See Charles Taylor, 'Political Theory and Practice', in *Social Theory and Political Practice* ed. Christopher Lloyd (Oxford: Clarendon Press, 1983), pp. 61–85.

21 Popper, 'The Myth of the Framework', p. 23. Unfortunately, Popper does not distinguish between moral relativism and cognitive relativism. His strictures are arguably more applicable against the latter than the former.

22 As Peter Laslett recognizes in 'The Conversation Between the Generations', in Laslett and James Fishkin, eds, *Philosophy, Politics, and Society*, fifth series (New Haven, Conn.: Yale University Press, 1979). Curiously, Bruce Ackerman defends a 'conversational' or 'dialogical' theory of justice as offering the best account of 'justice over time' even while acknowledging that future people cannot, in the nature of the case, possibly participate in that conversation. See Bruce A. Ackerman, *Social Justice in the Liberal State* (New Haven, Conn.: Yale University Press, 1980), pp. 221–2. See also n. 30, below.

23 See my 'The Picaresque Prince: Reflections on Machiavelli and Moral Change', *Political Theory*, 12 (November 1984), pp. 521–36.

24 I take it that the paradigmatic act of injustice, according to our lights, is one in which one person (group, class or generation) intentionally deprives another of what is rightfully theirs, i.e., to which they can justifiably claim a right. Of course, the concept of 'right' is itself a relatively recent addition to the language of morals. See A. I. Melden, *Rights and Persons* (Berkeley and Los Angeles: University of California Press, 1977), esp. ch. 7; and Richard Dagger, 'Rights', in *Political Innovation and Conceptual Change*, ed. Terence Ball, James Farr and Russell L. Hanson (Cambridge: Cambridge University Press, 1988), ch. 14.

25 Bertram Wyatt-Brown, *Southern Honor: Ethics and Behavior in the Old South* (New York: Oxford University Press, 1982), pp. 3–4.

26 See the arguments advanced in defence of slavery by Chancellor Harper and J. H. Hammond in E. N. Elliott, ed., *Cotton is King* (1860; repr. New York: Negro Universities Press, 1969); by Thomas R. Dew in *The Pro-Slavery Argument* (1852; repr. New York: Negro Universities Press, 1968); and by George Fitzhugh, *Sociology for the South, or the Failure of Free Society* (Richmond, Va.: A. Morris, 1854) and *Cannibals All! or Slaves Without Masters*, ed. C. Vann Woodward (1857; repr. Cambridge, Mass.: Belknap Press, 1960).

27 Wyatt-Brown, *Southern Honor*, p. 402. Cf. also Mark V. Tushnet,

The American Law of Slavery, 1810–1860 (Princeton, N.J.: Princeton University Press, 1981).

28 For an elegant explication and defence of the claim that 'ways of life are sharply coherent', see Stuart Hampshire, *Morality and Conflict* (Cambridge, Mass.: Harvard University Press, 1983), ch. 7, esp. pp. 148–9.

29 William Faulkner, *Intruder in the Dust* (New York: Modern Library, 1948), p. 194.

30 That our present-day standards of justice might require us to compensate our unfortunate black contemporaries does not, of course, affect my point. For it would be we who would be acting justly by our lights, even as we recognize that our ancestors were not necessarily acting unjustly by theirs. At the very least, we need to draw a distinction between 'past injustices' which were recognizable in principle but disregarded in practice by ancestral perpetrators and those which were not and which accordingly can be seen as such only through the wisdom of hindsight. The failure to draw this distinction and to trace its moral implications mars even the most incisive discussions of reparations for past wrongs. See, *inter alia*, Robert Nozick, *Anarchy, State, and Utopia* (New York: Basic Books, 1974), p. 231; Boris Bittker, *The Case for Black Reparations* (New York: Random House, 1974); and George Sher, 'Ancient Wrongs and Modern Rights', *Philosophy and Public Affairs*, 10 (1980), pp. 3–17.

31 M. P. Golding, 'Obligations to Future Generations', *The Monist*, 56 (1972), pp. 85–99; Michael Walzer, *Spheres of Justice* (New York: Basic Books, 1983).

32 See the exchange between Walzer and Dworkin in *The New York Review of Books*, 21 July 1983, pp. 43–6.

33 Golding, 'Obligations to Future Generations', p. 90.

34 Ibid., p. 97.

35 See Walzer, *Obligations* (Cambridge, Mass.: Harvard University Press, 1970), Part I.

36 Walzer, *Spheres of Justice*, p. 313.

37 Ibid., p. 314.

38 Cf. Clifford Geertz, *Local Knowledge* (New York: Basic Books, 1983).

39 Walzer, *Spheres of Justice*, p. 314.

40 John H. Schaar, 'The Question of Justice', *Raritan* 3 (1983), pp. 107–29.

41 Walzer, *Spheres of Justice*, p. 319.

42 Ibid., p. 29.

43 G. W. F. Hegel, *Philosophy of Right*, trans. T. M. Knox (Oxford: Oxford University Press, 1967), p. 11.

Index

Ackerman, Bruce 190n.
Adair, Douglas 170n.
Adams, Willi Paul 171n., 174n.
Adcock, F. E. 166n.
Althusser, Louis 8, 163n.
Antifederalism 47–8, 55–9, 60–7,
  68–70, 71, 170n., 172n.,
  173n., 174n.
Appleby, Joyce 170n.
Aquinas, Thomas 27, 166n.
Arendt, Hannah 92–4, 95–6, 102,
  104, 106, 107–9, 110, 111,
  175n., 178n., 180n., 181n.,
  183n.
Aristotle 26–7, 49, 83, 84, 85, 96,
  118–19, 146, 149, 167n.,
  188n.
Augustine 49, 149, 170n.
Austin J. L., 6, 96
authority 20, 106–21
  and conceptual change 107–10
  distinction between *in* authority
    and *an* authority 115–16, 118,
    119
  emotivist view of 106–7,
    110–15, 121
  epistemocratic view of 106–7,
    110–11, 115–20, 121
  functionalization of 108–9, 110,
    111, 113–14
Avineri, Shlomo 184n.
Ayer, A. J. 111

Bachrach, Peter 88–9, 176n.,
  177n.

Baier, Annette 187n.
Bailyn, Bernard 169n., 171n.
Balzac, Honoré de v, 2, 18, 161n.
Bambrough, Renford 188n.
Banning, Lance 168n., 169n.,
  170n., 171n., 172n., 173n.
Baratz, Morton 88–9, 176n.,
  177n.
Barrett, William 183n.
Barry, Brian 139, 140, 186n.
Bartolus of Saxoferrato 49
Beard, Charles 173n.
Beattie, Alan 165n., 167n.
Beck, Nathaniel 187n.
Begriffsgeschichte 9–10
Bell, Daniel 118, 183n.
Bentham, Jeremy 101, 131, 134,
  136, 147, 185n.
Berlin, Isaiah 25, 165n.
Bernholz, Peter 185n.
Bernstein, Richard J. 188n.
Beyme, Klaus Von 165n.
Bhaskar, Roy 179n.
Bittker, Boris 191n.
Bolingbroke 38–9, 52, 54, 167n.
Böll, Heinrich 2, 161n.
Boulton, James T. 168n.
Brailsford, H. N. 166n.
Brutus 56–8, 60–6, 68–70, 74, 172n.
Burke, Edmund 41–2, 168n.,
  173n.
Burtt, E. A. 175n

Cartwright, Dorwin 88, 177n.
Cervantes, Miguel de 1

1. conceptual history as reformulation of history of ideas

2. concepts and organizing space (p.10) ... see ~~the~~ notebook

3. root metaphor of civic body entails medical imagery (2a)

    A. organic   B. contractual
       a) medical
       b) disease

3. Republicanism in ratification debate 11.42,